HOW TO BUILD A STOCK EXCHANGE

"A rare phenomenon – succeeds in both demystifying an object with a technical and arcane history and being a genuine delight to read. It is an authoritative account that demonstrates exactly why stock markets should not be left to financiers and economists."

Liz Mcfall, University of Edinburgh

"A superbly written and urgent book which makes complex issues lucid. If you want to enjoy finding out how we got to where we are now, and what's wrong with our financial system, read Roscoe."

Martin Parker, University of Bristol

"Much in the way that the early Methodists pondered why it was that the Devil had all the best tunes, before using this as inspiration for writing toe-tapping hymns, Philip Roscoe, in this excellent and entertaining book, seeks to develop a counter-narrative to the stories that have been produced by and about the financial system. These stories give it a power and authority way above its station and that have been proved to be both damaging and destructive. Drawing on a wide range of sources, including from his pre-academic career in the foothills of the financial system, Roscoe tells alternative stories of finance to emphasize how its institutions are all too human inventions that are highly fallible but also open to reinvention, if only we make sufficient effort to understand them and, importantly, to think carefully about ways in which they might be rebuilt."

Andrew Leyshon, University of Nottingham

HOW TO BUILD A STOCK EXCHANGE

The Past, Present and Future of Finance

Philip Roscoe

First published in Great Britain in 2023 by

Bristol University Press
University of Bristol
1–9 Old Park Hill
Bristol
BS2 8BB
UK
t: +44 (0)117 374 6645
e: bup-info@bristol.ac.uk

Details of international sales and distribution partners are available at bristoluniversitypress.co.uk

British Library Cataloguing in Publication Data
A catalogue record for this book is available from the British Library

ISBN 978-1-5292-2431-3 hardcover
ISBN 978-1-5292-2432-0 paperback
ISBN 978-1-5292-2433-7 ePub
ISBN 978-1-5292-2434-4 ePdf

Cover design: Nicky Borowiec
Front cover image: CurvaBezier/Adobe Stock
Bristol University Press uses environmentally responsible print partners.
Printed and bound in Great Britain by CPI Group (UK) Ltd, Croydon, CR0 4YY

FSC
www.fsc.org
MIX
Paper | Supporting responsible forestry
FSC® C013604

To Jane, with love

Contents

Acknowledgements

This book has been written at a strange time, in a world locked down then emerging into war and crisis. Writing a book is never easy, but it is even more difficult under such circumstances, and thanks are even more heartfelt. Several of the people named below I have never met, yet I have come to depend on them in ways I would never have expected.

Let me start with Paul Stevens, my editor at Bristol University Press. This book would not have come to be without his encouragement and support. I thank him and his colleagues, especially Kathryn King, Georgina Bolwell, Ruth Wallace and Emma Cook, who have helped along the way. I have benefited enormously from the thoughts of Shona Russell and François-Régis Puyou, who read the full draft and generously commented, as well as the comments from the Press' anonymous readers. I thank my colleagues and friends at St Andrews, across the university, for providing a sustaining environment where a project like this can still happen.

The book began life as a podcast, and this endeavour – far more arduous than I had anticipated – was supported by a wide community of scholars and colleagues, especially Susi Geiger, Juan Pablo Pardo-Guerra, Andrea Lagna, Yuval Millo, Daniel Beunza, Toby Bennett, Kristian Bondo Hansen. Heidi Moore and Aditya Chakrabortty helped give the podcast some Twitter daylight. Everyone who tweeted: without your kind words and constant retweeting, I probably would have abandoned the project.

Here also, I would like to thank my JCE colleagues for their support and encouragement – Liz McFall, Carolyn Harding, Taylor Nelms and Jose Ossandon especially. Long may the WhatsApp group keep buzzing! The book's title came from Chris Wellbelove; there is something mischievous about writing a 'how to' book that never says how to. Thank you.

The project that forms the core of the narrative, a history of London's small company stock exchanges, was generously supported by a Leverhulme Trust Research Fellowship. I am grateful to the Trust and to my interviewees, who gave me their time, memories, documents and photographs, and especially to my friend David Coffman, who opened doors and made introductions, and the Jenkins family, without whose support the project would never have succeeded.

I thank you all, and the community of scholars on whose shoulders this book stands. Errors and omissions are mine alone.

Prologue: A Bad Kind of Magic?

'The Slave Ship', or 'Slavers Throwing Overboard the Dead and Dying, Typhoon Coming On', is Turner's great masterpiece. It is a swirling mass of colour and rage, held together by a lowering sun. Red, ochre, orange, the sea smashing from the left, foaming, boiling, the whole picture askance. In the background, a stricken ship, sails furled, ploughs through the spume. In the foreground, horror: a severed black leg, manacle attached, a feast for hideous fishes and circling gulls; hands reaching up; irons somehow floating; the water carmine to match the sunset. It is not easy to look at.

The painting was first exhibited in the Royal Academy in 1840. It evoked the whole brutality of the slave trade, but it referenced one event in particular: the Zong Massacre of 1781, when Luke Collingwood, captain of the slave ship Zong, ordered the drowning of 133 of his captives.[1] Through the efforts of abolitionist Granville Sharp, the massacre came to be emblematic of the horrors of slaving and helped to galvanize the public to the abolitionist cause. Sharp heard of the Zong Massacre from freed slave and campaigner Olaudah Equiano and, recognizing its rhetorical and political possibilities, compiled a weighty dossier that now rests in the archives of the National Maritime Museum. In this way and that, the massacre has been expropriated ever since, as a symbol not of tyranny but of salvation, of the narrative that allows Britain to take credit for abolishing a practice that it had done so much to establish. The ship has been borrowed as well. Turner's critics complain that his painting makes the viewer complicit in the atrocity for the sake of sensation, while a recreated Zong – the most infamous of all slaving ships, a floating gaol that had dawdled up the coast of Africa for a year before even setting off across the Atlantic – sailed into the Thames for a 2007 celebration of the vote that abolished slavery.[2]

Poet Marlene NourbeSe Philip's cycle 'Zong!' seeks to remember the killings differently. A tone poem of fractured and seemingly random words, it forces the listener to struggle to make sense of a happening that never can be understood. This, she writes, 'is the closest we will ever get, some two hundred years later, to what it must have been like for those Africans aboard the Zong'.[3] The poem's words may be fractured, but they are not random.

They come from another source, a bland and prosaic account of the legal hearing that followed. This was not a murder trial, you might be surprised to discover, but rather, a civil case, 'Gregson vs Gilbert'. The massacre became the basis of an insurance claim, and when the underwriters refused to pay, the slavers – the Gregsons – took them to court. Philip's poem draws on this document, a found text, corrupt, polluted by the murderous rationality of the law.[4] The text – the only surviving public source for the Massacre – is a place of silences: 'Where the captain of a slave ship mistook Hispaniola for Jamaica, whereby the voyage being retarded and water falling short, several of the slaves died for want of water and others were thrown overboard, it was held that these facts did not support a statement in the declaration....' It comes from a collection of legal reports published in 1831. The editor responsible for the compilation was a barrister and a legal scholar, a member of London's Inner Temple. His name was Henry Roscoe.[5]

To tell the story of 'Gregson vs Gilbert' is to go back to the commercial world that developed at an astonishing speed during the 18th century, centring on Liverpool, a provincial market town in North West England. The Zong Massacre is, as the literary scholar Ian Baucom made clear in his monumental *Specters of the Atlantic*, an event that is both singular (although 133 people, thrown overboard, one by one, over the course of three days, is also 133 singular events...) and typical. It is typical because it epitomizes a new kind of finance capital that had grown more than anywhere in Liverpool, and that had propelled the sleepy market town to a position of such pre-eminence in the Atlantic trade that it could consider itself one of the world's leading commercial centres.

The career of William Gregson, owner of the Zong and one of Liverpool's foremost slavers, exemplifies the possibilities that Liverpool offered in the 18th century. The son of a porter, Gregson started out as a ropemaker but rose to be one of its most distinguished citizens, becoming mayor of Liverpool in 1762. His rapacity was unequalled: during his career he invested in 152 voyages. 'Even in the desolate world of slave statistics', writes the historian James Walvin, 'these are astonishing figures.' Gregson's voyages carried 58,201 Africans, 49,053 of whom survived to landfall. By that account – and we shall return to accounts shortly – 9,148 perished.[6]

Mayor William Gregson would have occupied an office in the Liverpool Exchange, a lavish building that was opened in 1754. The Exchange existed both as a physical monument to newfound wealth and power and also as a political organization devoted to the furtherance of the city's economic growth. Slaves never travelled through Liverpool, but no one was innocent enough to suggest that the city's newfound prosperity was due to anything but slavery. The merchants themselves, the bankers and lawyers who served them; shipbuilders expert in the specialized design of these floating gaols; ropemakers, gun makers, ironmongers churning out gratings and manacles, sellers of victuals and rum; corrupt publicans who plied the sailors with drink and press-ganged them into service on the slave ships – the most hateful, hazardous and destructive occupation on the seas – all of this was driven by slavery. The city's influence and prosperity followed the new roads and waterways inland, shipping manufactured goods from Manchester to Africa, via Liverpool, and American cotton back to Lancaster. Slavery powered the economy of North West England, and everyone knew it. Those commissioning and designing the Exchange did not shy away from this fact, decorating its exterior with carvings of African heads.

As Liverpool's commerce boomed, so the city enjoyed an explosion of culture. It became international in outlook as well as trade; the Exchange building's piazzas of white stone were just one expression of a growing fascination for all things Italian. So energetic was this passion that it has been argued that the British romantic notion of the Italian Renaissance came from Liverpool.[7] Liverpool's cultural transformation was led by one man. He was William Roscoe, father of Henry Roscoe, barrister and transcriber of the Zong hearing, and great-grandfather of my great-grandfather.

Unlike William Gregson, who left few traces in the archives, Roscoe was famous. He is now remembered as one of the city's founding fathers, commemorated in plaques, street names and a fine little pub called the Roscoe Head. He was a leading intellectual figure: his biography of Lorenzo de' Medici brought him admiration from Horace Walpole and comparisons with Edward Gibbon, spreading Liverpool's identity as a cultural centre across the world. He wrote a children's poem (originally for my great-grandfather's grandfather), titled 'The Butterfly's Ball', which was admired by the King. He was known most of all as a leading abolitionist, and author of three long poems condemning slavery. These were a great popular success, although to the modern ear they are turgid. (A snippet: 'Come thou, and weep with me substantial ills;/And execrate the wrongs, that Afric's sons,/Torn from their natal shore, and doom'd to bear/The yoke of servitude in western climes,/Sustain.'[8]) He was even a Member of Parliament for a crucial year, which allowed him to vote for the abolition of slavery in 1807, although he faced riots and hostility on his return to Liverpool.

And yet… Roscoe's first profession was that of lawyer, and by the age of 46 he had made enough money to retire to Allerton Hall, a stately home outside the city. His art collection included a then unfashionable Leonardo da Vinci. In 1800 he took up a partnership in a distressed banking firm run by his friend Thomas Clark and set about righting it. (He never succeeded: the bank eventually failed and ruined him.) What did he bank? What contracts did he draw up? Liverpool's economic engine ran on slavery. Roscoe's huge legal fees, his banking commissions, his stately home, his Leonardo – all would have been tainted by its stench.

He would have certainly shared a cultural and social milieu with the Gregsons and their peers. Among the institutions that sprang up in Liverpool at the time was the Athenaeum, a subscription library that served, and still serves, as the meeting place for the city's merchant elite. Gregson's son-in-law, George Case, bought a large house next door to it. Roscoe was one of the Athenaeum's founders and his library was the foundation of its extensive collection. One of Roscoe's close friends was a Matthew Gregson. The slave merchants did as good 18th-century burghers would do: giving money to the right causes, improving and developing the infrastructure of the city. It seems likely that my great-grandfather's great-grandfather knew these men well, conducted business with them regularly, took their subscriptions to his civic schemes, and welcomed them at his cultural events. Indeed, in 1784, just months after the Zong hearing, and a few months before John Gregson – the next generation – became mayor, Liverpool held its Oratorio Week celebrations with theatre, shows, an art exhibition and a masked ball. Baucom speculates that the Gregsons attended the ball; I speculate that they also attended Roscoe's exhibition of Italian art, another highlight of the festivities and the first such exhibition to be held in Liverpool.[9]

***

Manacled and enslaved bodies never set foot in Liverpool. For that city, slaving was a *financial* endeavour, a sanitized mirror-world of lists and ledgers. The Liverpool merchants – and lawyers and bankers – invented a system of credit that allowed them not only to greatly speed up the circulation of capital around the slave triangle, but also to benefit from interest on that capital as it flowed. The physical trade, as is well known, operated in a triangular fashion. Manufactured goods were shipped from Liverpool and Bristol to West Africa where they were bartered for people. These Africans had been penned in slave factories subsidized and staffed by the British government, often under the aegis of the Royal African Company, a London-based 'joint stock company'. Slaves were transported across the Atlantic – the hellish Middle Passage – and then handed to factors who supervised the auction for a commission. The final leg of the journey saw this money converted into goods for import, such as sugar, rum and cotton, and returned to Liverpool for sale.

The problem with this system, at least for those trying to profit from it, was that it was slow and risky. Too much capital was tied up in material goods, circulating at the pace of the breeze, vulnerable to shipwreck, piracy, and, in the case of the human cargo, death, disease and insurrection. The Liverpool merchants' solution was to use credit in the form of bills of exchange. These were notes promising to pay the bearer a certain amount, plus interest, which could be redeemed by an associate of the issuer, or, in fact, anyone who trusted the issuer's guarantee. They were certainly not a new technology. They had emerged organically with the growth of trade in the late Middle Ages and had spawned a whole new industry. By the 14th century the first banks had been set up by wealthy individuals; the Medici dynasty, which so fascinated William Roscoe, opened its bank in 1397. Bank owners could afford to redeem the bills and take the risk of default for a commission (or, in the Middle Ages, an exchange rate speculation), or perhaps offer their own bill that would be accepted widely on the basis of their reputation. Networks of branches allowed merchants to deposit in one location and withdraw elsewhere, without problems of transporting gold or precious goods. These bank notes enormously expanded the money supply and with it the possibilities for circulation and profit.[10]

The Liverpool innovation was to tie these financial instruments to human souls. The factor would sell the slaves for hard cash and then, having taken his commission, return an interest-bearing bill of exchange by the next ship to Liverpool. The factor had

> ... not so much sold the slaves ... as borrowed an amount equivalent to the sales proceeds from the Liverpool merchants and agreed to repay that amount with interest. The Liverpool businessman invested in the trade had, by the same procedure, transformed what looked like a simple trade in commodities to trade in loans.[11]

The recipient of the note, who wanted his money sooner to reinvest in more ventures, had simply to cash it at the bank. The bills, like modern bonds, circulated among investors at a discount to face value. Many bonds offered three years of credit, and in boom time three years is practically forever: so much additional money to be made before the loan has to be repaid!

The Liverpool bill bond market became so liquid and reliable that in due course the merchants began to pay the African vendors with bills of exchange as well, a change that required the Africans to adopt a cash economy and a colonial form of accounting marked in cowrie shells. The slaves, writes Baucom,

> ... functioned in this system simultaneously as commodities for sale and as the reserve deposits of a loosely organized, decentered, but vast trans-Atlantic banking system: deposits made at the moment of sale and instantly reconverted into short-term bonds. This is at once obscene and vital to understanding the full capital logic of the slave trade.

The cowries, meanwhile, were said to feed on the bodies of slaves murdered out at sea, adding a ghoulish allegorical flourish to these new forms of economic circulation.[12]

Capital, as theorists in the tradition of Marx have argued, is desperate to jump from the earthbound circuit of production to a situation where it can multiply upon itself. That's the heart of financial capitalism, then and now: the search for ways of setting speculative capital free to flow more quickly and generate higher returns.[13] By this account, it is not just the slave ship that sits at the heart of the trade, but also the banking house, its heavy architectural solidity in rusticated stone underpinning the circulation of credit around the Atlantic. Credit is enmeshed in dense social chains of guarantee and underwritten by the merchants' knowledge of and trust in each other. It is why I feel a little uncomfortable about William Roscoe's social standing and I feel *very* uncomfortable about his bank; when he entered the partnership in 1799, it was at the behest of London banker Sir Benjamin Hammet, who held some £200,000 – a vast sum – on deposit.[14]

Slaves therefore existed simultaneously in two places, as bodies in the stinking, corporeal holds of the gaol ships and also as tallies – 'specters', in Baucom's terms – in the clean and disembodied realm of accounting ledgers. They represented two kinds of value: one of embodied labour not yet exploited, and the other a speculative financial value that rested on the Gregsons' balance sheet until it could be realized at auction in the Americas. Their speculative value was locked into place by insurance, another financial technology closely related to the social networks and the financial institutions of the city. Liverpool's slavers had quickly realized that the only means of surviving frequent total losses was through mutual support and the pooling of risk. Insurance formalized this practice but had an unexpected consequence: by underwriting the economic value of a person it also made concrete their existence as an economic object, a chattel or form of property. Insurance makes speculative value real.

Insurance takes us to the heart of the Zong Massacre. As Captain Collingwood, incompetent or deranged, or both, found himself unlikely to land a cargo of slaves, he sought to crystalize that speculative value by murder. If the slaves had died of natural causes, or landed sick and unsaleable, it would have resulted in a loss for Gregson's syndicate. But by the maritime insurance principle of 'general average', if part of the cargo had to be jettisoned to save the ship, all stakeholders would pay their share. And so, on the flimsy justification of navigational error and water shortage, he instructed his crew to hurl overboard 133 men. It took three days, even if the final 10, grasping what little agency they had left, chose to throw themselves voluntarily into the ocean. Captain Collingwood's actions cleaned up the embodied – traumatized, sick and filthy – aspect of these persons cum commodities, catapulting them headlong into the realm of speculative value, of capital already made real by the insurance contract.

Marlene NourbeSe Philip's cacophonous words make as much sense of this as anything: it is senseless. I would like to say that is why the insurers refused to pay, but Henry Roscoe's papers show a legal system unconcerned with the lives and deaths of slaves. Finding that they should have a bad market for their slaves, argue the lawyers for the insurers, the slavers took these means to transfer the loss from the owners to the underwriters. The Gregsons' lawyers begin, 'it has been decided, whether wisely or unwisely, that a portion of our fellow creatures should become the subject of property. This, therefore, was a throwing overboard of goods, and of part to save the residue.' Lord Mansfield, presiding, concedes the matter to be 'a very uncommon case', and rules that the claim is unsupported by evidence and worthy of a second hearing. 'It would be dangerous', says Justice Buller, 'to suffer a plaintiff to recover a peril not stated in the declaration!'[15] See what is not contested: the morality of slavery, the existence of property rights, the act of murder.

★★★

Fast-forward two hundred and twenty-seven years. It is 2008. The global financial system is on the verge of collapse. The US government injects $182.5 billion into AIG, one of the nation's great insurers, which pays out to Wall Street creditors at 100 cents in the dollar, a direct transfer of wealth from US taxpayers to the richest stratum of society. This is another moment of financial magic, of a strange speculative alchemy that made some fortunes and sold others into economic bondage. The role of the insurance company had been to make speculative value real, just as it had been in 1781, only this time the state intervened to *keep* that value in place.

For most of the decade, Wall Street had been engaged in a gold rush, buying and selling bonds built from the mortgage obligations of US citizens. These were interest-bearing notes, similar in purpose to the slavers' contracts, although of a dazzling complexity. We will come back to the detail later. For now, it is simply enough to observe that the bonds washed out the gritty particularity of individual mortgages and local circumstances, representing the debts in ways that were statistically and scientifically knowable. The bonds, like the slavers' notes, circulated through the global economy, free from the constraints of bricks and mortar, shorn of the complexities of borrowers' lives. The other fact to hold on to is that the higher the risk, and therefore the rate, the more profits could be made on the deals. The demand for high-risk mortgages led to a massive explosion in lending, a moment captured by the movie *The Big Short*: two wide-boy, white mortgage salesmen in a tacky country club in Florida, boasting of their loans to migrants unable to read the small print and unaware of the interest rate rises just around the corner. In real life, too, predatory lending was directed disproportionately at Black and Latino communities previously excluded from mainstream mortgages.[16]

Through the same statistical alchemy these hybrid deals offered the banks an 'irresistible arbitrage opportunity'.[17] A true arbitrage is a risk-free profit – free money – but this one was only risk-free for those constructing the deals. At the other end of the trail were poor Americans, whose adverse credit ratings and lack of financial skills made them easy prey for the issuers of mortgages so constructed as to lock them into economic bondage. Their future repayments were sold on, packaged and repackaged, underwritten by insurance. Sophisticated financial instruments backed by novel ways of measuring and counting – the 'Gaussian copula', soon to be known as the formula that blew up Wall Street – allowed the solid value of suburban America's tidy homes and its steady stream of hard-won weekly wages to cross to the realm of speculative financial circulation.[18] This financial alchemy was too much even for the most imaginative of financial engineering to sustain. One of Michael Lewis' characters in *The Big Short* shrieks: 'The more we looked at what a CDO [collateralized debt obligation] really was, the more we were like, Holy shit, that's just fucking crazy. That's fraud. Maybe you can't prove it in a court of law. But it's fraud.'[19]

Looking at the slavers' notes or these predatory mortgage bonds, it is easy to let outrage blind us to more structural factors. The prosperous elites of 18th-century England and 20th-century Wall Street had gained their great wealth at the expense of others, less powerful and less fortunate. The collapse in housing markets from 2007 to 2008 tore the veil of calculative rationality from these mortgage bonds. What remained, however, was not the particularity from which they had been extracted but rather its spectres, ghosts of optimism and prosperity flitting through empty houses and half-built estates. The bonds turned out to be phantasmagorical money, simply disappearing. Giant global institutions found themselves labelled 'zombie banks', economic corpses resuscitated by the public purse. Here, too, as anthropologist Taylor Nelms points out, there is a genealogy of metaphor that links back to the Atlantic trade. The figure of the zombie, rooted in Haitian voodoo, mingles our fears about speculative capital with its murky origins in the Caribbean, fashioned 'at the violent confluence of slavery, colonialism, and the emergence of capitalism as a system of speculation and an outgrowth of the early modern Atlantic cycle of trade.'[20] Where earlier zombie imaginings hinged on fears of automatons and industrial production, contemporary zombies invoke consumption, dislocation and excess: a dark parody of the plantations first of all, and now the speculation of high finance. Spectres, alchemy, zombies, phantoms – our imaginings speak of a bad, dark magic under the bright surface of finance.

There are no such things as zombies. Finance is a machine, one that we have made in our own image. It may be a triumph of the modern imagination, but it is also solidly grounded. Its very immateriality demands a robust material infrastructure. The magic of speculation, like that of a stage conjurer, relies on physical props. The magic is, in the end, artifice: the finance of the Atlantic triangle was not magically apart but written onto beaten and enslaved bodies. Finance exists in account books, in wires, cables and screens as much as it does in narratives, speech and talk. It is embedded in its institutions and these have histories and geographies. Its story is fundamentally Western and colonial, an ideological and material project. In our time, it is not just Jeff Bezos and company's good fortune, commercial acumen or even hard-hearted rapacity that has made them so extraordinarily wealthy, but a set of structural, institutional and material changes centring on a particular kind of institution: the stock exchange.

Stock exchanges play a central role in contemporary life. They are always newsworthy: a hedge fund collapsing, Wall Street under attack by an army of private investors, an entire nation crippled by debt repayments, or another bank bailed out by government. Yet, despite their importance, they are little understood. Textbooks tell us that stock exchanges exist to allocate capital efficiently, to fund growing businesses and to provide rewards for entrepreneurs. But these explanations scarcely match news stories that show finance as chaotic and agonistic, our own lived experience of financial markets as influencing the very shape of our polity, or the popular narratives that paint finance as macho, gendered and exclusionary. Has finance somehow gone wrong? Critiques of finance, from both friend and foe, often hinge on the claim that finance has lost its way – perhaps because it has been detached from its 'proper' purpose, funding productive industry or managing risk; or perhaps because its culture has gone awry. Perhaps finance is *not free enough*, with regulations and tariffs getting in the way of the unlimited expansion of contracts. For critics, there is always a golden age, whether in the past or the utopian future.

I would like to suggest otherwise: finance and its institutions are part of modernity, as much a part of our world as industry. Like industry, finance is a social technology sustained by us. We have made it and we can remake it. The stock exchange is the factory of finance: we can choose between dark satanic mills and gleaming, safe and productive workplaces; between oppressive and collaborative, exploitative and mutually enriching. At least, we can try, although we might also discover that the best kind of stock market is none at all.

To build something, or refashion it, you have to know how it works. You must sweep aside the illusion and banish the spectres. This book will take the stock exchange apart, showing the cogs and wheels that sustain the magic. We will explore the material and technological underpinnings of the market, from the technologies of the early Industrial Revolution, through the 19th century, to the fibre-optic cables and lightspeed processes of contemporary stock exchanges. Stock markets are full of people, and we will explore how bodies flow through this amazing money machine. We will see how exchanges co-evolved with the institutions of modernity and helped make nation states possible: how they bankrolled whole countries and paid for wars. We will unpick the stories we tell about finance, and show how they make some things possible and prevent others; just as stock markets are embedded in historical, political and technological trajectories, so they are also entangled with narratives and ideologies. Stories, as we shall discover, make worlds. Where better to begin than with one of the most prominent of all, a neoliberal fairy story, a morality tale concerning the purpose of stock exchanges.[21] It asks – who are stock exchanges *for*?

1

Why We Should Care about Finance

In 1976 two professors from the Simon Business School at the University of Rochester in the USA, Michael Jensen and William Meckling, introduced a new phrase to the lexicon of management ideology. 'Agency theory' referred to the relationship that the directors of a firm have with the shareholders, that they act as 'agents' to the shareholders who are 'principals'. Jensen and Meckling saw the firm as a network of contracts, nothing more. The scholars suggested that owner-managed firms offered better returns to shareholders than firms with salaried managers, and that they did so because in the case of owner-managers, the interests of capital and management were neatly aligned. They therefore proposed that managers should be made owners – given a share in the firm. Fourteen years later, with Jensen now at Harvard Business School, these ideas were entering the mainstream. Jensen and his colleague Kevin Murphy penned an influential *Harvard Business Review* article with the strapline 'it's not how much you pay, but how'. How indeed? Chief executives, they urged, should be granted the option to buy shares at knockdown prices if certain targets were reached. 'On average, corporate America pays its most important leaders like bureaucrats', they blustered.[1] The complaint about being paid 'like a bureaucrat' is not a gripe that executives are paid as badly as bureaucrats, because, by 1990, chief executives were already paid vastly more than public servants; it is that bureaucrats are paid *irrespective* of their organization's financial performance. Max Weber, who early on recognized the importance and power of bureaucratic organization, saw this security of tenure as crucial to the disinterested discharge of bureaucratic responsibility.[2] But it did not convince Jensen and Murphy. 'Is it any wonder then,' they continued, 'that so many CEOs act like bureaucrats rather than the value-maximizing entrepreneurs companies need to enhance their standing in world markets?' This was just what America's 'most important leaders' wanted to hear, and chief executives would hardly contradict esteemed business school academics who told them that they were, in fact, underpaid:

> Are we arguing that CEOs are underpaid? If by this we mean 'Would average levels of CEO pay be higher if the relation between pay and performance were stronger?' the answer is yes. More aggressive pay-for-performance systems (and a higher probability of dismissal for poor performance) would produce sharply lower compensation for less talented managers. Over time, these managers would be replaced by more able and more highly motivated executives who would, on average, perform better and earn higher levels of pay.[3]

Without the verbiage – 'Are CEOs underpaid? The answer is yes.'

Agency theory provided the intellectual underpinning for a new class of super-chief executive, whose incentives are all too well aligned with those of their shareholding paymasters, committed to the 'tough choices' that will increase short-term earnings, often at the expense of long-term performance. It is a modern morality tale – to quote the anthropologist Karen Ho – that situates shareholders as victims of managerial sloth and cupidity, needing to be rescued by bankers in the name of 'shareholder value'. As stock markets and remuneration packages began to reward executives for increasing returns on shrinking assets, thus driving up the financial ratios that power share prices, so corporations turned to the strategies that we know today: global outsourcing of manufacturing, often to areas where health and safety concerns and environmental standards are weaker; erosion of worker rights and stepping back from collective responsibilities such as pension provision; gig work and aggressive strategies for maximizing productivity for those who do remain in work. Sociologists Gerald Davis and Suntae Kim put it well:

> Blockbuster Video, which operated over 9,000 stores in 2004 and employed over 80,000 people, has been displaced by Netflix, which streams videos over the Internet, rents capacity on servers owned by Amazon, and employs a mere 2,000 people. Whereas the conglomerate firms of the 1960s and 1970s sought to straddle the Earth, the contemporary share-price-oriented firm seeks to dance on the head of a pin.[4]

The outcome has been steadily rising inequality, both of income and opportunity, with those at the top of corporations earning vast sums while everyone else finds their share eroded. It is not just gig workers and outsourced labourers who suffer, although they suffer most; there is plenty of evidence that white-collar workers and professionals are subject to the same pressures and uncertainties, from the 'purposeful Darwinism' that Amazon deploys to keep its executives overperforming, to the steady ratcheting up of pressure on public sector workers and even academic researchers.[5] An ultra-competitive, quasi-evolutionary theory of work organization lies behind Jensen and Meckling's fanciful claim that fitter, better-performing executives would eventually drive out the wasteful, lazy ones.

Other things have changed, too. As the financial sector's share of national revenue and profits has grown at the expense of manufacturing and other more traditional industries, so, too, have the career aspirations of our most talented youngsters moved. Careers in the productive economy are unfashionable compared to those in technology and finance. Four decades ago, bright young people wanting to change the world might have joined a non-governmental organization (NGO) or the United Nations (UN). Now they found a start-up and chase an IPO – an initial public offer, when the firm launches on a stock exchange and new shareholders' money rains down on founders and early investors. Even the chief executives of manufacturing corporations are bored of the minutiae of production. Firms have become increasingly involved in financial activities – take car manufacturer Tesla's 2021 purchase of $1 billion worth of cryptocurrency – and the doing of 'deals', a rhetoric of business that is firmly embedded in exchange rather than production, and now freely circulating in the political sphere. Moralized discourses of finance 'giving back' have opened new vistas for finance. So-called 'philanthrocapitalism' targets social impact projects, with returns triggered when the target population hits certain milestones. Society is turned inside out: prison inmates, young offenders or members of whatever social stratum is considered undesirable become recast as potential investments, no longer costs but profit centres. Sometimes the action shifts away from productive activity altogether: 'platform' businesses such as Uber and Airbnb invest huge resources drawn from shareholders purely to secure a monopoly position, and at the same time engage in a speculative financial business plan that centres on lucrative offerings on the stock exchange.

The 1970s and 1980s – the very period that gave rise to this shareholder capitalism – saw not a resurgence of individual shareholder democracy but a sustained shift to institutional ownership. In 1952, for example, although 90 per cent of the US stock market was held by individuals, these stockholders represented a mere 4 per cent of the population. In 2018 roughly half of the US population held stock, but only one-third of the market was directly owned by individuals. The picture in the UK is similar, with a prolonged fall in direct ownership of shares.[6] In other words, although many of us are invested in the financial market system, we do so indirectly through a new class of intermediary institutions, insurance and wealth management companies. This concentration of voting power in the hands of a few huge fund managers has only sharpened the commitment to shareholder value.

It is no surprise that the contemporary corporation, disciplined by external pressure, actively pursues what economists call 'rents'. These are profits derived from monopoly positions, comfortable contracts or ownership of scarce resources. Geographer Brett Christophers argues that *every single one* of the 30 largest companies quoted on the UK stock market receives rents: 'rent is what the companies are all designed to generate; rent is their shared raison d'être, and rentierism is embedded in their individual and collective DNA.'[7] Rent is nothing new: Thomas Piketty pointed out that rentier economies flourished in the past, especially in the late 19th century, in the world of Balzac, Austen and Trollope, where social status, annual income and total assets were linked by such a cast-iron formula that a character could infer the whole from a statement such as 'in possession of £10,000 a year'. What is new is our acquiescence to the return of this rentier economy and our blindness to the unfairness, even violence, that lurks beneath its surface. Piketty shows us that a rentier economy is characterized by rigidity and lack of social mobility, as the return on capital will always be higher than the return on productive economic activity.[8] Historically, corporate rent was backed by colonial and military might: India's railways, for example, were financed on such egregious terms that British investors received a century of rents, guaranteed by the Indian taxpayer. In modern times the pursuit of rent remains a moment of unfairness and extraction, facilitated by regulation, political influence and sheer financial power.

The stock exchange is in the thick of these transformations. It is the fulcrum through which extractions and inequalities are enacted, a pivot point in the siege warfare between those who have capital and those who do not. Chief executives of these giant firms are remunerated for delivering shareholder value in the form of steadily rising share prices and dividend streams. Investors like predictability, which fundamentally clashes with the notion of risk inherent in an entrepreneurial business. According to the textbooks, entrepreneurs earn money *because* of risk. Generating predictable, long-term, above-average profits is only possible by taking a share from someone else: establishing a monopoly over supply and overcharging customers, paying wages below an acceptable level, avoiding taxes, health and safety, or passing on environmental costs. This is how our finance-driven economy works: gig workers carry all the risk, as do self-invested pension holders, while their employer carries none; when mortgages are rolled together and sold on, risk moves away from the lender but a chunk of profit remains; and, in the case of the 'social impact bond', it is the recidivist who shoulders the real risk of these novel financial arrangements. When polluting industry shifts to the Global South, it is citizens there who carry the costs, not to mention the environment itself. Problems manifest close to home, too. The abject failure of the privatized energy market in Britain, now unable to cope with a supply crisis and promising a winter of hardship not seen since the end of the Second World War, is a story that begins with the privatization of British Gas in 1986 and British Petroleum in 1987 (we pick this up in Chapter 5). In the summer of 2022, as I review the final draft of this book, the media announces that Britain faces a drought while two-and-a-half billion litres leak from the water system daily. We have finally exhausted a nature-given water buffer that has allowed companies to underinvest and overextract, passing their costs on to the environment.[9] These things and more – these are why we should care about finance.

★★★

Drought is an apt metaphor. Fernand Braudel, one of the great historians of the 20th century, argued that the eruption of finance capital as a dominant economic form is always a sign of economic autumn.[10] It is the browning of business' leaves where once there was green; a decadent, golden display of decay in place of purposeful, shooting vigour. It is an era in which a loss-making taxi firm – a taxi firm! – can be worth nearly $100 billion, more than the GDP of Luxembourg. It is not only the present moment that witnesses these kinds of transformation. Theorist Giorgio Arrighi understood this process of flourishing and decay to be iterative, with century-and-a-bit cycles of capitalism each culminating in a period of exuberance in the financial economy. There was, he writes,

> a Genoese cycle, from the fifteenth to the early seventeenth centuries; a Dutch cycle, from the late sixteenth century through most of the eighteenth century; a British cycle from the latter half of the eighteenth century through the early twentieth century; and the US cycle, which began in the late nineteenth century and has continued into the current phase of financial expansion.[11]

The Liverpool-based transatlantic triangle underpinned the British 'long century', kick-starting the British Industrial Revolution with demand for manufactured goods and the cash needed to establish new factories and infrastructure.

Such theorists see finance's flight to immateriality as an inevitable step in the evolution of capitalism. As returns on productive activities begin to tail off, so finance finds ways to feed off itself, accelerating and detaching from the 'real' economy. We witness, writes Fredric Jameson, 'the withdrawal of profits from home industries, the increasingly feverish search for new kinds of profits available in financial transactions.... Capital itself becomes free-floating, it separates from the concrete context of its productive geography.'[12] There is something unreal about this new form of accumulation, something hollowed out, exhausted and feverish: 'spectres of value ... vying against each other in a vast, worldwide, disembodied phantasmagoria ... capital exhausts its returns in the new national and international capitalist zone and seeks to die and be reborn in some "higher" incarnation, a vaster and immeasurably more productive one.'[13] These are the 'spectres of the Atlantic' that Baucom traces through the slavers' accounting books, or the phantasmagorical images of predatory mortgages, flitting between traders' terminals in Wall Street.

The notion of finance as spectral, somewhere else, somewhere 'other', is surprisingly common. Theorists often reach for Gilles Deleuze and Felix Guattari's concepts of 'nomads' and 'war machines' roaming in 'smooth space' to capture how capital flows above and beyond nation states and geographical boundaries, disembedded from the world and unchecked, often perceived as hostile in its intent, conducting a class war of the global elite (them, elsewhere) against the rest of us, now and here. Fernand Braudel thought of the economy as multitiered: above the elementary economy of subsistence production, above even the market economy of industrial production, there exists the 'zone of the anti-market, where the great predators roam and the law of the jungle operates. This – today as in the past, before and after the Industrial Revolution – is the real home of capitalism.'[14] Even great Marxist theorists are not immune from machismo characterizations of the financial world.

There are two problems with all this. The first, as I have already made clear, is that finance is embedded in institutions – of which the stock exchange is the preeminent example – and these institutions are themselves bound up with material architectures and technologies as well as social practices and bodies. If finance is a spectre, it is the kind that flies from wires in the theatre; the zombie that walks by cogs and wheels, not occult inscriptions.

The second problem is that Marxist theorists are just too serious. Over the last few years I have presented my research many times. I have tried to position it as a focus on the innovations and possibilities of finance, or on the diabolical expropriations of which it has been guilty. All these are valid. When I tell the stories, however, they always come out the same way. Often, they are just funny, the characters as eccentric and ridiculous as one might find in any other office or profession. Some are thoughtful and virtuous, some hardworking and dull, others vainglorious and hubristic. For all the extraordinary technical invention, there is nothing really new. Sometimes things work, and sometimes they do not. Sociologist Donald MacKenzie shows us how engineers' efforts to get prices from New York to Chicago at the speed of light are thwarted, periodically, by the tides in Lake Michigan and by the rain.[15] These same things that bedevilled navigators in renaissance Europe. Tides, rain, and bandits troubled them too. From that nuisance came modern banking. In more recent times we see the best paid, biggest brains on the planet, the self-anointed 'Masters of the Universe', sending the international police to a London suburb so that they might arrest an autistic man still living with his parents. This 'Hound of Hounslow' (we will come back to him in Chapter 13) was charged with bringing the US markets to a halt. One can scarcely believe it to be possible.

Finance is often a theatre of the absurd. It is our failing that we take it so seriously, and that in doing so we have let it get out of hand. By presenting finance as a monolithic entity taking over the world, we perversely dignify it. It works! The machine does what its dastardly commanders tell it! Yet the distinguishing characteristic of finance, both in my research and in my lived experience, is its *ineffectiveness*. It is disorderly in nature and teeters around failure, narrowly averted most of the time, occasionally catastrophic. Despite its disastrous consequences – its central role in environmental catastrophe, inequality, the hollowing out of productive industry and the nation state – finance is hardly the stuff of the grand plan, the global cabal. Some of it is good, some bad; it is the summed-up outcome of complex histories, technological developments and the many-sided ambitions and projects of its protagonists. It is also wrong to claim that finance is simply amoral. As we will see throughout this book, financial markets have their own moralities, specific to their situation, embedded in culture and in the architectures and technologies of the markets. Even financialization, as the anthropologist Kimberly Chong has shown, is an ethical position.[16]

Where finance *does* truly succeed, I think, is in its ability to tell a story about itself. Its greatest strength is rhetoric. Finance is a cultural phenomenon as much as it is a material one. And if finance's success, its power, comes from its ability to make us take it seriously, laughter is the method of critique we need.[17] How else can we face a figure like Elon Musk, in whom finance, culture and technology so thoroughly fuse? Actually-existing finance is a comedic affair. Take the Royal Bank of Scotland (RBS), in 2007 the largest corporation in the world, commandeering an RAF flyby and a royal visit for the opening of its new office complex in a business park outside Edinburgh, an office in which Fred Goodwin, the chief executive, would berate cleaners for vacuuming the boardroom carpet against the weave. It is hubristic, and ultimately disastrous (by 2009 the bank was bust, Goodwin stripped of his knighthood) but also just plain funny. The difficulty, of course, is that at the same time finance is not funny at all. For all Musk's oversized social media-friendly persona, many investors who followed him into cryptocurrency lost fortunes. RBS' new office was funded by the bank's enthusiastic participation in the mortgage bond market, which condemned the UK to a decade of austerity. The Zong trial, the slavers' credit notes and the horrors that underly them: absurd and incomprehensible, but not funny. We must tread lightly. But humour can do one thing at least: it can help us make strange a phenomenon that has become so normal in our world.

★★★

This is my story too. The final weeks of 1999, the closing moments of the long and tumultuous 20th century, and in many ways a pivotal moment of our story, found me sitting in a scruffy office in then still scruffy Southwark, across the water from the steel and glass of the City of London, patiently compiling a section of book excerpts for the Christmas issue of the stocks and shares magazine that employed me.[18] It was all there, snippets from 'The Art of War', from Benjamin Graham, from Edwin Lefevre, even (forgive me!) Tom Wolfe. The editor was delighted, for it filled several pages very cheaply and did something that an entire issue's worth of stock reporting could not have done. It conveyed a sense of the excitement and danger of the markets, and that any punter reading the magazine and in possession of some corporate paper belonged to a continuum of financial buccaneers stretching right back to the dawn of finance – the warrior! The speculator! The 'Master of the Universe'!!!

Critics fret that we have been unable to transcend 'the limits of financial imagination'.[19] In 1999, however, that imagination seemed unlimited. History had ended, the existential threat of nuclear war had receded, the twin towers still stood, and Tony Blair's New Labour government had not yet lost its shine. The move to a more financial economy, with all that it entailed, had not really started to bite; at least, we had not yet noticed. Globalization pointed to a world of open borders. Ideas were grandiose – technological optimism, prosperity, freedom – and British cultural iconography saw no contradiction between the Europhilia of Joanne Harris' *Chocolat* and the 'Cool Britannia' of Geri Halliwell's dress. We – at least the parts of the UK that were invited to the party, mostly metropolitan or suburban, educated and increasingly affluent – stood at the head of nearly a decade of continuous economic growth, cheap money and a stock market boom that ran to the spring of 2000. Once again, business school academics were in the thick of it. I have somewhere a book by a pair of Swedish business guru-academics called *Funky Business: Talent Makes Capital Dance*.[20] On the book's cover they butted their bald, bespectacled heads. Marx was right, they reckoned: the workers had finally taken hold of the mechanism of production.

It is my story, then, because I inhabit the later pages of the book, a younger, plumper, naive version of myself, an autoethnography so thinly remembered that it borders on fiction. But also because it is my book, the sentences laboriously picked out, word by word, an effort in world-making, for *writing*, as even a foolish 20-something stocks and shares hack knew perfectly well, is always also *doing*. Finance depends on this ongoing work of storytelling, 'the constant reweaving of a phenomenally complex shared fiction about social value, a network of mutually supportive … stories about the world'.[21] Alongside the everyday fictions of the dollar bill, the mortgage bond or even the crypto hoard there is another tapestry of imaginings, of futurity and possibility that shapes the economic domain.

The texts I so carefully assembled into the magazine's Christmas section were snippets of 'financial print culture', a literary form that emerged in parallel with the excesses of high finance in the 1980s. It is epitomized in the journalistic genre by Michael Lewis' *Liar's Poker* and in the fiction of Tom Wolfe's *Bonfire of the Vanities* and Oliver Stone's film *Wall Street*. This mode of narrative has done much to entrench the position of finance as a complex, risky endeavour, necessarily the preserve of male, white elites. Through business autobiographies such as Donald Trump's *The Art of the Deal* it has shaped the political framing of the contemporary world. Not even literary fiction escapes. Literature scholar Paul Crosthwaite argues that capitalist logic subsumes every cultural space; the encyclopaedic novels of David Foster Wallace, Thomas Pynchon and Iain Sinclair offer a literary reflection of the all-knowing, all-consuming market.[22] The stock exchange is ubiquitous – not just an institution embedded in history, geography, politics and ideology, but also an idea and an ideology. It is a story, and if we want to change it, we must tell a better one.

It has been said that capitalism's strength lies in its realism, that it corrodes the imagination through 'an attitude – a grim identification of the rule of markets with necessity, practicality, and hard-nosed common sense'.[23] William Roscoe, abolitionist and banker, showed that need not be the case. Although he was horrified by the cruelty of the bodily trade, he could not escape the patterns of capital that underpinned it. He owed his legal practice and his bank to that capital. The very livelihood of his city depended on it. Yet he voted for abolition and faced physical reprisals for doing so. He tackled slavers' manacles with words and – of all things – poetry. It strikes me that Roscoe's position was not so far from that of the critical academic in a contemporary business school: seeking to give voice to the injustices that flow directly from the system that pays our salaries. Alas, he was much braver than us. We play the game, warily, ironically, but we play it all the same. He faced the slave trade and, at great personal cost – beaten by dockers, forced out of Parliament, eventually bankrupt – helped to destroy it. He had principles. Do we, in the business school? I am not so sure.

As our world faces crisis on crisis, we scholars bear part of a collective responsibility for the trouble our discipline has caused. Agency theory, human capital theory, asset pricing and financial economics, cost-benefit analysis, scientific management – so many moments of modern misery owe their origins to the business school.[24] These ideas fail because they are determined to do things at arm's length, trying to construct a dispassionate science of administration abstracted from particularity.[25] I would like to try something different, something a little bit 'gonzo', a more-or-less telling of stories as the best way we have of finding our moral compass in this complicated world. Stories of success and failure; of innovation and accident; of generosity and meanness; stories told with fascination, sometimes with affection, sometimes with shame. We do not have long to make amends, but there may yet be different ways of doing, if only we can discover them and give them voice, telling better stories about how the world might be. It will be difficult, but that is not to say we should not try.

PART I

How the Markets Became

2

From Future Pigs to Present Prices, a Chicago Story

'Heedless of all these things, the men upon the floor were going about their work. Neither squeals of hogs nor tears of visitors made any difference.... It was all so very business-like that one watched it fascinated. It was pork making by machinery, pork making by applied mathematics....' So wrote Upton Sinclair of the huge stock houses in 19th-century Chicago.[1] *The Jungle*, Sinclair's muckraking exposé of industrial pork production and exploited labour, takes us to the beginnings of a new kind of market, a distinctively modern, technological, Chicago affair. By the early 20th century, Chicago was the biggest railway hub in the USA and the gateway to the agrarian West. At its peak this heartless pork-making by applied mathematics chewed its way through 13 million animals every year. Caitlin Zaloom, an anthropologist who has studied the growth of Chicago's financial markets, writes that the 'disassembly line' was 'an important inspiration for a later industrialist, Henry Ford, who mimicked this orderly model of death and dismemberment in his automobile plants. His admiration focused particularly on the meatpacking industry's refined division of labour, the intricate order behind the foaming rivers of blood that ran through the slaughterhouses.'[2] The stockyards supplied canned products across the USA and gave rise to appalling environmental conditions closer to home:

> ... the residents would explain, quietly, that all this was 'made' land, and that it had been 'made' by using it as a dumping ground for the city garbage. After a few years the unpleasant effect of this would pass away, it was said; but meantime, in hot weather – and especially when it rained – the flies were apt to be annoying. Was it not unhealthful? the stranger would ask, and the residents would answer, Perhaps; but there is no telling.[3]

The stockyards created immense wealth: so much money, so much energy, so much filth. All called for civic action, and April 1848 saw the foundation of the Chicago Board of Trade. Its founders were prominent businessmen and politicians, and it was set up to enhance the city's stature, cementing Chicago's position as a national centre for trade. They built a headquarters in the centre of the city and sought to shape the urban architecture in such a way that products could flow in and out more easily; visiting Chicago you sense that that it was not built as a city for people. Nonetheless, as the Board's influence spread, and with it the volume of trade, members encountered a problem. America is big, the Midwest vast. Even with modern communications it takes a while to get around, and in the late 19th century, things travelled much more slowly.

Chicago's other great interest was in grain, and the Board sought to streamline the processes of this trade. River barges hauled the grain to the city, where new machinery helped to move the bulk commodity into huge storage towers, or elevators. Standard measures and qualities allowed the stored grain to be traded by way of warehouse receipts, only being moved when it was needed. Still, there remained obstacles to profitable commerce. In the case of grain there was a natural temporal mismatch between supply – the annual harvest – and constant demand. Merchants profited from buying the grain, storing it and reselling it, but at the same time they tied up capital and exposed themselves to the risk of changing prices. To deal with this problem, a new kind of contract appeared. In 1851 and 1852 members began trading 'to arrive' contracts, where counterparties agreed a present sale for future delivery. These were futures contracts, the deal made at a discounted price to compensate for the risk that was being traded alongside the corn. There was a similarity between the structure of these deals and the slavers' bills of exchange. Futures trading had been practised in the bourses, or stock exchanges, of Antwerp, Amsterdam and London since the late 17th century, but the model for Chicago's contracts came from Liverpool, where the cotton traders employed similar devices to manage risk and free up capital.[4] Their form has shaped futures trading ever since and makes another link in the grim genealogy of contemporary high finance.

The grain futures were still, at this point, contracts directly made between counterparties and based on the expectation that goods would arrive. Yet the beauty of these contracts was that they could be traded absent the physical commodities to which they referred. Despite their name, goods never actually had to arrive, and the contracts could be settled in cash. They were 'derivatives' – a kind of security derived from, or based on, something else. As soon as the financial contracts were unhitched from the commodities that they represented, a speculative market began to develop. Alongside those who needed to buy and sell winter wheat or pork bellies stood those who had no interest in supplying the commodity or consuming it but sought to make a living purely from the fluctuating price of the contract. So many new speculators began to participate that the Board was forced to impose formal regulation, and in 1865 it introduced standard terms, margin deposits and restricted futures trading to members of the exchange. These are common characteristics of contemporary futures markets, and once again, the Board followed the lead of the Liverpool Cotton Brokers Association, which regulated its futures market in 1864.[5] Self-regulation was only partially effective, however, and futures trading remained a specialist and somewhat disreputable occupation.

Fernand Braudel and Fredric Jameson wrote of capital's ever-present urge to disassociate itself from the cumbersome materiality of trade or productive industry and to circulate more swiftly in the realm of financial abstraction. So it was in 19th-century Chicago. Speculation is tricky if you have actual commodities to deal with, and almost impossible if those commodities are heavy, perishable or in need of feed and water. The new security, made up of legal contracts rather than bristle and oink, could be passed around much more easily. The market could bring a thousand bushels of wheat into Chicago without moving them from Kansas, could sell them to a man in New York, to another in Baltimore, and to a third back in Kansas who actually intended to use the grain. Markets bend space by transacting in the simulacra of commodities. They compress time, too, selling the summer's harvest while it is still under the snow of the plains. Contracts proliferate, circulate, are bought and sold, then settled by cash; fortunes are won or lost, and all the while the grain lies in the elevator. The Board flourished and speculators, unconcerned with the hard business of raising pigs or growing wheat, soon come to dominate the market, their capital making them far more influential than simple buyers and sellers. Not everyone thought this a good thing. Frank Norris' classic Chicago novel *The Pit*, published in 1902, concerns one such speculator and his attempt to corner the wheat market – that is, to own the rights to every bushel of wheat in the entire nation. Norris portrays the battle of man versus market as an elemental affair, the swashbuckling trader against the forces of nature herself. In fiction, hubris reaps its reward, while in real life the legitimacy of the speculators remained deeply suspect until early in the 20th century.

***

Capital cannot fly unsupported, despite what its keenest supporters and fiercest critics might say. The new market depended on a material infrastructure that spilled out throughout the western plains: the city's stockyards and grain elevators, the canals and railways, and the telegraph, its cables laid alongside the spreading railways and corralling a whole nation's agriculture into a single room. In fact, it was the new technology of the telegraph that made the market possible, just one of many market transformations driven by technological progress.

Sociologist Alex Preda has investigated how developing methods of communication reshaped markets into the structures that we recognize today.[6] Before the advent of the stock ticker, markets had been jumbled up. Merchants mixed stock trading with other ventures, even as markets spread across the Atlantic. Preda quotes a letter, from one Richard Irvine, of New York, to J.A. Wiggins, in London, in 1872. The author slips a few choice stock quotations into a communication concerning equally choice apples, peaches and oysters:

> We have shipped to you care of Messrs Lampard and Holt, by this steamer, the apples you ordered in your favour of the 20th September last. We are assured that peaches and oysters are of the best quality, and trust they will prove so. Below we give you memo of their cost to your debit.

In other words, here is some fruit, some fish, and here is the bill. Irvine continues:

> We think it is well to mention that First Mortgage 6% Gold Chesapeake and Ohio Railroad bonds can now be bought here to a limited amount at 86% and accrued interest. They are well thought of by investors, and were originally marketed by the company's agents as high as 14% and interest. We enclose today's stock quotations.[7]

When we seek early market technologies, we find letters like this. The letter holds the market together and at the same time tangles it up with all sorts of extraneous material. Our apples and peaches are good, says the merchant, so try our railroad bonds.

The jumble did not stop there. Irvine would have purchased the bonds at the New York Stock Exchange, an institution that ran two different markets simultaneously, one formal and one informal, one regular and the other chaotic. Traders of the formal market – called the Regular Board – sat inside the exchange, wearing top hats and tailcoats, and called out prices in a prescribed order. Those in the informal market – the Open Board – stood in the street where they mingled with the general public. Most of the business was done in the street. But letters, promises, noise and chaos worked; they made up a market powered by social relationships. At the very least, they were fit for purpose, if that purpose was hanging on to clients and keeping business going, and they suited merchants mixing – as many did – stock trading with a more general inventory. But persistent worries about market manipulation, whether in the USA, Europe or Great Britain, were symptomatic of concerns on the part of outsiders that real participation in the market required an actual physical presence in the market's places.

The stock ticker changed everything. Invented by an engineer named Edward Calahan, who had himself started out as a market messenger boy, the ticker tape used the telegraph network to transmit prices, tapping them out on a long roll of paper, those same paper streamers thrown onto returning astronauts and sporting heroes in the heyday of the 20th century. Despite technological difficulties – jammed wheels and batteries comprising large jars of sulphuric acid – the ticker quickly caught on. By 1905, 23,000 brokers' offices subscribed to the ticker. These offices were spaces for investors to gather, to gossip and to consult the code books necessary to decipher the orders transmitted across the tape. Preda gives one example, 'army event bandit calmly', which somehow translates as 'Cannot sell Canada Southern at your limit, reduce limit to 23.' Brokers' rooms became part of the market's place and remained a feature of stockbrokers' offices until relatively recently – my colleague Yu-Hsiang Chen visited Taiwanese brokers' rooms just a few years ago, and found a social technology in its final days, slowly being displaced by electronic messenger services, apps and the internet. Back in 1902, Norris highlights the moral ambiguity of speculation through a sharp, unflattering description of a broker's room. It is a place of ruin, filled with nondescript, shabbily dressed men with tired eyes and unhealthy complexions, as the telegraph key clicks unsteady and incessant in the background.[8]

The ticker brings the market into being in a completely new way. It chatters as the market buzzes and falls silent as trading slows. It moves relationships away from people and into machines. We no longer need to trust that our apple and peach seller is giving us good investment information when we can simply read the tape. It opens up the market. There are no longer insiders, those able to mingle in the street or sit top-hatted on the Regular Board, and everyone else, always disadvantaged by an outsider status. Now everyone can participate on a relatively equal basis, although the ticker also gave rise to the phenomenon of bucket shops, which we will come to in the next chapter. The fact that the ticker was a machine, the high-tech of the day, made the markets seem objective and rational. It cast speculation as scientific and reputable as opposed to a game of chance. Its chatter and arcane codes provided a new space for thinking about and representing market action. The stock market classic *Reminiscences of a Stock Operator* by Edwin Lefèvre (the very same included in my Christmas share-pickers' selection) talks at length about learning to read the tape, a task Lefèvre regards as being the necessary basis for any success: the tape can show the market 'up close', even from a distance.[9] Often, the tape is Lefèvre's metaphor for the market as a whole. The tape does not care why, he says, or the business of the tape is today, not tomorrow. Literary scholar Peter Knight notices

> how often the dramas of Wall Street are illustrated (both visually and verbally) not with noisy scenes of crowds and mass hysteria but with small-scale scenes of concentrated reading. Again and again these tales of fortunes won and lost are depicted in their most dramatic moments by scenes of men (and it is nearly always men) poring over the ticker tape that pours into the waste paper basket.[10]

Lefèvre's fictionalized hero, Jesse Livermore, epitomizes the discipline, concentration and cool, masculine detachment necessary to master reading the tape. His task is to discern patterns in the chatter, to ascertain meaningful action from market noise. Those who lacked the superhuman concentration necessary to manage these numbers in their minds could draw graphs, and the stock-picking strategy of technical analysis, or 'charting', still popular today, has its roots in the stream of prices emerging from the tape. Reading the tape, investment manuals asserted, was a scientific mechanism of forecasting; those wishing to engage in the market have to treat it appropriately, casting away notions of a market built out of personal relationships and instead participating at a distance, through proper, technical practices.[11]

For this new scientific forecasting to even be possible, time itself had to be organized. In the chaos of the open board, where messenger boys carried news on paper slips, market time had been 'ragged', with 'irregular intervals, parallel times, and holes', disrupted and discontinuous.[12] The ticker imposes time. It brings speed and direction into the market. It is suddenly possible to say that a stock is going up or down; that it is moving swiftly or slowly. New kinds of speculative practice become possible, chasing a price movement, or sparking action where there was none. Preda records an anecdote of a group of speculators dropping orders for Southern Railway into a quiet market:

> When all these trades appeared on the tape and in such an absolutely dead market, it did look as if something had started. Here was a chance for some of the thousands of people sitting around hundreds of tickers all over the country to get a little action. Outside buying orders started to come into the crowd; in a few minutes Southern Railway was up a point and a half.[13]

The ticker transcends space, turning a chaotic, confused cluster of market*places* into a single, orderly, measured market. Its regular patterns live on in the scrolling horizontal stock price displays that you see outside buildings or rolling across the bottom of television screens. In our present time, when market trades are completed in microseconds, the gently rolling ticker is an epistemological absurdity, but it remains a universal representation of the stock market.

All the same, the ticker's aura of rationality and objectivity was only superficial. For Knight, the 'mechanised, depersonalised financial imaginary in this period is continually haunted by the glimmerings of a quasi-human intentionality – sometimes conspiratorial at other times supernatural – behind the invisible hand of impersonal market coordination'. The machinelike trance into which the speculator sinks as he reads the tape is that of the oracle rather than the technician. He is hypnotized, and possessed, entering into the realm of 'free-floating capital' with 'specters of value … vying against each other in a vast, world-wide, disembodied phantasmagoria.'[14] The market is both rational and occult, the ticker tape not so different from the 'talking boards' and other tools of the séance, so popular in 19th-century society. The phantasms of the market, its bad magic, lurk not far behind the reliable, scientific mechanism of the ticker.

★★★

In those miserable hogs, and the (almost) equally miserable workforce that hacked and scraped in a systematized division of labour that would have horrified Adam Smith's impartial spectator, we see the beginnings of the Chicago Board of Trade, soon to become one of the mightiest financial markets on the globe. New rules, measures and contracts made possible a speculative trade in financial instruments only indirectly related to the underlying commodities. The reliable, automated stock ticker made market time regular and became a new site for market action: speed and direction are suddenly visible, and with them profit. It encouraged a new persona in the market, the cool, ruthless market speculator, whose self-discipline and objectivity allowed him to triumph over weaker adversaries, dimly discerned through the chatter of the tape.

Chicago became a national market not just because goods arrived on railways; information followed the same tracks. The ticker had created a new entity, the 'market', but this market still needed a place. Buyers could not, in the end, meet sellers purely within the confines of the tape. As the railways and the telegraph system brought the economic world into Chicago, the Board of Trade provided such a place, a series of increasingly huge trading rooms housed in a succession of ever more grand buildings. So connected, the market became a single entity, its tendrils running out from the great metropolis until they encompassed the whole globe. The pit gave Norris' book its name, and he characterizes it as a monstrous whirlpool, a force of nature; the speculator, in seeking to tame the market, is wrestling an elemental power. A more prosaic metaphor, admittedly one out of reach of a 19th-century novelist, might be that the pit was the processing unit of the humming human computer that made the market work. Its signals *were* the market: orders went into the pit, and prices came out.

The pit was a simple structure, an octagonal stepped ring set into the floor. At first traders had stood in crowds in the Board's trading room, but it was hard to see over the heads of the crowd so some took to moving furniture and climbing on desks to get a better view. In 1870 this workaround was formalized and the octagonal pits were first introduced. The pits formed the heart of a new building in 1885, a monument to the civic power of finance with figures of Agriculture, Commerce, Fortune and Order decorating the trading room. Soon, trade outgrew the architecture and the Board commissioned a new building, the Art Deco monolith that still looms over LaSalle Street. The pit-powered trading room dominated this building too. It was a vast open space, as designers by now understood that uninterrupted lines of sight were crucial to the functioning of the market. The world flowed into the room through the newest communication technologies imaginable: the telegraph, pneumatic tubes, even telephones. The new building, completed in 1930, manifests the industrial modernity and bling of Art Deco: as Zaloom cannily notes, machined-finished, stylized images of plants and flowers bear the same relation to nature as the futures contracts, one step removed from the real thing.[15] We might say that the building's form represents the existential presuppositions of the business at hand; its architectural imagery is far more concerned with the mechanical processes of commodity production and transport than the earthy business of growing things that lies behind them.

These stepped, octagonal spaces were soon found across the world. Their basic organization had changed little by the time Zaloom and others visited them in the 1980s and 1990s. A bell sounded to open and close trading, deepening liquidity by compressing orders into a short period of time. Every bid or offer – every attempt to buy or sell – had by law to be shouted out into the pit. Runners brought orders into the pit and carried trade records out to be stamped and recorded, while traders did battle to outwit their fellows and take home a profit. A pit trader did not need to know economics or commodity forecasts. Those things were translated into the orders pouring in from outside. They simply knew how to trade. They read faces and sought fear or weakness in the shouts of their rivals. It was enormously physical work, pushing, shouting and gesticulating, using a complicated system of hand gestures that had evolved over the previous century. A trader buying would turn his palms to his body, while palms out signalled a sale. Fingers could denote the final unit of the price; everybody knew the rest of the number so there was no need to count it out each time. The prices that returned from the pit to the outside world necessarily lagged behind the sharpest prices in the centre of the melee, but flow out they did, back through the ticker and into the brokers' rooms of the nation where the real-life counterparts of Livermore and Jadwin waited, ready to take their chance. Photographs of trading pits towards the end of the day invariably show a confetti of dealing slips and messages, the physical detritus of the passage of prices through this extraordinary human computer.

Zaloom notes the sheer size of some of these men, some big enough to be American football players, others with built-up soles – a cobbler in the building's basement fitted deep heels to the shoes of shorter traders. Traders talked about learning to control their voices, sharp enough to carry across the pit but not so sharp as to show panic, and to coordinate their shouts with jumps and looks. The rhythms of the pit signify rising or falling, and the ambient noise shows the depth of trade. Trading must be immediate, intuitive: 'In training their bodies as instruments of both reception and delivery of the underlying information of market numbers, the first step is learning not to calculate.'[16] This anti-rationality is more akin to the tape-reader's trance than the dispassionate and rational speculator, and an essential connectedness with the rhythms of the markets had always been the *sine qua non* of the pit trader. In Norris' novel one protagonist would 'feel – almost at his very finger tips – how this market moved, how it strengthened, how it weakened. He knew just when to nurse it, to humor it, to let it settle, and when to crowd it, when to hustle it, when it would stand rough handling'.[17]

Of course, such primal, embodied trading demands a personality to match, and Zaloom found the traders constructing for themselves hyper-masculine, profane, even debauched behaviours. She records arguments and even physical fights, as does the sociologist Donald MacKenzie, who visited Chicago's pits in 2000. One trader showed MacKenzie his spectacles, covered with flecks of spittle after a day of trading; another recalled that he could lift his feet off the ground and be suspended between the bodies of those pressed against him. Traders may not have been friends, but they worked together day after day, year after year. Their knowledge of each other's habits and tactics was the basis of their trading: 'In the pits,' writes Zaloom, 'social information is founded in deep knowledge of the local environment. Traders organize trading strategies with the situations and motivations of their particular competitors and compatriots in mind.'[18]

It would be a mistake, however, to think of this scrum as anarchic. The trading pits were organized and governed by complex social norms and procedures. More senior traders, often those prepared to commit to bigger, more risky trades, worked their way to the front of the pit where they enjoyed better visibility and the advantages that came with it. Traders had to be prepared to take on losses, dealing with brokers or fellow market-makers struggling to unload a position, a favour that would be reciprocated another day. Those in the pit would respect its politics and status, organizing themselves according to its invisible hierarchies. But most of all, those in the pit would honour their bargains even though these were simple, spoken agreements. Failure to do so, or indeed to comply with any of these routines, would result in exclusion from future trades. In a now classic study the sociologist Wayne Baker showed how these behavioural patterns governed the ideal size of a pit; while economic theory would suggest that a bigger crowd would provide more liquidity and better prices, Baker showed that social controls failed if the crowd became too large, and the whole pit suffered.[19] Such social controls were necessary to protect the integrity of the central characteristic of the market, unchanged for a century and from which all else follows: the acceptance of a spoken trade as a solid contract.

Both Zaloom and MacKenzie caution us not to romanticize the pits. Scratchy voices and worn-out bodies, financial ruin and even tragic stories of suicide formed the background hum to the in-your-face noise of the pit itself. Moreover, it is not clear how cleanly the human computer worked. 'The subtle webs of reciprocity and trust needed to keep open outcry trading flowing smoothly,' writes MacKenzie, 'could turn into informal cartels that operated to the disadvantage of other pit traders or external customers.' Social relationships, the very things that kept the market running, might all too easily lead it away from the longed for – although never achieved – goal of efficient market function.[20]

You can see this world, perhaps a caricature but still well observed, at work in the finale of the 1980s comedy *Trading Places*. The verbal deals made by the heroes are concrete enough to bankrupt the villains after a failed corner in frozen concentrated orange juice, of all things. There are clocks and bells, runners and time stamps, and when trading ends, a deserted pit strewn with paper. There are off-colour jokes about stress and ulcers. Some things are wrong. It is impossible to imagine that two strangers could elbow their way to the centre of a pit and trade with total strangers, but it remains a sharp portrait of a technology that had persisted fundamentally unchanged for over one hundred years. A confluence of political change, economic development and new technologies created the pits, in the Board's grand trading rooms and elsewhere, and we will later see how another political moment, together with new and better technologies, made the trading pits redundant. For now, we have taken the first step in de-mystifying the stock exchange, peeling back the surface of the illusion to show it as an institution embedded in history, technology and the often quite banal concerns of businessmen in an earlier age. Our next task is to explore the complex and uneasy relationship of nation states and stock exchanges, a story that takes us back to the hubbub and grime of 17th-century London.

3

King William's Overdraft

On 6 May 2010, the day of the General Election in the UK, Prime Minister Gordon Brown was voted out of power and 13 years of 'New Labour' dominance in UK politics came to an end. The country, still reeling from the near collapse of the global financial system and tired of petty squabbles among the government, moved for change.

It was neither a decisive defeat for Brown, nor a victory for anyone else. David Cameron, leader of the Conservative Party, looked set to form a minority government. Stock markets seesawed with anxiety, posting big losses on the morning after the election. Markets like certainty, the pundits said, so Cameron did something else: he made Nick Clegg and the Liberal Democrats party a 'big, open and comprehensive offer' to share in a coalition government. Such moments matter. Political commentator John Rentoul, writing in the *Independent*, wonders how things might have gone differently; he sketches out an alternative story where Clegg joins forces with a Labour Party revived by new leadership. 'If Clegg had made a different choice,' he writes, 'we would be living in a different country now: slightly better off, with better public services, and probably still in the EU.'[1] Probably. But I am not sure that Clegg *could* have said no.

My recollection of those moments is the extraordinary prominence given to the sentiments of the financial markets. It seemed that the force driving politicians to set up this bizarre, ideologically incompatible coalition – one that would ultimately destroy the Liberal Democrats as a third party in British politics – was not a concern to properly serve the British electorate and represent its wishes, but an overwhelming need to pacify the markets. This was certainly how it was reported during the tense days that followed the election. In *The Telegraph* on 9 May: 'The Conservatives and Liberal Democrats last night sought to reassure financial markets that they are close to agreeing an economic deal that would allow David Cameron to take power.'[2] On 10 May, *The Financial Times* reported that 'both the Conservative and Liberal Democrat leaders want to strike a deal as soon as possible to reassure both the public and the financial markets that a stable government can be formed quickly.'[3] It seemed undignified, these leaders scurrying to shake hands to keep the market happy, especially as the most pressing problems stemmed from the collapse of some of the country's grandest financial institutions, and the multibillion pound sticking plaster that had been pressed over the cracks – chasms – in the nation's financial system in order to stop the whole collapsing. In short, Britain was broke: the only source of money was international borrowing accessed through the bond market. This playing to the market, the posturing of politicians and the chatter, reportage and commentary that flowed across our pages and screens was just schmoozing the bank manager to avoid having the nations' house repossessed. In reassuring the markets that it could meet its debt repayments, the British government was forced to promise a financial parsimony that manifested itself in a decade of austerity. It would seem reasonable, then, to ask how financial markets came to be so important, and how it came about that 21st-century politicians trembled in expectation of their pronouncements.

The truth is that things have never been otherwise.

London's market is much older than Chicago's. The historian Anne Murphy takes note of the spectacular interlude that sparked London's very first stock market boom: in 1687, the triumphant return of Captain William Phips' treasure hunt, his ships sailing up the Thames laden with silver salvaged from Spanish wrecks in the Caribbean. Shareholders received fifty times their initial investment. The dissolute Duke of Albemarle, who had partially funded the expedition, received a vast pay-out. London went stock market crazy.[4] The ingredients necessary for a boom were already in place: an affluent population, especially merchants whose opportunities for international trade were hampered by a drawn-out war with France; a small number of joint-stock companies such as the East India Company, the Hudson's Bay Company and the Royal African Company, with shareholder registers closed to newcomers and which regularly paid dividends of up to 50 per cent during the period. Murphy's work in the archives suggests that in early 1690s, eight joint-stock firms – those mentioned above, as well as the Linen, Glass-Makers' and White Paper Companies, and the Company of Copper Miners – formed the core of the market, with a growing number of smaller enterprises of varied quality.

A great deal happened in a short space of time. According to Ranald Michie, an expert on the history of the London Stock Exchange, the end of the 17th century witnessed a massive increase in stock trade. 'Before 1689,' he writes, 'there were only around 15 major joint-stock companies in Britain, with a capital of £0.9m, and their activities were focused on overseas trade, as with the Hudson's Bay Company or the Royal African Company. In contrast, by 1695 the number had risen to around 150 with a capital of £4.3m.'[5] This represented a five-fold increase in capital over as many years. Twenty-five years later, during the boom that became known as the South Sea Bubble, a further 190 entities were proposed, hoping to raise £220 million from overexcited shareholders; that fantastical figure, had it come to pass, would have represented a 220-fold increase over three decades. Of course, London's first stock market bubble was followed by London's first stock market crash, and many found their fortunes abruptly reversed. The caricaturist William Hogarth took a break from his usual subject matter of drunkenness and debauchery to draw a hideous satire on the bubble (the 'South Sea Scheme'). It featured a merry-go-round with a prostitute and a parson, a housewife and a hunchback and a Scottish laird on a horse with the face of a fat child; elsewhere, a monkey dressed as a gentleman, and Honesty being broken on a wheel while Lady Luck is hacked to pieces by a devil with a scythe. Less was never more for Hogarth. The market was accused of having been overcome by female temperaments, and women took much of the blame: 'We have been ruined by whores; nay what is more vexatious, old ugly whores!', ran one headline.[6]

A joint-stock company is simply what we would call a corporation, a legal entity with shares that can be traded independently of the firm. Among the earliest was the now-notorious East India Company, set up by Queen Elizabeth I's Royal Charter on New Year's Eve in 1600. As Michie points out, the financial structure of these firms suited risky endeavours in overseas trade or finance rather than steady commerce at home, and the stocks remained specialist investments. There were legal problems, too. Financial assets were still construed as a kind of debt and therefore understood as 'choses in action', a legal category attached to the person of the debtor and not easily transferable; the sociologists Bruce Carruthers and Arthur Stinchcombe, who have written on the topic, identify a John Bull, who traded 13 times between 1672 and 1679, as the most active trader in Royal African Company stock.[7] Dutch merchants had already found ways round these obstacles, however, and when a Dutch king, William of Orange, ascended to the English throne in 1689, laws and practices swiftly changed. The absorption of Lex mercatoria, or medieval merchant law, into English law accompanied by specific regulatory changes – Carruthers and Stinchcombe cite the Promissory Note Act of 1704 – made financial contracts freely tradable. Brokers and jobbers began to use standardized contracts, making the business of trading more straightforward. But the problem remained that few would actually want to buy these securities: they were too illiquid, exotic, too risky. Murphy agrees: even in the years from 1691–93, the height of the very first boom in stocks, trading volumes remained relatively small, focused on a handful of corporations, and conducted by a relatively small group of sophisticated merchant-traders.

The situation changed in 1693 when the government launched its national debt, a permanent but transferable, interest-bearing security. Until this time, government debt had been short-term, borrowed when the need arose and paid off when it fell due. But the new King William had taken England into a protracted and ruinously expensive conflict with France. The country's public expenditure almost trebled over the period 1689 to 1702, and the Exchequer suddenly found itself in need of large sums of money. What was worse, Parliament had not yet learned the virtue of parsimony, and the nation's creditworthiness was deteriorating in the eyes of its subjects. In 1694 the Million Adventure Lottery raised £1 million, but the most important innovation was the incorporation of the Bank of England in 1694. The sole purpose of this joint-stock company was to lend the government money: £1.2 million in return for £100,000, plus a fee, annually. This was an 8 per cent annual return, offered with a reasonable degree of security, at a time when war rendered other kinds of merchant trade impossible. The offer to subscribe for the shares opened on 21 June 1694, and the books were filled by 2 July.

Other offers followed. The Bank lent more and more, although by 1697 shareholders were refusing to fund the government further. In 1698 the government offered out the franchise (in today's language) to exploit India, and a New East India Company was set up after promising to lend the government £2 million of shareholders' money. The old East India Company did not take to its new rival, steadily outcompeted it, and merged with it in 1709. The South Sea Company was a similar endeavour, a joint-stock company with a trading monopoly over South America and an obligation to lend huge sums to the government. We can think of money going through the corporations like a pipe – from private shareholders into the firm and out the other side to the government, with interest payments flowing back the other way. Where the government stock remained relatively illiquid, the shares of the corporations could now be easily traded. Volume grew – not only shares, but also a flourishing market in lottery tickets and annuities. To give an idea of the expansion in trade, 1720 – the height of the stock market boom – saw 22,000 transactions. Compare that to Mr John Bull and his 13 trades just 50 years earlier.

Investors understood that these stocks were effectively government-backed, making them a much safer bet; when public confidence in the national credit declined, a secondary market allowed cautious investors to sell at a discount to the more confident, who carried the risk in the expectation of additional return. New financial organizations such as insurance companies and banks, which needed to generate returns on capital held but at the same time remain able to draw on it, started to buy and sell the stocks, as did merchants holding cash between adventures. The joint-stock companies had formed an essential conduit between the needy Exchequer and the fat purses of the English merchant classes. The national debt was born, and London's stock market emerged as an essential adjunct to government policy, a primitive money-laundering device for the bellicose national government throughout the 18th century: 'by the middle of the eighteenth century', writes Michie, 'the Bank of England, East India Company, and the South Sea Company had lent some £42.8 million to the government.'[8]

***

Every market needs its 'market-makers'. These are the individuals who stand between producers and consumers, smoothing out irregularities in supply and demand, transporting goods and establishing a marketplace. By their very existence, their *willingness* to buy and sell, they constitute the market. They might be the stallholders in a Saturday grocery market, the car dealers who set up shiny motor villages on the outskirts of the city, grain dealers in the 19th-century Midwest, or energy traders shipping crude oil across the globe. Stocks and bonds, although less material, are no different. Carruthers and Stinchcombe have shown that liquidity – the basic precondition of a functioning market – is a considerable organizational achievement. It depends, they argue, on the existence of three mechanisms: continuous trade of some kind, the presence of market-makers who are willing to maintain prices in whatever is being traded, and the presence of legally specific, standardized commodities. We have seen the last of these three conditions met: the creation of securities, the trade in which was both legal and desirable. Now we need to find our market-makers.

London's market flourished precisely because of a crowd of buyers and sellers, often merchants who began to speculate alongside their other activities. As Murphy notes, the skills of a merchant were highly transferable to the financial markets. Someone who traded stocks became known as a stockjobber (a title that lasted until October 1986!), snarkily described by Dr Johnson in his dictionary as 'a low wretch who makes money by buying and selling in the funds.' Daniel Defoe claimed that jobbers who manipulated the market risk only their reputation, which was 'generally already lost', and their souls, 'which trifle is not worth mentioning'.[9] London's commodity markets centred on the Royal Exchange, and the traders settled there, but they were numerous, noisy and disruptive, and their stocks did not have the cache of the more visible commodities of the Exchange. They were soon thrown out and began to gather in the nearby spaces, especially Jonathan's Coffee House, and Garraway's, both located on the city's Exchange Alley, a dangerous place of pickpockets and unscrupulous dealers.

Rudimentary news outlets developed, with almanacs and price lists circulating alongside handbills and other such material. One John Castaing established a list of stock prices in 1697 and the London Stock Exchange is often dated to this moment.[10] But these printed news sources would have been unreliable and out of date, no substitute for physical presence in the noise and hubbub. Traders came from all over Britain, and even from Holland, to set up in the market. These jobbers and their strange offerings, their trade seemingly beyond the limits and even capacities of the law, were an uncomfortable phenomenon for a society that associated wealth with the solidity and immobility of land. Conventions fell away: women, especially spinsters and widows, could participate in this market on equal terms. Their contemporaries simply could not understand a market that traded continuously in financial abstractions. An anonymous diatribe from 1716 catches the flavour of popular opinion:

> ... the vermin called stockjobbers, who prey upon, destroy, and discourage all Industry and honest gain, for no sooner is any Trading Company erected, or any villainous project to cheat the public set up, but immediately it is divided into shares, and then traded for in Exchange Alley, before it is known whether the project has any intrinsic value in it, or no...[11]

Regulation proved ineffective. The 1697 Act to limit the numbers of jobbers had achieved little, so Parliament tried again. The Barnard Act – promoted by Sir John Barnard and passed in 1734 – aimed to 'prevent the infamous practice of stock jobbing'. Although the Act was almost entirely ineffective, it did have the consequence of rendering 'time bargains' as illegal. Classed as gambling debts, they were now unenforceable through the courts, which meant that the traders themselves had to develop a code of self-protection.

A first attempt at shutting out undesirables came in the form of a subscription-based club that, in 1761, took over Jonathan's Coffee House as their sole place of business and excluded non-members. One such non-member successfully pleaded in court that he had been unfairly shut out of the market, and the clique was broken open. In 1773 another group of brokers opened a building on Threadneedle Street on more legally favourable terms. Michie notes that:

> ... admission to this building was on payment of 6d per day, so that all could participate if they wished ... if a broker attended six days a week all year the cost would be £7.80 per annum, which was remarkably similar to the £8 which was to be paid to Jonathan's. Clearly that offer had made a group of the wealthier stockbrokers realize that they could personally profit by setting up an establishment for the use of their fellow intermediaries and then charging them a fee for its use.[12]

Ironically, the same circumstances that had made the Threadneedle Street site available to the jobbers challenged its dominance: the expanding Bank of England, now managing the government debt, was constructing its own buildings including a rotunda, which rapidly became a popular venue for the trading of stock. The market took over and disrupted the Bank's space, filling it not just with jobbers but also pickpockets, street sellers and prostitutes. Would-be customers were enjoined to walk into the melee and 'call out lustily' what they wanted, and would immediately be surrounded by brokers.[13] Although London's Stock Exchange had established a building and closed its ranks, the market overspilled its walls, still ragged, chaotic and noisy.

Nor is the story one of continual, steady progress. The economic historian Philip Mirowski found that the English share market actually contracted during the course of the 18th century. Share turnover relative to shares issued fell almost continuously from the early 1700s to the 1750s, while

> prices generally rose from 1710 to 1720, plunged precipitously for a few years and then were essentially stationary from 1725 until around 1755. … After some expansion in the 1760s prices fell continuously from the late 1760s to the mid-1780s, a period generally identified as one of unprecedented expansion in the English economy at large.[14]

Business found its money elsewhere: not least in the enormous inflow of capital from the transatlantic slave trade and its cycle of diabolical human credit.

***

If, in 2010, Messrs Cameron and Clegg cowered in the face of the market's demands, we can at least see that this is nothing new. The stock exchange evolved as an instrument to support government, but on its own terms. As the outsider status of London's new jobbers shows, some contemporaries found these new trading practices hard to swallow. That has not changed, and the relationship between markets and states is also a struggle over the accepted norms of market practice. From ancient times, thinkers have tried to distinguish between legitimate trade in things we need and the pursuit of profit for its own sake, between the 'productive activity' of growing or making and the notion that money can 'breed upon itself', as Aristotle put it. We see this in characterizations of jobbers as wretches, vermin and villains, and in the Barnard Act's attempt to ban 'time bargains'. Stock markets create a liminal space beyond the jurisdiction of nation states, rendering lawmakers impotent and unsettling society. At the same time, stock markets are always in need of the law, and sometimes they must work hard to secure its support.

Chapter 2 explored how the concentration of agricultural power and communication networks on Chicago led to the formation of the Board of Trade, and then rapidly to the advent of 'to arrive' contracts. These allowed trading in abstract representations of agricultural commodities, and in doing so offered farmers the chance to protect themselves against changes in the price and the weather. As in London, where jobbers had been trading in time – those bills of exchange – since the 17th century, the market gave rise to a class of professional speculators, and at the end of the 19th century trade in financial abstractions exploded. Jonathan Levy, the University of Chicago historian who has chronicled the legal wrangling over derivatives trading, states that 8.5 billion bushels of wheat were sold at the New York exchange between 1885 and 1889. During the same four years, the city consumed only 162 million. Levy shows how derivatives trading only became legally, and morally, acceptable after a long dispute – a culture war over the soul of the market.[15]

At root, the dispute came down to a few core principles. The first was the question of gambling. Traders – known as scalpers – had developed a technique called 'setting off', allowing them to settle a deal at any point before the agreed delivery date; they did so when the price moved in their favour. Setting off was just another step in an evolution of contracts that had begun with abandoning physical exchange and instead swapping 'elevator receipts', tickets representing grain in one of the city's many silos. Soon enough the traders abandoned all pretence of a physical commodity. This begged the question of what they *were* trading: the winds of Minnesota, rather than its wheat, according to one grain handler. Court cases pursuing settlement hinged on just this point – a transaction could only be legitimate if there was a genuine intention to transfer the goods. Speculation for its own sake was too close to gambling, and the courts were often unwilling to distinguish between those who had a legitimate interest in risk management and those who simply sought to make money from trade. It did not help that many of the speculators themselves were unconvinced that options trading contributed to the common good. As one senior member of the Board put it, in 1888: 'Did you hear what Charlie [Charles Hutchinson, president of the Board] said? Charlie said we're philanthropists! Why bless my buttons, we're gamblers! You're a gambler! You're a gambler! And I'm a gambler!'[16] That the speaker was Hutchinson's own father cannot have strengthened his arguments.

This was not just a moral issue. It was also a dispute between those involved in the growing and shipping of physical commodities, and the pit traders. It was about the very nature of work. According to the farmers, the ability to set prices for crops grown on the land was a right 'as old as civilization', a right of which they were now being cheated. They sought to contrast the toil of cultivation and the heft of their products with the ephemeral, speculative abstractions that circulated in the pit. Theirs was a labour, while the work of the pit was a game of chance. The speculators responded by stressing the mental efforts involved in their work, and emphasizing its role as a responsible risk management practice. Here they echoed the promoters of life assurance in the USA who had faced similar moral objections to wagers on time, life and death.[17] The traders also offered a more pragmatic defence: the genie was out of its bottle, and the abstractions could not be un-thought. If the pits were closed by US legislators, these spectres of commodities would simply circulate elsewhere. The futures market had forever uncoupled the productive and financial circuits of the economy. 'In the pits,' writes Levy, 'speculative trade in incorporeal things stood newly naked before the wider public.'[18]

Ironically, it was the public's involvement that led to an eventual settlement of the dispute. The growth in futures trading had been accompanied by the rise of so-called 'bucket shops', betting establishments where the public could trade on the fluctuations in commodity prices.[19] Like the brokers' rooms, the bucket shops received prices by ticker, but no orders were fed back to the pits, and the public betted against the proprietor's book. The shops also catered to small farmers seeking to insure themselves against changes in prices or failures in the weather and whose orders would have been far too small for the scalpers to take seriously. Although the bucket shops differed from the exchanges in as much as the customers really were betting – engaged in a zero-sum contest with the proprietor who stood to lose if they gained – the shops eroded the distinctions between gambling and speculation, and with it the legitimacy of the formal exchange. Bucket shops operated at the margins of legality, changing names and addresses regularly, keeping few records, and even asking customers to sign a slip expecting actual delivery of the goods – the expectation of delivery being the Board's main defence against accusations of gambling. Stories abounded of rash young men ruining themselves and their employers by excessive wagers.

Historian David Hochfelder writes that the game really was rigged: bucket shops employed low margins and 'wash sales' to squeeze money from their customers. In a 'margin trade', the speculator puts down just a percentage of the overall trade value as a deposit and is effectively loaned the balance by the broker. Should the stock price move against the trade, the percentage deposit will decrease, and the broker will demand further capital, a 'margin call'. We will encounter this practice throughout the book. In 19th-century Chicago it was exploited by the bucket shops that deliberately set low margins, which would wipe out customers' positions on relatively small price fluctuations.

Because the customers gambled against the house, not the market, their orders could never affect the actual prices. The shops, however, *could* trade on the market and did so to their advantage. If they noticed a worrying building up of orders, they would simply place their own orders on the exchange, drive the price up (or down) and 'wash out' the unfortunate customers. These 'wash sales' even got a mention in Lefèvre's *Reminiscences*. Despite all of this, the shops capitalized on the public's inability to differentiate between them and the Board, to the point where the bucket shops were drawing large volumes of trade away from their more 'legitimate' cousin. The Board's attempts to persuade the courts to recognize the distinction between the bucket shops' gambling and their own philanthropic speculation met with little success, with courts taking the view that the Board officials were more interested in avoiding competition than establishing moral probity.

Eventually the matter was settled. C.C. Christie – a bucket shop magnate – sued the Board of Trade over a deal with Western Union Telegraph Company that prohibited the distribution of prices to the bucket shops. This legal argument centred on property rights to prices, and in 1905 the case arrived in front of Chief Justice Oliver Wendell Holmes of the Supreme Court. Holmes' decision went against the shops. He held that they were sites for gambling, while the pit traders were legitimate dealers and 'setting off' constituted a legal delivery. Moreover this kind of speculation 'by competent men', he said, 'is the self-adjustment of society to the probable'. At a stroke, derivative trading had become not only legitimate but also desirable in the eyes of the law, and Holmes had legally articulated a new role for the markets – managing risk – that became increasingly important as the 20th century drew to a close. At a stroke is perhaps an exaggeration: Hochfelder reckons that the litigation had 'cost the Board about $120,000 and had spanned 25 years, 248 injunctions, 27 jurisdictions, 20 cities, and 11 states.'[20]

★★★

Nation states, then, have an uneasy relationship with financial markets that goes right back to the emergence of modern political systems. It is uneasy because states often seem to need markets more than financial markets need states. Yet that is a very selective reading: states provide the legal infrastructure within which markets flourish, and throughout the history of stock markets it has been states that provided much of the impetus for the growth. Back in Europe, it was the war with France at the end of the 18th century that finally secured London's dominance as a financial centre, both through the damage done to European bourses and the enormous demand for money on the part of the British government. By 1790 the national debt, barely a century old, stood at £244 million. In the USA, the massive 'Liberty Loan' bonds of the First World War turned those bucket shop gamblers into legitimate market participants. Stock exchanges emerge from a history of speculation, of booms and busts, of technological innovations like the ticker, the telegraph and the railway. But laws, technology and investment crazes do not quite a market make: as we saw in the pits of Chicago and the coffee houses of London, they need people, too, a densely choreographed social ritual that allows a stock exchange to function.

4

Mind Your Eye!

Let's step back to a different time. Imagine an enormous room, capped by a vast dome. At 100 feet in height and 70 feet in diameter it was said to be of a kind with the basilicas of St Peter's in Rome and St Paul's in London. This was the great trading room of the London Stock Exchange, known as the Old House. A blue-mottled marble faced its walls and pillars and the wags called it 'Gorgonzola Hall' after the cheese. There was not much furniture, just a few rickety shelves, and throughout the hall, ramshackle chalkboards covered in figures. Each firm of jobbers occupied a particular spot on the Exchange floor, where the chalkboards marked their 'pitch', while the brokers spent market hours in their 'boxes' at the edge of the floor. Business stayed in the family, and these pitches and boxes were often passed from father to son. Women were not allowed even to set foot on the floor of the House. During trading hours as many as 3,000 people jostled under the dome, manning these pitches or circulating through the crowds. Images show men in dark suits and ties, white shirts, hatless, in an attitude of ease, standing in groups, chatting or strolling.

There were games. One etching shows young jobbers, wearing proto-hipster beards and frock coats, competing to throw a roll of ticker tape over a bar fixed high up in the dome. And there were pranks. Whatever the weather, every self-respecting member of the Exchange would come to work with bowler hat and rolled umbrella. On a rainy day it was entertaining to unfurl a brolly, fill it with a confetti of shredded paper and roll it back up again. There were nicknames as sophisticated as the japes: one man was named the Chicken, another the Lighthouse because he was 'always moving his head around and it reminded people of the light flashing on the top of a lighthouse'. Then there was 'the Tortoise … he was a little bit round-shouldered, he always wore a bowler hat, brown suit, carried his umbrella and his nose would remind anybody that he was a tortoise. And he used to walk very slowly through the market.' One short, very ugly man in the mining market was affectionately named 'Don't Tread In It'. When business was slow, on a Friday afternoon, songs would burst out: the jobbers would sing the Marseillaise to a supposedly French colleague and slam their desk lids – the clerks had old-fashioned schoolroom desks – as cannon. Three thousand male voices raised in song together, echoing under the dome: noise, camaraderie and xenophobic 'banter'. A bygone age, a different world, but not that long ago. The Old House closed in 1966, the same year that England last won the football world cup.[1]

Stock exchanges, it is clear, depend on technology, buildings, commerce, the twists of history and the whims of the state. But they also depend on social interactions, habits, relationships and customs. They are, or have been until very recently, filled with bodies. I described the trading pit as a human-powered computer, taking the information that flowed into the exchange as buy and sell orders and turning it into prices; a computer powered by voices, shouting, pushing and shoving.

That was Chicago. London's trading, although every bit as ruthless, had a more gentlemanly exterior. In Chicago those trading for speculative profit were known as scalpers. In 20th-century London, they were still called 'jobbers'. Their occupation had evolved alongside the Exchange itself, and they traced a genealogy to the 17th-century merchant stockjobbers of Exchange Alley, those low wretches so deplored by Dr Johnson. The jobbing system was 'single capacity', meaning that jobbers traded on their own account and executed orders for brokers, while brokers dealt with clients. This was thought to prevent jobbers taking advantage of clients, while at the same time introducing much-needed speculative liquidity into the market.

London's trading was ambulatory. While the Chicago men crammed into a stepped pit and yelled orders at each other, the jobbers strolled across the floor of the House and chatted to their counterparts, standing eye to eye as they squeezed their rivals into the toughest bargains possible. Specialization was tied not to individual pits but to areas on the floor that serviced different sectors. There was the government broker, trading gilts in the smartest part of the house, the mining market, and the unfortunately named kaffir market, trading the stocks of Southern Africa. Jobbers stood at pitches comprising little more than notice boards. Larger firms might carve out an established pitch by a wall or a pillar, furnishing it with makeshift shelves and even a seat. Smaller firms simply had to stand among the crowds. The boards listed the stocks traded, names engraved onto magnetic strips, an attempt to give some sense of permanence to the seemingly temporary stalls. The jobbers 'expected to be there tomorrow', as one put it. A junior trader, known as a 'blue button', would be in charge of marking up prices in red or blue crayon, next to the opening price, lettered in black. The boards themselves might be put to strategic use, updated a little more slowly than prices moved, obscuring market action and helping jobbers take a turn.

The Exchange retained a staff of top-hatted 'waiters' whose function was to ensure the smooth running of trading. One of the many problems was keeping track of people in this great crowd, especially the brokers who stalked the floor in search of the best price for their clients. The waiters used speaking tubes like those found on old ships to speak to brokers, first blowing through the tube to make a whistle that summoned someone to the other end. If a broker could not be found a number would be illuminated, and it was up to the individual to spot their number and raise their hand. A waiter would point them to the telephone room or the meeting room where they were required. Telephones were located in booths around the outside of the hall and had a movable floor that sunk down when the user stepped in, flicking out a marker to show that the booth was occupied. The waiters managed the circulation of bodies around the room, preserving the rules of conduct in the seeming chaos. They even conducted the dreaded 'hammerings'. These ceremonial moments of public shaming and bankruptcy saw firms that could not meet their obligations shut down by the blow of two gavels and the partners' assets turned over to the administrators.

The business of buying and selling was conducted according to a complicated verbal etiquette set out at length in the Stock Exchange's *Code of Dealing*. Here is an example, from the sociologist Juan Pablo Pardo-Guerra's study:

> 'What are XYZ?' Answer: '125.8.'
> Broker: 'I am limited I'm ½p out in 250.'
> Jobber: 'I could deal one way.'
> Broker [hoping for the one which will suit him]: 'Very well, you may open me.'
> Jobber: 'Give you ½p.'
> Broker: 'Sorry, I'm a buyer at 127½.'[2]

It is unintelligible to us, but perfectly clear to the jobber. No agreement has been reached, and no deal done. Traders had to use a particular form of language to avoid being snared in an accidental bargain: you might say 'I'm only quoting' to make this clear, just as a lawyer might raise a point 'without prejudice'. Prices could be quoted in fractions of a pound, 'seven fifteen-sixteenths to over the figure … a very complicated effort', says one. Dealing was, until 1971, conducted in pounds, shillings (s) and pence (d), making already complex arithmetic devilishly so, and jobbers needed enormous mental aptitude for numbers and prices – not only conducting deals but also remembering who would buy and sell at what price. Jobbers were obliged to quote and deal if a broker wished, and so it was wise to have a sense of who needed what on the floor. Like the traders in the pits, jobbers did not need to know the prospects for a company or the long-term economic forecasts for the nation. They simply needed to know who wanted to buy, and who wanted to sell. All the information was 'on the floor', says one broker, 'eye contact, sweat, movement. You could always tell from the eyes of the junior trader whether his boss was long or short, and how badly they wanted to get out of their position'.[3] Says a jobber, 'I felt I used to know, when a dealer came up to deal with me; I used to be able to read him, the sort of business he had … the way they walked sometimes, whether they went twice round a pillar.'[4]

Like Chicago, London worked on the principle of the spoken deal. Trading was a matter of promise, transacted at the moment it was spoken, even if it was settled much later. The entire social infrastructure served to reinforce the primacy of this bargain, epitomized in the London Stock Exchange's motto, *Dictum meum pactum*, 'My word is my bond'. Deals, once made, were almost never cancelled by the Exchange, which took the attitude 'pay and be paid' – the rule is on the side of the seller, and in order to ensure that jobbers were paid for stocks sold, they must always pay for stocks bought. The aim of the jobber was therefore not to hold stock, but to pass it on as soon as possible, limiting risk and keeping commission flowing. Prices were continually in flux. Written reports flowed long behind the deals made by jobbers, spilling first onto the boards and then to the newswires and the settlement clerks who worked termite-like in offices located beneath the trading floor. Throughout the day, Exchange officers came to the pitches and collected prices, which hardened overnight into the print of the Stock Exchange's *Daily Official List* and *The Financial Times*, but by the time these printed records were made, the verbal transactions of the market itself had left them far behind. The slowness of record-keeping made 'My word is my bond' of paramount importance, because the market could only function if spoken agreements were honoured, even if the deal caused one counterparty considerable financial pain. Sanctions were informal and effective, and anyone who defaulted on a bargain would have great difficulty making another. There was a kind of schoolboy justice, too. One anecdote recalls a leak from the *Sunday Express* and the dealing that followed, the problem solved by a false news story left on the editor's desk; embarrassed faces and wasted money reprimand enough for an offence that would nowadays attract police attention and might even lead to prison.[5]

★★★

The Exchange had an apprentice-based career system that welcomed cockney sparrows as well as the younger sons of the old elite. Boys from the East End rubbed shoulders with graduates of august Oxbridge colleges: 'I like talking to you', an old jobber told one young Balliol man, "cos you're the only bloke in the market, wot I talk to, wot talks proper.'[6] Nonetheless, while jobbing – often seen as a kind of bookmaking by participants – demanded trading acumen and offered opportunities to those with working-class origins, the Exchange preserved in microcosm the nuances of the British class system. Old Etonians drifted towards the posher firms, the gilt-edged brokers, while the lads from Hackney and Islington sought out opportunities in the less grand stretches of the market. At the top of the heap were the brokers, and at the top of the brokers' heap were those dealing government stock, or gilts. Smartest of all was Hoare, Govett, formerly Hoare & Co, the government's own broker. It was, writes journalist Martin Vander Weyer,

> the fiefdom of Kit Hoare – a City gent from the school they knocked down to build the old school, as it were. A splendid pirate [who] would have boarded any ship, according to a contemporary, he did business on a nod or handshake, never wrote anything down, and contrived to be on the inside of all the lucrative deals of his day – if necessary gathering intelligence by wandering the corridors of merchant banks, pretending to be lost.[7]

The possibility of meritocratic success did not extend to women, however, and Michie records the details of the struggle to secure equality of access to the institution.[8] In 1966 – the same year that the Old House was closed – a Miss Muriel Bailey, highly commended brokers' clerk, sought membership of the Exchange in order to apply for position as partner in her firm. To be a partner, one had to be a member, and to be a member, one had to be a man. Miss Bailey, who had run one broker's office throughout the Second World War and in subsequent years had built a substantial client list, considered this an unreasonable obstacle and applied for membership all the same. The Council of the Stock Exchange agreed to support her application so long as she promised not to set foot upon the trading floor, but the membership resoundingly rejected this proposal. That was in 1967. At least the membership proved to be consistent in its bigotry, in 1969 rejecting the membership of foreigners, defined as 'those not born in Britain', and voting against the admittance of women again in 1971. Nor should the Exchange itself be entirely exempt from scrutiny. In 1962 it had refused to accept a listing application from automotive firm Fiat, presumably on the grounds of being too Italian.[9] Only in January 1973 did the membership consent to allowing female clerks to become members, and even then it took until the summer of that year before rules banning them from the trading floor were abandoned. Miss Bailey, by now Mrs Wood, was elected to the membership in January 1973, aged 66.

There is something of the sacred and profane about these exclusions – particularly the suggestion that Miss Bailey should not step on the hallowed ground of the trading floor. Men who wished to join the priestly order of jobbers had to serve a lengthy apprenticeship, working through clerical and junior status until eventually they became a dealer, then partner. Brian Winterflood – a central character in our story – was one such lad. Now in his 80s, he is a short, jovial man, still full of energy. He is known for his anecdotes, as well as his opinions – he was an outspoken supporter of Brexit – and is unerringly generous to the press. They treat him well in return, filling diary columns with stories about his long career. Sometimes these verge on the shameless, like Winterflood passing off a recent finger amputation as frostbite sustained on an Arctic cruise. Despite his pleas, the paper reported, the ship's doctor refused to operate and Winterflood had to be treated on *terra firma*.[10]

My lunch with Winterflood was a spontaneous affair. I was waiting in Wins' (as it is known) trading room, watching in awe as the traders, sleeves rolled, surrounded by dirty coffee cups and nodding donkey desk ornaments, surfed the waves of numbers flooding through their screens. Winterflood and I were supposed to be meeting in the office, but he did not show up. Stacey, from the front of house, appeared. Mr Winterflood had called: he could not find a parking place near the office, so he was going to pick me up instead. The lads on the trading desks – gender roles are still very much alive in the City – joked about the gaffer keeping a picnic hamper in the back of his Rolls, but neither materialized. Instead Winterflood took me to a favourite spot – a stripped-down Italian restaurant in now-smartened Southwark – where he could chat to the staff like an old friend, sip a blend of Angostura bitters and ginger beer he called 'Gunner', and park his modest executive runabout on the disabled badge space outside. On a second meeting he recounted a recent encounter with an unknown item on a cruise ship menu – *poivron*. He can read most French menus, he told me, but was stumped by that. Still, he didn't believe the Philippine waiter who claimed that 'Poivron' was a region of France. The secret ingredient turned out to be leeks. Brian Winterflood, arch-Brexiter, is a most amusing man.

Winterflood is a legendary figure in the smaller company market world. His career has tracked the markets' ups and down more closely than anyone; his name is, in fact, almost synonymous with small company trading. Growing up in a suburban household in Uxbridge, West London, his arrival in the City was the gift of a generous school teacher, who asked him what he intended to do for a living.

'I said I don't want to drive a bus – because my father was a tram driver', he recalls, 'what I would like to do is to make some money.'

'Well', replied the schoolmaster, 'if you want to make money you should go to where money is made. I have a friend who is a partner in a stockbroking firm and I wonder if you would want to go up the City.'

'Yes, I would', replied Winterflood, without thinking more. And so one of the most influential men in the small company world began his career as a messenger at the very bottom of the heap.

'Thank God I did start there', says Winterflood, 'running round the City, getting to know the City, getting to know the people. It was magical, absolutely magical.'

If you weren't cut from the right cloth it could be hard to get on. Winterflood remembers coming back from National Service to find that one of his contemporaries at the brokerage, excused service, had been elevated to the partnership:

> I was a sort of running mate to another blue button who happened to be The Hon somebody or other … when I came back I saw him half-way up the partnership list … and I thought, 'This is the wrong side of the fence for me, because I don't know anybody and I have no silver spoon'.

Winterflood found a place in a jobbing firm instead, where opportunities were available to those without the requisite background. Would-be jobbers began as messengers, then 'red buttons' and 'blue buttons', each colour of badge denoting an increased level of seniority and certain powers and responsibilities. Established jobbers wore no buttons and junior employees would have to remember who was who, lest they disgraced themselves by speaking out of turn to a senior member. Blue buttons ran messages between jobbers and brokers, as well as marking up prices on the boards. They asked questions and learned from their employers who doubled as tutors and mentors, sponsoring the careers of juniors and preserving the future of the Exchange. Another East End blue button, Tommy, whose memoires were captured by historian Brian Attard, recalled his attachment to Pat Durlacher,

> a jobber out of this world … he didn't mind me asking questions. He didn't mind telling me what he'd done. He didn't mind telling me why he's changing the price without doing any business in it. … I think he's one of the best there ever were … his foresight seemed absolutely tremendous. … He was never afraid to cut the book if he thought it was wrong and he was never afraid to build the book up if he thought it was right and he could make a good turn out of it.[11]

Eventually, after several years of long hours and low pay, checking bargains with longhand arithmetic and slide rules, learning how to manage the firm's 'book', and picking up the etiquette of the House, the lucky ones were promoted to 'dealer', able to trade for the first time. The moment of appointment was a theatrical Stock Exchange ritual, the young dealer sent up from the floor to the partners' office to be given a badge. Tommy recalls his transition to 'authorized clerk' with awe:

> I was called into the partners' room and they said, 'How would you like to become a dealer?' I said, 'I don't know'. I was absolutely dumbfounded. Where I come from I couldn't have anticipated anything like this. So I said 'I'd love to, I'd love to have a try.' So I was authorized, and I'll never forget the first morning.

There was no ceremonious anointment-by-partner for Winterflood. 'I had a particularly nasty senior partner', he remembers.

> He was a moody so-and-so and he used to gamble every day on the horses, his life was terrible, he ran off with another woman. The day that I got authorized to go on to the floor of the Exchange, he puts his hand in his pocket … and he says, 'All right Winterflood, now you are authorized', and he took his hand out like that and he gave it to me, it was my badge, my authorized badge. And he said, 'Mind your fucking eye.'

'Mind your eye' is an old expression meaning 'take care'. It is often translated into comical dog-Latin: *mens tuum ego*. Winterflood remembers the sudden responsibility of holding a trading book as an authorized dealer in a partnership, trading with the partners' own money and, moreover, their unlimited liability. Partners took a keen interest in their own property and the menacing presence of the waiters' gavels:

> It was good looking over everybody's shoulder when they were [trading], but when the senior partner says, 'Mind your fucking eye', I mean you are terrified. … I remember when he came back from a bad day at the races, which was the bookie outside the Exchange, he would sit in the pitch and say, 'What have you done?' I would say, 'Well not a lot Sir, but there are one or two things that you might like', and he goes across and looks at the page, I say 'Have you noticed sir, so and so', and he said, 'It only pays for the bad ones.'

This process of apprenticeship served to reproduce the social structures that held the Exchange together, years spent learning who was who, and what was what, before being allowed anywhere near the money. Eventually it was possible to buy a 'nomination', a seat on the Exchange, and become a member. One could then embark on a career proper, building a reputation in a particular sector or for a particular strategy: a specialist in Tanganyika Concessions, a specialist in insurance, an expert in arbitrage, in contango, a bull or a bear, depending on one's personality, skills and good fortune. Eventually one might, like Winterflood and the jobber Tommy, earn a place in the partnership and begin to pass on these skills to the next generation.

It was the process of apprenticeship, as well as the distributed structure of the London Stock Exchange's membership, that made the institution so extraordinarily durable and yet simultaneously so conservative and resistant to change.

★★★

In Chapter 2 we explored the birth of the Chicago Board of Trade, seeing how agricultural markets and a confluence of railways, telegraphs and civic ambition led to the formation of early derivatives markets. From the beginning, these markets were economic entities driven by commercial concerns; it is only later, when Justice Holmes opines that speculation 'by competent men is the self-adjustment of society to the probable', that such matters achieve a moral mandate too. Chapter 3 explored how London's market coalesced from the disorganized trading in the coffee shops of Exchange Alley. London's market, like that of Chicago, flourished at the intersection of commercial and political concerns. Where the Chicago Board of Trade was linked to the city's prominence, the London Stock Exchange gathered momentum as a vehicle through which the new national debt could be bought and sold, churned through the shareholdings of the new joint-stock companies, the Bank of England and the East India Company in particular. London's traders became the point of passage between the nation's Exchequer, greedy for funds to fight foreign wars, and the bulging pockets of merchants looking for a reliable and safe return on their capital.

We have, in other words, begun to sketch out the material, political and historical entanglements that go into the making of a stock exchange. We have seen how stock exchanges (and derivative exchanges) are commercial concerns, driven by the business interests of their members. They are also dependent on the state for support and legitimacy, which often tempers the entrepreneurial zeal of the exchanges. By the 1960s and early 1970s – while the jobbers still sang the Marseilleise – the London Stock Exchange had fallen on hard times. As in the 18th century, a nation in need of funds offered such high returns on its debt that equity investing looked unappealing. Regulation had made small-scale flotations impossible, while the government was using the London Stock Exchange as a regulator, a quasi-public role that came to preoccupy the Exchange's managers and justified their refusal of Fiat's listing. As a consequence, there was little business, and members had little flexibility to pursue new opportunities. Member firms saw capital and skills lost through retirement, while high levels of personal taxation made it difficult for individuals to recapitalize their partnerships. This led to a decade of consolidation. Across the UK, regional exchanges were wound up and their business absorbed into the London Stock Exchange. In Scotland, the stock exchanges of Glasgow, Edinburgh, Aberdeen and Dundee, artefacts of the 19th-century boom in the shares of railways and shipbuilders, were consolidated into a single Scottish Stock Exchange in 1964, and then closed in 1973. The London Stock Exchange's member firms also merged. In 1960, 405 firms held memberships of the London Stock Exchange; by 1970 only 223 remained, although the number of partners remained almost constant.[12]

When the good times did come back, these few firms would find themselves in a stronger position for want of competition, but for now members held other jobs and scrabbled to make ends meet. Winterflood and his wife ran a small bric-a-brac shop named Fludds in Valance Road, at the end of Petticoat Lane. Others did worse: Winterflood recalls meeting a colleague selling carpet squares – 'not even whole carpets, carpet squares!' It is hard, now, to believe that finance could have been so impoverished a profession. Jobbers would talk about making their daily 'two and six', the cost of the train journey to work and home again. The Exchange seemed set in its ways, hidebound. Its member-owned structure held back change and its social conventions remained static; only in the 1960s, suggests Attard, was it possible for a working-class boy to imagine being admitted to the partnership. Elsewhere, the revolutions of the swinging sixties were seen only in the sartorial innovations of the younger traders: soft collars, Cuban heels, sideburns and mohair suits. 'We were the leaders of change', said one, 'when I look back on it, I looked a total prat. But I thought that it looked good.' A decade earlier, even these would have been unacceptable: as a messenger boy in 1953, Winterflood stepped on to the exchange floor without the regulation black shoes and was driven away by cries of 'Brown boots! Brown boots!'[13]

In January 2017, just after his 80th birthday, Brian Winterflood rang the Stock Exchange bell to call time on his career. The man who ran a bric-a-brac shop to make ends meet is now a multimillionaire, able to charter a private jet to his holiday home in Corsica or spend the winter in a Floridian holiday village where there is line dancing every evening. Winterflood Securities – Wins – the firm that he founded and sold in the early 1990s but ran for many years after, is reported to have made £100 million in 2000.[14] How did such a change in fortunes come about? How did these impoverished market-makers go from metaphorical rags to very real riches in the space of two decades? The answer to those questions lies in another extraordinary transformation of finance.

5

God Bless Margaret Thatcher

Under the great dome of the Old House, close to the edge of the floor: here we would have found the postwar boom in the shares of dog tracks, and here we would have found a remarkably tall man, one Sidney Jenkins, sometimes known as 'King of the Dogs', reputable dealer in all shares leisure-related. On 1 April 1960 – April Fool's day – Sidney Jenkins and his son Anthony formed S. Jenkins & Son Ltd. Sidney's son John started work as junior in the early 1960s. It was, says Anthony, 'a family firm and everybody knew one another. We knew when people had families and passed their driving tests, and they were good days.'

The firm specialized in leisure stocks, dog tracks and the holiday camps – Butlins and Pontins – that boomed in the days before cheap air travel opened up the beaches of Spain to the British public. This was often described as the 'spivvy' end of the market, but it lacked the defining characteristic of spivviness – financial sharp practice. Sidney Jenkins may have been 'King of the Dogs' but his business affairs were solidly managed. His firm had a good reputation and deep personal connections to the directors of the companies whose stocks they traded. Jenkins had a horror of overtrading and the 'hammerings', when gavels wielded by the Exchange's top-hatted waiters sounded the end of a jobbing firm. He plied his risky trade with care; the firm never borrowed money or stock. 'Father's attitude was "I like to sleep at night",' says Anthony. 'We earned a good living out of the business and the staff all did well, and Father's attitude was "Why should I over-trade?" That was something that he was always frightened of. You've got to remember also, Father saw a lot of hammerings, a lot firms went broke in his time.'

People remember the Jenkins family for two things: for being tall, and for being decent. One former broker's boy remembers going down to the floor on his first day unaccompanied – an unusual occurrence – and looking helplessly at the crowd: 'I was sort of wandering around, a little bit lost, and a very tall man bent down and said, "Your first day, sonny?" and I said, "Yes sir". He said, "How can I help?" and I told him, and I showed him the list of prices I'd been obliged to collect. That man was Sid Jenkins.' The family were generous to a fault: 'If you had a charity that you wanted to raise something for,' said another broker, 'they'd often put a bucket in the middle of the floor on a Friday afternoon and fill it up, or make people fill it up.' In all, they had a good name, and on the floor of the old Stock Exchange, that mattered.[1]

These anecdotes capture the state of London's great Stock Exchange at the onset of the 1980s: tight-knit but a little threadbare, small-time, careful – the kind of world that tidied the books every night and slept soundly on the takings, however meagre. Sidney Jenkins died in 1981, and Anthony briefly became senior partner. A year later Anthony's younger brother John took over the role. John specialized in dealing 'over the counter' – stocks that did not even have a listing on the London Stock Exchange. Jobbers were able to trade these stocks under an exemption offered by the Exchange, so long as they obeyed the rules of 'matched bargain' trading. As John explained,

> In those days you were not allowed to have a position in [an unlisted stock] at all, so you would have a list of buyers and a list of sellers and you would have to try to knit them all together. And at the end of the day whatever you bought you had to sell, you could not go short or long, so you had to be completely flat and I used to love doing that. … I reckon this is back in the early 80s. … I could make a grand a day out of those, which was matching, matching and matching. Nobody else wanted to do it, nobody else wanted to fill the forms out, run round and you would fiddle about in those days, would the client take 1,049? Well, I know he wants to buy 1,000 but will he take 963? And then you would have to piece it all together and do it. … But for a grand a day, in those days!

A thousand pounds a day – rich pickings indeed. That was in the early 1980s, when S. Jenkins & Son Ltd was still the smallest firm of jobbers on the Exchange. In 1984 this same tiny firm made a *million pounds* in *five minutes* of trading. In 1986 it sold out to investment bank Guinness Mahon and thence to Japanese banking giant Nomura. In 1987, the firm – now a trading desk in a global bank – lost £10 million in a day's trading and clawed most of it back over the following few. Something, it seems, had changed.

The period from the late 1940s to the end of the 1960s had seen sustained gains in productivity and quality of life on both sides of the Iron Curtain.[2] These came from an expansion of industrial employment as agrarian workers moved to the cities and took up jobs in factories. An economist would call this extensive growth, adding new factors of production, rather than intensive growth, getting more out of the same resources. In the liberal West a political-economic settlement centring on the Bretton Woods Agreement of 1944 secured the USA's global economic leadership, with the dollar exchange rate pegged to gold and other currencies pinned to the dollar. New institutions such as the International Monetary Fund and the World Bank came into being as international banks that facilitated this transatlantic structure. Weaker economies could hold dollars in their reserves as a source of financial stability. Fixed exchange rates and a strong dollar, as well as cheap, imported oil, in part guaranteed by exploitative political pressure on the producers in the Middle East, meant good times for those at home in the USA. International currency flows led to a growth in global financial markets, and by the 1970s US regulators had become increasingly inclined to laissez-faire practices, even condoning the growth of huge overseas dollar-denominated currency markets located in London. These 'Eurodollar' markets, strategically overlooked by both British and US regulators, brought the dollar the depth and liquidity needed to establish it as a global reserve currency, and for Britain, the economic benefits of hosting these markets and their infrastructure. They were the beginnings of today's global offshore network and were hugely successful. Even Soviet Russia joined in, with $60 billion deposited in safety and anonymity.[3]

These good times could not last. International and now ungovernable financial markets pressured the overinflated dollar. In 1971, the USA abandoned the gold standard and tried instead to devalue the dollar to improve prospects for its exports. This, in turn, caused massive collateral damage to those developing world countries holding dollars in their central reserves. Since many of them produced oil, they clubbed together and put the prices up. The Shah of Iran remarked that 'the industrial world will have to realize that the era of their terrific progress and even more terrific income based on cheap oil is finished.'[4] Multiple economic shocks followed across the West, with Britain one of many countries struggling through a toxic combination of recession and inflation – from January to March 1974 the country even endured a three-day week as coalminers, whose wages had been eaten away by inflation, went on strike and coal-fired power stations ran short on fuel. We should add to this a slow decline in the influence and popularity of postwar Keynesian economics, which now seemed unable to cope with these kinds of crisis, and in its place, a growing vogue for free market, monetarist policies of the kind advocated by Friedrich Hayek and Milton Friedman. The free marketers were radical and organized, seekers of individualist utopia inspired by the writing of Ayn Rand. Their ideas spread. In 1979, the Federal Reserve under Paul Volcker adopted an explicitly monetarist – anti-Keynesian – policy that forced dollar interest rates upwards, leading to a rush of capital back home to the USA and a stinging recession everywhere else.

With ever less value to be had from industrial production, capital began to circulate through the financial economy. In these circumstances capital becomes increasingly self-referential: rather than investing in productive assets, it invests in debts, derivatives and other kinds of financial instrument.

It dislikes financial assets sitting quietly on balance sheets and seeks to parcel them up and move them around. Such assets become an end in their own right and commercial arrangements are reshaped to produce them. Wall Street discovered new concepts – like securitization and financial engineering, a phrase that subtly places financial models and debt securities in the same category as railways, bridges, factories and other sturdy trappings of industrial production. This was the beginning of our own era of financialization, and in the mid-1980s it looked like the glimmer of a new dawn, at least for those on the right side of the fence.

Current free trade historiography holds that Margaret Thatcher's Conservative government tore down sacred cows, ripped up the rule books and hacked through red tape to turn London into a global financial powerhouse. The following, published in 2020, is typical: 'Things were due a shake-up. And who better to shake things up than Mrs Thatcher? The old boys' network had to go, with regulation slashed to allow competition to flourish.'[5] In truth, the government displayed a remarkable timidity in targeting the financial sector, and if the government's policies transformed London, they did so as an accidental consequence of one of the earliest reforms the new government had made.[6] In 1979 the Conservative government scrapped legislation that restricted the flow of capital in and out of the country. These 'exchange controls' even limited tourists' holiday money. They had been designed to preserve the stability of Sterling and were part of the postwar financial settlement, which had centred on Bretton Woods and the gold standard. Now that settlement was collapsing.

Sir Nicholas Goodison, then chairman of the London Stock Exchange, remarked that that exchange controls had done great harm to Britain as a financial centre.[7] Ironically, the greatest beneficiary had been the Exchange itself, as currency controls had made it impossible for overseas investors to deal in the shares of British companies, and protected the jobbers and their comfortable, fixed commissions. Trading UK 'blue chips' (the biggest firms on the market) was a lucrative business, with big orders and low costs, so brokers in New York and elsewhere began dealing the shares of British companies as soon as exchange controls were cancelled. Their firms already had offices in town: during the 1970s many international businesses had opened up shop in London, lured by the growing international securities and 'Eurodollar' market. They could cherry-pick the large orders and deliver them cheaply, undercutting the London jobbers who were bound by the fixed commission regime. The London Stock Exchange was now in trouble, losing its lucrative trade to foreign competition and still bound to offer fixed prices on smaller, less cost-effective deals. Without cross-subsidy the jobbers were left in a difficult situation, and they pressured the Exchange to reform its rules. The Exchange was willing but, in another ironic twist, the Conservative government became the main obstacle to progress. In

1979 the Office of Fair Trading (OFT) had taken the Exchange to court over its restrictive practices. Goodison tried to open up negotiations but the government, fearful of what the tabloid press might say, declined. As the Exchange defended itself against the OFT's legal assault, it became ever more entrenched in the systems of single capacity and fixed commissions, exactly what the government hoped to reform.

In 1983, however, Thatcher won a second election victory. 'The Iron Lady', as she was now known, had a mandate for more confrontational policy. The newly appointed Secretary of State for Trade and Industry, Cecil Parkinson, was amenable to negotiations with the Exchange, and a deal – the Goodison–Parkinson Agreement – was agreed. Minimum commissions would be abandoned. Single capacity would have to follow soon afterwards because the ability to negotiate commissions would swiftly cut out the middleman – the jobber – as brokers simply did deals between each other. The deadline for these reforms was set three years into the future, for 1986. Monday 27 October was the day singled out for London's 'Big Bang'.

Until that point the London Stock Exchange had operated in an idiosyncratic manner. Its 'single capacity' prevented brokers from trading on their own account or settling deals in their own office away from the Exchange floor. Jobbers could settle deals for brokers but never met clients. The system, which had evolved alongside the Exchange itself over the course of two centuries, elegantly prevented profiteering. Brokers never had the opportunity to offer their clients anything other than the prices available from jobbers, while these latter were forced to offer good prices as they competed for business. Single capacity and fixed commissions were part of a package that allowed the Exchange to act as a regulator, maintaining standards of dealing with ordinary investors, as well as a trading institution. The downside was that dealing was expensive for customers and that the market could only be accessed by brokers offering advisory services, whose own rules and costs ruled out participation by the everyday punter. Here we can agree with the pundit quoted above: 'it was all terribly, terribly cosy'. It was, says Andrew Beeson, then a small company stockbroker and more recently chairman of investment bank Schroders, a comfortable 'cartel'. In 1985, the prospect of life outside the cartel may have seemed unappealing, even terrifying. Again, hindsight helps us see things in a different light: when I meet Beeson the city grandee – tall, elegantly tailored and immaculately spoken – in the executive suite of the bank, with its discreet lighting, Chesterfields and 'old masters', it seems that those fears had been unnecessary.

In fact, this should alert us to another vital aspect of the sociology of markets: those who have carved out profitable positions try hard to hold onto them. If they manage, these advantages soon become normalized, 'congealing' into the organization of markets, so that, as the sociologist Greta Krippner so neatly puts it, 'congealed into every market exchange is a history of struggle and contestation. … In this sense, the state, culture, and politics are *contained* in every market act'.[8] At the time, however, things looked less comfortable: the Exchange found itself open to foreign competition, with firms forced to cut their commissions to keep business. In order to survive in this newly deregulated financial jungle firms needed to be bigger, wealthier, and able to integrate a much wider range of services. The reforms to single capacity trading and commissions were, therefore, accompanied by a third ruling, allowing Stock Exchange members to be owned by foreign firms. But what had these firms – some tiny enterprises like S. Jenkins & Son Ltd and others not much bigger – to offer that could possibly interest global investment banks?

***

The 1980s was a time of political violence and industrial unrest. News reports of the 'Battle of Orgreave', 18 June 1984, showed police charging on horses, raining truncheon blows down on the heads of protesters, a few of whom threw bottles and rocks in retaliation. This unexpected and disproportionate show of force, more akin to a dictatorship than a democracy, broke the spirit of the miners. Thatcher's reforms gutted industrial Scotland, the coalmining North East of Britain, coalmining and engineering Yorkshire and South Wales, the steelworks of the Black Country and the potteries of Stoke. In Wapping, the decaying dockside heart of East London, print workers scrapped with the police as Rupert Murdoch undertook to break the unions in return for permission to purchase *The Sun* tabloid newspaper. This was a class war, between the working classes in centres of industrial production and the newly propertied class of shopkeepers and small-time entrepreneurs that Thatcher had brought into being across the nation. Underlying it was a broader project to shift political power away from workers and to those who owned assets – from labour to capital.

The destruction of the unions through confrontation – the armed repression of the miners' strike at Orgreave and the print unions in the 'Siege of Wapping' – was only one weapon at Thatcher's disposal. The other, much more effective in the long run, was to greatly enlarge those on the moral side of capital, the property-owning classes. This she did. Her political followers were exemplified by 'Sierra Man', worker turned property owner, polishing his car on the drive of his recently purchased council home.[9] 'Sierra' refers to the Ford Sierra, the archetypal affordable, mid-range family vehicle of the time. The postwar social contract of solidarity and mutual protection came to an end alongside the economic institutions that accompanied it. New thinking scoffed at collective action – 'there is no such thing as society', said Thatcher, parroting the free market economist Milton Friedman – and worshipped instead individuality and family values. Its disdain for the state, also inherited from Friedman, saw national ownership of assets – be they council houses, infrastructure, heavy industries or utilities – as wasteful and undemocratic. The government needed to rid itself of the state-owned industries that it had inherited, inefficient, bureaucratic behemoths needing nothing less than a good dose of private enterprise and market discipline to knock them into shape.

Through a series of huge privatizations the government sold shares in these institutions – now corporations – to members of the public, often at knockdown prices that guaranteed a quick profit. No one seemed to be unduly bothered by the fact that, as citizens, they had already owned the assets that had just been sold back to them, nor that by abolishing the principle of cross-subsidy through a nationalized industry they would make it possible for private enterprises to scoop up lucrative parts of the business while abandoning the rest, a recipe for long-term exclusion and unfairness. Nor indeed by the fact that that an industry committed to maximizing shareholder returns would inevitably underinvest, leaving a failing infrastructure for future generations, and that in the longer term private enterprise would be unwilling and unable to compete with cheaper foreign labour and that many of these corporations would simply close, leaving a wasteland of post-industrial despair over much of Britain.

Quite the reverse. The privatizations were seen as manna from heaven, pound notes raining from the sky, and generated a huge popular interest in the stock market. A new category of investor was born, and Sierra Man could add a few British Gas shares to his ever-growing collection of assets. This new investor even had a name, Sid, carefully chosen to capture the new Tory demographics. It suggests a midlife everyman, a baby-boomer edging from a life of toil to one of property-owning prosperity. The government commissioned a series of ingenious television adverts for the new share issues. Sid is the protagonist. We never meet him, but simply hear a series of strangers passing the news of the latest offer with the catchphrase, 'If you see Sid, tell him.' The messengers are postmen, milkmen, men in country pubs, old ladies out shopping, all pillars of the emerging, Tory-voting, economic majority. Regional accents abound. As these very ordinary men and women pass the message to the ever-absent Sid, it becomes quite clear that it is intended for you, the viewer, whoever you may be. Economic times, they were a-changing, although not as much as that: the advert's final voice-over, advising a telephone call to the appointed broker – the patrician N.M. Rothschild & Sons – is offered in a cut-glass, upper-class English accent and the established order holds firm.

For those on the floor of the Exchange, these deals really were manna from heaven. The first big issue was the British Telecom flotation, offered for sale in November 1984. While lucky investors made a few hundred pounds, the jobbers made a killing. Although many of the jobbing firms were still quite tiny, the government broker scattered riches without discrimination.

S. Jenkins & Son, smallest of all, received almost the same allocation as the larger firms, despite its complete lack of experience in the telecoms sector.

'The boys heard about this BT issue coming up', says John Jenkins,

> and they went up and saw the shop broker and said 'We want to have a go at this'. We had no track record at all in British Telecom, nothing, or any electronic business, nothing at all. They went and saw the shop broker and all of the market makers were issued with the same amount of stock ... 900,000 shares in British Telecom, which we sold first thing on the morning of the float and we took *nearly one million profit.*

'We actually finished up with something like 950,000 shares', says John's brother Anthony,

> and when you think that Akroyd and Wedd, all the large people, got 1.4 million, for a little tiny firm of our size to get 950,000 was absolutely amazing because we got all these profits. But at the same time I wasn't entirely happy with this because whatever bargain you've got you are still at risk.

Jobbers who signed up to the issue had to pay for the stock the next day, whether they sold it or not. 'If anything happens to Maggie Thatcher,' thought Anthony, 'or if another war breaks out then its pay and be paid with this sort of stock.' But it is hard to find much sympathy with Anthony's predicament, or to believe, in view of the tectonic shifts in British politics and the sudden explosion of enthusiasm for the market, that these jobbing firms took any real risk at all. The British Telecom issue was the most profitable bargain that anyone in the Exchange could remember, ever. More issues followed: British Gas in 1986, Rolls Royce and British Petroleum (BP) in 1987. (The public offer for BP, closing in October 1987, days after the biggest market crash of the century, did justify Jenkins' worries. Underwriters, especially in the USA, lost hundreds of millions on the deal.)

Thanks to the relaxation of Exchange rules on foreign ownership, the treasure chest that 1980s London had become lay open to all. It offered a bridgehead for US firms looking eastward and European or Australasian firms looking west. Here was an opportunity to gain entry to the august London Stock Exchange, a closed shop for 200 years. The easiest way to get a seat on the Exchange was to buy a firm that already owned a membership, and bidders circled. Foreign buyers found the jobbers with ledgers fattened by the profits of these public issues and snapped them up at inflated prices. S. Jenkins & Son was sold to Guinness Mahon, which was soon bought by the Japanese bank Nomura. Beeson's firm was bought by Grindlays Bank in 1984, and the whole was almost at once consumed by ANZ. Kit Hoare's

Hoare Govett, most gilded of the gilt-edged brokers, was sold early on to Security Pacific, not just a US firm, but one from Los Angeles with interests in 'real estate', of all things. Even if the amount offered did leave 'pound signs bouncing up and down behind the eyeballs'.[10] Indeed, the sums at play were extraordinary by the standards of the time. Security Pacific paid £8.1 million for its 29.9 per cent stake in Hoare Govett, while

> Barclays linked up with the jobbers Wedd, Durlacher and the brokers de Zoete & Bevan, forming eighties stalwart BZW. Citicorp teamed up with three brokers, Vickers da Costa, Scrimgeour Kemp Gee, and J. & E. Davy, while its US rival Chase Manhattan contented itself with two, namely Laurie Milbank and Simon & Coates. Even the chairman's own firm, Quilter Goodison, sold a 100 per cent stake to the French bank, Paribas, in 1986.[11]

It took the jobbers by surprise. '1980 was a very difficult period …' says Beeson. 'Four years later, suddenly someone was going to pay us £11 million. You know, [pay] all the partners for this business and we thought that Christmas had come.' Note Beeson's phrasing: 'pay all the partners'. Not the staff or the shareholders, but those who happened to be standing at the top of the escalator in October 1986. Big Bang did more than dismantle a system that had been in place for 200 years. It completely destroyed the social infrastructure of the City. The old firms had run on the partnership model. Jobbers traded with the bosses' money; they had to 'mind their fucking eye' and wince inwardly as the partners ran their careful fingers down each day's tally. Apprentices earned little but could work up the ladder to a seat on the Exchange and a place in the partnership where they would be comfortable, secure and one day even wealthy. Everyone's interests were focused on the long term: if the firm went broke, everyone lost.

Big Bang tore this apart. The partners became rich almost overnight and took with them the spoils that might have gone to future partners. There was no longer any reward in long service. Time-served dealers drifted away and youngsters, often with university educations, ruled the roost. They traded long hours at screens before dashing to exclusive wine bars or the BMW dealership; less middle-aged than Mercedes and more accessible than Porsche, the BMW had become the young city slicker's car of choice. Firms that did well were those that catered to the traders' tastes, often fronted by flamboyant entrepreneurs: Richard Branson's Virgin, Anita Roddick's The Body Shop, Terence Conran's Habitat and Paul Smith's expensive-but-fashionable suit shops all flourished in the centres of global capital. At the same time, the pressures of work had risen enormously, with traders working hours that could not have been imagined just a few years previously.[12] These youngsters were tasked with making as much money as they possibly could, seemingly irrespective of the risk. The bonus culture replaced the partnership culture, and institutional memories of harder days faded quickly or simply walked out of the building. What was worse, there was a fundamental clash in corporate culture between the new arrivals and the incumbents of the Stock Exchange, with often tragic consequences for the former jobbing firms. In one firm, recalls Winterflood,

> The senior partner was saying to the other partners, they had just received a bid of £12 million, 'Gentlemen, we have been kissed by the Holy Ghost', and they are all rejoicing. And within twelve weeks it did not exist, it did not exist. They really had been kissed by the Holy Ghost! That was the Americans, they came in like the Fifth Cavalry and they thought they knew everything and they didn't, they certainly did not understand our culture and it cost them a fortune.

Who cared! It was boom time: the three hundred and fifty-seven days that followed Big Bang marked a peak in the City's fortunes, the very height of the 1980s bull market.

To keep on rising, stock markets need a steady stream of money. Much of that money came from private investors, these newly minted Sierra men, taking their life savings from under the mattress – or at least out of the building society – and hurling them into the ever-rising stock market. Sierra women too. That the market stopped rising barely a year later came as a great shock to many – not just to the private investors, but also a new generation of freshly wealthy, young financial professionals who did not have the life experience to know that investments can go down as well as up. On Black Monday, 19 October 1987, they did just that. But before we bring the 1980s to a close, we must get to grips with a distinctly new phenomenon – the strange science of money.

PART II

The Spectacular Science of Money

6

Finding Prices, Making Prices

'An Experiment on a Bird in the Air Pump' hangs in London's National Gallery. Painted in 1768 by Joseph Wright 'of Derby', it is extraordinary, luminous. I try to creep up on it, so as to take its figures by surprise. They are gathered around a glass jar. It contains a parakeet, whose life is being brought to a premature and unpleasant end by the extraction of air from the chamber. Light spills out of the painting, catching the faces of the onlookers in movement; we cannot see the source, for it is obscured by what appears to be a brain in a vat of liquid. Two boys concentrate on the experiment, while the young couple to the left have little interest in the wretched bird. A man, an enthusiast, wild haired, wrapped in a red dressing gown and a shirt open at the neck, is pointing to the jar and declaiming to the watching boys. His other hand hovers above the brass mechanism and winding handle of the air pump, a precision instrument of its time, set in a heavy, ornate, wooden frame. Two young girls are visibly upset by the suffering; one covers her eyes with her hand while the other clutches her sister's gown for support. Another man comforts the girls. He is pointing to the bird. We can imagine him saying: 'Come now, this is science. Put away your childish sadness and take heed of our remarkable demonstration.' Another boy, his face a mixture of malice and sorrow, is shutting up the birdcage hanging from the ceiling, while to the far right an older man rests his chin on his walking stick and stares at the apparatus with an unfocused, pensive gaze. Stepping back from the painting we can see the trappings of wealth: the rich finery of the clothes, the polished wood furniture and expensive apparatus, the heavy fresco plasterwork of a doorway in the background. The moon shines pale through a large sash window. It is a country house spectacle. These details are hidden in the half-darkness, away from the extraordinary chiaroscuro Wright achieves with the lamplight.

Compare this to another of Wright's masterpieces, 'The Alchemist, in Search of the Philosopher's Stone', painted in 1771. Again, the canvas is lit by light emanating from a glass vessel, and the light catches faces in movement, but the setting is utterly different. The light, much hotter and brighter than the gentle lamp of the country house, boils out of a vessel. This is set on a tripod, its stem bound into a metal pipe running into a peeling brickwork chimney. It illuminates a room that resembles a church with Gothic arches built of plain stone; in the background the moon shines through a mullioned Gothic window. A man kneels by the vessel. He is old, grey-haired, with a thick long beard, wrapped in a scruffy robe. His gaze is directed at the ceiling, so that his face, illuminated from below, appears in an attitude of prayer. He is surrounded by the scattered junk of alchemy: pots, vases, scrolls and a globe. Behind him is a writing table, and two surly faced boys chat and point at the kneeling man. The sole, incongruent trace of modernity is a clock shown clearly in the middle of the picture.

The pictures capture the 18th-century transformation in science, from a secretive, quasi-mystical, solitary pursuit to an expansive social practice based on demonstration. Wright's two very different visions not only picture the birth of modern experimental science, but also give us a metaphor that helps us understand the practice of finance. On the one hand we see the entrepreneur discovering prices through lonely and even haphazard sallies into the market, groping in the dark for the light of price efficiency; on the other the gentlemanly, public spectacle of experimentation with its accompanying materiality and sociality – instrumentation, expertise and collective agreement about the outcome of what constitutes a correct price. To be crude, the first is an economic conception, the second a sociological one, and we can use this metaphor to help us answer a question that must vex us if we are to get to the heart of financial practice: what is in a price, and why does it matter?

Let me pursue the analogy. The alchemist, pursuing his solitary work in the laboratory, happening by accident on the magical luminescence of phosphorus – by boiling urine, apparently – is roughly how finance thinks it works. Individual traders, some informed, some noisy, battle for profits, and their atomized, individualistic actions bring prices into line. Traders take risks, and through mechanisms such as option pricing theory learn to handle those risks; they are big beasts that are rightly rewarded for their bravery and their hazard. The other painting is an experiment, a public demonstration in which the laws of nature are temporarily suspended to effect a particular outcome. It is a piece of theatre, combining the very latest in technology and knowledge to demonstrate a fact. Although it seems rudimentary to us, the air pump was a cutting-edge technology of the mid-18th century. The pumps misbehaved, and in practice the outcome of the experiment was not as predictable as all that. Nothing changes – ask any experimental scientist about the day-to-day practicalities of working in a laboratory and you will hear stories of knocked benches and malfunctioning equipment. It is such a struggle to get these things to behave. Tiny cells have a wriggling, delinquent agency, while the complex instruments of contemporary big science have personalities all of their own, and whole careers are spent tending them. Experimental science is a messy, prolonged process; if not country house entertainment, it is a theatre of kinds, a spectacle of proof that is ratified among learned professors at conferences and in the pages of academic journals.[1] So it is with finance. It is a collective activity, the preserve of the well-educated, affluent, social elite. The process of testing and experimentation rolls onward as the markets follow the sun around the globe. Financiers, like scientists, debate: they meet in luxury hotels – the 21st-century equivalent of the country house – to settle arguments, developing new kinds of practice and new ways of making money.

We can push the comparison further. Sociologists of science have argued that scientific facts are assembled in networks of instrumentation, of practice, of social relationships and institutional hierarchies. If we ask what is in a fact, they will answer: all of these things. Facts do not lie around, partially invisible and waiting to be discovered, but are assembled laboriously through the efforts of scientific specialists. They are fragile, held in place by those same efforts and mechanisms, and maintained only as long as those networks hold together. Facts are *made*.[2] This is not to say that facts are any less factual. If we are aware of the laborious rigour that surrounds their production we will take them all the more seriously: facts are not opinions precisely because of the very great difficulties involved in their assembly. But after a while facts become naturalized, settled, domesticated. They are taken for granted, and the arduous circumstances of their production left behind. Such a process is necessary if science is ever to move forward, or we would be forever reinventing our most basic findings. Facts become, in the words of Bruno Latour, 'black boxed' in instruments and practices. It is only when things go wrong that we reopen and reexamine the content of these boxes.[3]

So it is with prices. The value of someone's savings portfolio or mortgage is an obdurately real affair, and to understand that prices are made is not to somehow lessen their status. But prices, like facts, are assembled through demonstration, instrumentation, sociality and expertise. What, then, is *in* a price? Everything: the wires, screens, the telegraph or ticker tape, the social rituals that bind exchanges together, the modes of calculation, the most innovative practices and knowledge of market participants, market regulation and vigorous lobbying, global political-economic shifts. All these things are rendered down into a vast collective agreement as to what something is worth. Rendered down and held in place for a day, a year, or a microsecond, before a new settlement emerges, and with it a new price.

Take LIBOR, for example – the London Interbank Offered Rate, a daily calculation of the basic cost of borrowing money. Donald MacKenzie, who has researched it in detail, suggests that LIBOR is interesting because it was for many years so thoroughly black boxed that it came to be regarded as a fundamental natural fact of the financial universe.[4] Banks lend each other money all the time. A network of screens supplies current buy and sell prices for debt, and dealers are skilled at inferring the likely cost of borrowing. In a highly routinized daily fixing, the LIBOR office asks the bankers how much money costs. Once a day, by 11.10 am, representatives of 16 selected banks phone an office in London's Docklands, passing on their best estimate. Sometimes, says MacKenzie, they forget, and the office calls them. Their suggestions are sorted in order, the top and bottom quartiles ignored, and the mean of the second and third quartiles is published at 11.45 am as the British Bankers' Association LIBOR. The process is all very rule of thumb, but it is also, as MacKenzie points out, sociologically robust. The banks' inputs are made public and subject to scrutiny, while excluding the top and bottom quartiles makes wildcard or overly aggressive suggestions redundant. It would take a concerted effort to distort LIBOR.

This simple calculation, routine and forgotten by 11.46 am each morning, serves as the basis for a whole superstructure of additional financial transactions. The prices of some $350 trillion of derivatives are indexed to the number. 'The importance of the calculation', writes MacKenzie,

> is reflected in the arrangements if a terrorist incident or other event disrupt the office in which I witnessed it. Nearby, a similarly equipped office building is kept in constant readiness; dedicated lines have been laid into the homes of those responsible for the calculation; a permanently staffed backup site, over 250 km away, can also calculate LIBOR.

Although LIBOR is thoroughly black boxed, the circumstances of its production rendered invisible, those circumstances remain important enough to demand not one but two replacement facilities in case of emergency.

LIBOR is a price, and it contains the state of all information about the demand and supply of global credit. Let's think of it through the analogy provided by those paintings. It is talked about – and used – as if it had been discovered by experiment, a natural artefact surfaced by the curiosity of financial man. This is – metaphorically speaking – the alchemist kneeling before his boiling pot. When MacKenzie explains its construction, however, we can see that the process is more like the public spectacle of the bird and the air pump. It draws in the material architectures of credit brokers with their voice boxes and whiteboards; the judgement of expert traders as to what they might be able to borrow and at what price; regular calculative practices kept clean by the daylight of transparency and the threat of reputational damage; and at the highest level, a sharp politics of inclusion and exclusion determining who is able to contribute to the fixing and who is not. It is a messy process, contested and unsettled. Rival standards come and go, scandals break out. It is also exclusive, secretive and hidden: financial facts, like any others, remain the domain of those expert and qualified enough to deal with them.

In 2012 a scandal broke concerning banks colluding to manipulate LIBOR rate. Traders were prosecuted and banks fined huge sums – Barclays alone incurring hundreds of millions of dollars in penalties from regulators in the USA and Britain. The UK investigation lasted seven years and cost £60 million. A class action from US homeowners proposed that the distorted rates had led directly to foreclosures and home repossessions and they sought damages accordingly. A casual reading of these again supposes the alchemist's view of prices, that there is one correct bank rate and that any deviation from it is incorrect. The price is out there in the darkness, a shadow waiting to be illuminated. It is hard, on this view, to work up any real outrage about an incorrect LIBOR fixing. It is wrong, but not *morally* so – it is more like a wrong answer in a class test. Traders must try harder!

Once we embrace the idea that prices are constructed, like experiments, in public theatres of truth, we then open ourselves to another realization vital in our understanding of finance. Prices are always *political*. Seen in a more sociological way, the traders' crime was not to create a price that was somehow wrong, but rather to distort a robust sociological process in pursuit of their own agenda, to use the social might and privileged position of the bank (we do not all get asked for our opinion on the best price of borrowing) to fatten their own bonuses. That is a crime that regulators should get worked up about even if, as one news report put it, LIBOR was the rate that nobody borrowed at. As a result of the scandal, the British Bankers' Association lost its stewardship of the rate, and at the time of writing financial markets are moving away from the measure to others that put less weight on 'expert judgement', with its attendant 'costs and risks'. Those words come from Andrew Bailey, governor of the Bank of England. The alchemist's ideal proves hard to dislodge.[5]

***

In fact, the march of finance over the last three decades has been driven by innovations in social and calculative practice that are often passed off as some kind of alchemy. During the final three decades of the 20th century the ingenuity of bankers knew no bounds, and a series of significant innovations transformed the shape of finance, and thus also that of the world we live in today. Where status and power had once accrued to certain *individuals* through their social and educational background, it now flowed through *networks* of financial practice, centring on different kinds of financial deal. Banks began trading on their own account and were increasingly involved in processes of what we have come to call 'securitization', a neologism signifying the making of securities (usually bonds) from other kinds of things; old-fashioned 'mergers and acquisitions' business was replaced by a new kind of financial project management, coordinating networks of institutions to raise and deal in vast sums of money.[6] In different ways, both styles of business invoked new kinds of financial products, backed by novel kinds of financial mathematics and demanding a complete change in the regulatory and cultural framing of finance. As always, bringing these into being was hard work.

Let us deal with securitization first. We saw in Chapter 3 how the Chicago Board of Trade grew to provide a speculative market in the future prices of agricultural goods. Chapter 4 recalled how disagreements over the legal and moral validity of futures trading found their way to the Supreme Court. The debate had centred on agricultural goods, and although Chief Justice Holmes recognized the speculators' practice of 'setting off', or settling deals in advance, it remained that the goods could be delivered if so desired. This legal distinction separated legitimate, legal speculation from gambling. Speculation on the future prices of financial securities failed this test. Financial securities could never be delivered, as they were nothing more concrete than claims on uncertain future revenue streams. Financial futures remained immoral, illegal and politically undesirable; they had been implicated among the causes of the disastrous financial crisis of 1929, still very much in the mind of US legislators.

The 1960s were hard for financial dealers on both sides of the Atlantic. London's exchange languished as the regulatory arm of an interventionist government. In the USA, regulated commodity prices offered little opportunity for speculation: traders were left sitting on the steps of the pit, reading their newspapers. In the face of this pressing need for new business the Board of Trade, together with the Chicago Mercantile Exchange (the Merc), worked hard to expand trading venues. As index-linked futures remained illegal, the Board focused its efforts on stock options. A stock certificate *could* be delivered and therefore options were *technically* legal, although highly unpalatable to Chicago regulators. Donald MacKenzie and Yuvall Millo trace this story, and how it led to the opening of the Chicago Board Options Exchange, or CBOE, in 1973.[7]

The first step was to establish the intellectual credibility of options trading. The Board employed lobbyists and lawyers to promote a new narrative about options trading, arguing that it was not wild and reckless gambling, but a credible, scientific activity. Just as the stock operators and ticker tape readers of the 19th century had invoked a veil of scientific rationality over their speculations, grounding them in the disciplines of statistics and the objective analysis of business statements, so the Chicago traders began to draw on the rhetorical resources of mainstream economics to justify their desired practices.

The idea that stock prices moved in a 'random walk' had been around for a century, first set out in 1863 by a Parisian broker Jules Regnault.[8]

Throughout the 1950s and 1960s a series of increasingly sophisticated analysis by mathematicians such as Benoit Mandelbrot, Harry Markowitz and Eugene Fama helped solidify the notion into what is now known as the 'efficient market hypothesis'.[9] The EMH, as it is usually known, claims that all available information (as well as a certain amount of 'noise') is encoded into prices; as information emerges in an unpredictable manner, so prices move in a stochastic dance. The theory put paid to the hopes of ever discerning the future of the market. It was simply unknowable. The patterns speculators such as the fictionalized Jesse Livermore had seen on the ticker tape were just fragments of noise, shaped by our behavioural disposition to see order where there is none. Markets would just have to get used to living in a world of uncertainty.

Such randomness of stock prices could only mean financial hazard. The traders argued that financial options could be traded as a means of protection against this, just as they were in dealing with changes in future weather and market conditions for agricultural products. None other than Milton Friedman penned a demonstration of the benefits of a currency futures exchange, for which he received $5,000 from the CBOE, perhaps $40,000 in today's money. But the supporters of options trading could, and did, go much further than simply emphasizing its utility.

The EMH is the foundation stone of today's financial orthodoxy. Around it has grown a thicket of theoretical and practical techniques, many of which date from the same period of intellectual ferment in the middle of the 20th century. One such was Harry Markowitz's portfolio theory, which underpins modern asset management. Another was option pricing theory. The startling innovation of three academic economists – Fischer Black, Myron Scholes and Robert Merton – option pricing theory has subsequently become recognized as one of the most important contributions of 20th-century economics. It brought Merton and Scholes the Nobel Prize in 1997, Black having died in 1995. The formula showed traders how to construct a portfolio that mirrored the option and therefore suggested an appropriate price. In doing so, it acted as an engine that *shaped* prices, organizing previously chaotic options markets in line with its predictions.[10] But the new mathematics also played an important *rhetorical* role in legitimizing the new kind of trading: 'the whole weight of orthodox modern economics could now be deployed against anyone still claiming options to be disreputable.'[11]

The CBOE, dedicated to options trading, was launched in 1973. There were other factors at play. Richard Nixon's 1969 election to the Presidency led to a change in leadership of the SEC (the US financial regulator) and a financial regime more favourable to options trading. Leo Melamed and others worked hard to bring about regulatory changes as well as a cultural one. But it was the technical solution to options pricing, published in 1973, and increasingly adopted by market participants over the coming years, that cemented derivatives trading as the engine of contemporary finance and shaped the financial paradigm that we live with today. This is a paradigm where finance is underpinned by complicated mathematics out of reach to anyone without postgraduate training in the mathematical sciences. It does not matter that at the heart of these sophisticated calculations is the experience and judgement of the trader, and that the core skills of the practice have changed far less than protagonists might like to suggest. If prices are political, then making prices is an act of power; the new science of financial economics stands gatekeeper over the markets, determining who can enter and profit, and who must remain outside.

The irony of the story, noted by MacKenzie and Millo, is that the kind of collective action necessary to bring legitimacy to options trading is completely alien to the assumptions on which the EMH is based: rational egoism and individual action. Bringing Chicago economics into being demanded a decidedly un-Chicago form of collaboration. The introduction of a financial logic that squeezed out traders educated on the market floor was only possible on account of the obligations and networks in which those traders had been immersed throughout their whole careers. But, as we have seen in previous chapters, markets depend far more on collective action, ritual and reciprocity than their most fervent supporters might like to admit.

★★★

The growth of mathematical finance, with all the gatekeeping it implied, helped to settle the great question of finance: who dines on whom? Who is predator and who is prey? Middle America, it seemed, fell into the second category. In the late 1970s and early 1980s, Wall Street's eyes lighted on mortgages as a source of possible opportunity. For people whose business was buying and selling debt, the cumulative amount owed by homeowners in the USA – following postwar decades of suburban growth that saw home ownership as a crucial part of the American dream – must have been mouth-watering. But there were certain problems. Government regulation during the same period had been heavily skewed towards the interests of the borrowers. According to Lewis Ranieri, the Salomon Brothers trader who pioneered commercial mortgage bonds, the mortgage became 'so perfect for the borrower that a large economic benefit is taken away from the other participants, including the long-term investor'.[12] Despite Ranieri's protestations, this was perfectly acceptable to the lender. Mortgage debt was owned by conservative, small-scale savings banks known as 'thrifts' (building societies in the UK), the business of which was offering low-risk loans on homes. Moreover, two giant government-sponsored bodies, Fannie Mae and Freddie Mac, underwrote a portion of these loans with the intention of expanding the pool of eligible borrowers and thus broadening home ownership.

These underwriting institutions also provided mechanisms through which loans could be passed on by the thrifts, with the aim of increasing the supply of money into the sector. They bought up loans and resold them in bundles as bonds, but the results were attractive only to specialist investors. As an investment, the mortgage had several problematic characteristics. It was small. It was attached to an individual, and therefore inherently unpredictable. Mr and Mrs Smith, the homeowners of the suburbs, might lose their jobs, or die, or remortgage. The last was a pressing issue, as regulation designed to protect homeowners allowed anyone to pay off a mortgage without penalty at any time. This 'prepayment risk' (named from the perspective of the buyer) made mortgages unattractive investments for pension funds, corporations and governments whose primary objective was long-term stability. If interest rates went down, rather than holding a more valuable bond investors would be left with cash returned by homeowners changing to cheaper deals, cash for which they would now struggle to find a lucrative home. Where most bonds rose swiftly as interest rates dropped, the price of mortgage bonds changed little: everyone knew the underlying loans would already be in the process of being redeemed.

In 1977 the Bank of America, in conjunction with Ranieri's team at Salomon Brothers, launched the first private mortgage bond. It was elegant in principle, if complex in actuality. The technique, which Ranieri dubbed securitization, was to collect many individual mortgages into a pool. The pool was divided into tranches, or slices. The lowest slice absorbed the earliest prepayments in return for the highest interest rates; with mortgages underwritten by Fannie Mae and Freddie Mac defaults also registered as prepayments. The middle tranche absorbed the next, and the senior tranche held the longest-surviving mortgages. The genius of this structure was that you did not have to know which individual mortgages fell into which tranche; they self-selected by virtue of paying up early. But you could now estimate how long it would take for each tranche to be paid off, and across the whole it was possible to have a robust, statistically informed understanding of the likelihood of prepayment (the risk) set against the promised interest returns. The bond mortgage worked as a device for standardizing and typifying, for translating the irregularity and grit of everyday domestic situations into a smooth and predictable flow of returns.

The bond was a knowledge machine, designed to convert one kind of knowledge into another, turning complex lived experience into statistically – scientifically – determined prices. Once this had been done the bond was now depersonalized, free-floating and tradeable. 'Thus standardized', writes Michael Lewis, 'the pieces of paper could be sold to an American pension fund, to a Tokyo trust company, to a Swiss bank, to a tax evading Greek shipping tycoon living in a yacht in the harbour of Monte Carlo, to anyone with money to invest.'[13] Backed by this epistemological apparatus, the credit rating agencies issued the highest level of creditworthiness to the senior bonds, treble-A, equivalent to the national debt of a healthy nation state. The interest payable on the super-safe senior tranche, while still low, was much higher than the equivalent return on government stock and therefore very attractive to pensions funds and public sector organizations. Bonds sold and the mortgage desk thrived.

Until Salomon arrived on the scene, mortgage lenders, terrified of losing the principal, were notoriously risk-averse. The bonds allowed them to shift risks from their books and simply retain the commission. Naturally, the reward (interest rate) for selling a high-risk loan was greater than for a safe one, and here the incentives for the thrifts aligned perfectly with those of the traders. Profits for those constructing the bonds arose from the difference between the interest received from borrowers and the interest paid out to investors. Monies out will always be lower than monies in as the diversified nature of the bonds makes them less risky than the original mortgages – interest payments on super-safe treble-A-graded bonds are very low indeed. But payments out, the interest on the bonds sold to investors, is largely fixed by market rates. The only way to increase the difference between inflows and outflows, or 'spread', as it was known, was to *lend* at higher interest rates, and to do that riskier loans had to be made, something the thrifts were prepared to do now that they could shift the risk elsewhere.

This higher-risk lending demanded a new technological apparatus. For a long time, lending decisions had depended on expert judgement, usually on the part of the local lender, whose representatives' on-the-ground knowledge assisted greatly in establishing who might have good credit. But expert knowledge offered only the binary choice: lend or do not. Assuming for a moment that risk and reward increase hand-in-hand, it follows that anyone who believes that they will be able to repay a loan at 25 per cent (or is desperate enough to try) is a riskier proposition than someone who can only pay 2.5 per cent. This is a self-fulfilling theory, as the good credit has already been filtered out at low rates; the less in need of money you are, the more cheaply you can borrow, while the poor seek out loan sharks and payday lenders.[14] A more carefully calibrated market in credit required another way of making loan decisions, and the technology of credit scoring that had emerged in the USA over the previous decades made it possible to issue such higher-risk, higher-reward loans.[15] Credit scoring had originally developed for the purchase of consumer items; applied to housing, it not only indicated the difference between good and bad credit risk, but also made it possible to distinguish between different degrees of credit risk.

Now, two significant barriers were overcome: the worry of losing the principal, and the difficulty of matching risk and return across a broad population of borrowers. Huge profits could be made from loans and financial operations that simply could not have existed a decade previously.

The Wall Street tail really did begin to wag the dog of Middle America. New mortgages led to a buoyant housing market, and this kept the mortgage bonds afloat. It seemed as if everyone was winning: the banks setting up the bonds and the investors buying them; the thrifts selling loans on commission but shedding the risk; and the eventual borrowers, able to buy a house in a rising market and take a hold of the American dream. And yet lines are drawn: who is weak, who is strong; who is predator, who is prey. These new kinds of deal, backed by arcane mathematics and the new science of financial economics, subtly shifted Wall Street's status relative to the rest of US society. They made finance elite and exclusive, closed to anyone without the necessary educational and cultural resources. They brought small lenders and homeowners across the nation into a new circuit of capital centred on Manhattan, one that the investment banks entirely dominated. If prices are a form of knowledge, and knowledge is power, then the one who decides how prices are made is the most powerful of all.

7

Where Real Men Make Real Money

Elsewhere, in the once staid world of merchant banking, another kind of predator was flourishing. Corporate raiders like T. Boone Pickens, Sir James Goldsmith and 'Tiny' Rowland became renowned, even glamorized, as ruthless hunters on the wide plains of capitalism. Their exploits shade into fiction. Sir James Manson, the scheming industrialist in Fredrick Forsyth's 1974 novel *The Dogs of War*, has their aura: 'He knew what the City was; it was a jungle, pure and simple, and in it he was one of the panthers.'[1] The fictional Manson and the real-life Rowland shared a colonialist disdain for the continent in which they conducted much of their business; as the piratical Manson put it, 'Knocking off a bank or an armoured truck is merely crude. Knocking off an entire republic has, I feel, a certain style.'[2]

If these real-life raiders were indeed hunters, their prey was more easily digested than Manson's. Throughout the 1950s and 1960s the conglomerate had become a fashionable organizational form. Companies bought other companies, creating empires of unrelated businesses, wherever managers felt that capital could be productively used. The conglomerate was a creature of its times, a product of managerial capitalism where business invested money in making and selling things, and the skills of managers were to do with organizing production and generating effective returns on capital from doing so. Conglomerates benefited from a favourable legal environment and tax relief on debt that made borrowing to buy cash-generative businesses a sensible choice. A cynical observer might also think that in an era where top rates of tax touched 90 per cent there was little to be gained from fat-cat salaries, and much more to be had from featherbedding the expense account. On this measure, the lean corporation of contemporary fashion has less to offer than a global empire complete with jets, golf resorts, celebrity hangers-on and the rest. (An aside, but I do not sense that the contemporary chief executive pines for the lack of private jet or chauffeured limousine. Perhaps leanness, like taxes, is for the little people.)

By the 1980s, the conglomerate era was over. Journalists delighted in mocking monikers – my favourite was always 'guns-to-buns Tomkins' applied to the giant group that owned both Smith & Wesson and Hovis Bakery. There was, indeed, little commercial logic to support such a ramshackle collection of holdings, and conglomerates found themselves unfashionable, their share prices depressed. This presented the raiders with an opportunity. They could buy the business for a significant premium on existing share prices, and thereby claim that they were returning value to shareholders. The amount they would pay would still be less than the value of the assets they had bought, and they could break the firm up, selling businesses and assets and keeping the difference. They grew bolder, their deals bigger, until a watershed moment. 'In 1978 the firm Kohlberg, Kravis and Roberts [KKR]', writes anthropologist Daniel Souleles,

> then called an investment bank, now a private equity firm, bought a manufacturing conglomerate, Houdaille for $355 million dollars. Not only was this four times more than KKR had ever bid to buy a company's stock and manage it privately but KKR only had 1/300th of the total price. The rest of the money they spent, the remaining 99.7% of the price of Houdaille, they made up with borrowed money, either in the form of capital from investors, or loans from banks.[3]

If, as geographer Sarah Hall suggests, securitization is one practice that maintains the position of financial elites, this is the other.[4] Investment bankers derive their power from the networks they can enrol around them, creating new financial structures that allow unimaginable amounts of money to be deployed in raiding the market.

KKR hit on a winning strategy. 'It is not often', says Souleles,

> that one can pinpoint and describe a new and durable way people get rich. But KKR's purchase of Houdaille with very little of their own money, and quite a bit of borrowed money, affords one such moment. KKR's innovation of the leveraged buyout [LBO] would set the standard the industry still follows today.[5]

The audacity comes in the innovation that the target firm should borrow the money to buy itself. Once imagined, this makes perfect sense. There is no way that a small investment banking boutique could borrow enough to buy a sprawling conglomerate. But the conglomerate can. It will issue bonds, and Wall Street traders led by Ivan Boesky had pioneered low-quality 'junk' bonds for exactly this purpose, risky and punitively expensive for the borrower. But if the borrower is the target company, who is to care – except, perhaps, for the employees, customers and suppliers of the conglomerate, who will eventually have to pay for this loan. The buyers can, however, offset the exorbitant cost of the debt against tax, and this meant that KKR could see value in the firm that the market could not. KKR's deal, printed on a huge and complicated chart that hung proudly in one executive's office, changed the rules of what was possible in a takeover; just the option pricing formula established a framework for subsequent trading innovations, so the LBO deal formed the basis of everything done in private equity since.

Raiders cut these conglomerates up and sold the pieces on. They closed down 'underperforming' firms. They restructured, moved employees around, or simply sacked them. Yet these moves were justified by the suddenly fashionable opinion that only the interests of shareholders mattered. Shareholders, the thinking held, were being denied their rightful share by featherbedding executives. Perhaps they were: the classic account of one of these deals, *Barbarians at the Gate*, paints a picture of RJR Nabisco's senior management as cocooned in a world of private jets and country club memberships, using the firm's incredible cash flows ($1.2 billion a year in the mid-1980s) to satisfy every whim. The book offers a litany of corporate excess: fleets of maroon stretch limos with chauffeurs in matching uniforms, a roster of top-class sportspeople on company retainers, and an anecdote about Rocco, the chief executive's German shepherd dog, being whisked away on a corporate jet to avoid punishment having bitten a security guard. 'A few million dollars, [RJR Nabisco's CEO F. Ross Johnson] always said, are lost in the sands of time.'[6]

In this hyper-masculine morality tale, plunging a firm deep into debt could be presented as imposing financial discipline on soft, pampered executives. At the same time, those executives were likely to receive substantial holdings of stock as a reward for making such changes; Jensen and Murphy had argued that we can only expect chief executives to work for shareholders if we make them shareholders too.[7] So the soft, pampered executives became wealthy, lean executives, the corporate raiders became even richer, and the pain of meeting debt repayments was felt in the warehouses and factories, or in the places where the warehouses and factories used to be. The RJR Nabisco takeover ended in disaster, the confectionary operations spoiled by poor management and cost-cutting, the once-profitable cigarette arm destroyed by tobacco litigation and the subsequent settlement.

The ethnographer Karen Ho argues that these new stories of shareholder primacy and principal–agent relations allow the shareholder to be 'positioned as the victim, denied his rightful role in the modern corporation by manager-usurpers. It is partly this notion of the wronged owner reclaiming his just rewards that has fuelled such righteous (and moralistic) activism for shareholder value'.[8] It is no coincidence that the rhetorical focus on shareholder value coincides with a broader move towards individual share ownership and the associated shareholder democracy, at the expense of collective action and organized labour. The focus on shareholder rights helped to deflect scrutiny from the phenomenon of most LBOs 'failing according to multiple parameters, from a decline in shareholder value itself to massive losses in profits, corporate morale, productivity, and jobs.'[9] But it was also the case that the things that were threatened (labour and jobs) were *already* losing their supremacy in the collective imagination of Anglo-Saxon capitalism. Wall Street was simply part of a bigger picture, a transformation in our conception of finance and, in turn, of finance's understanding of itself. Of course, the bankers were happy to help matters along, especially while they made a killing doing so.

★★★

The more refined, scientific and arcane finance becomes, the less refined and otherworldly are the characters that represent it. Michael Lewis' characters in *Liar's Poker* are 300lb mortgage traders devouring five-gallon cans of guacamole; the traders of *Inside Job* are cocaine-fuelled degenerates who charge sex workers to expense accounts; most famous of all is Michael Douglas' reptilian raider Gordon Gekko, his face and a speech burned into our economic consciousness. The phrase 'Master of the Universe' comes from Tom Wolfe, who journeyed to the 1980s heart of the market, the trading room at fictional broker Pierce & Pierce:

> a vast space, perhaps sixty by eighty feet, but with the same eight-foot ceiling bearing down on your head. It was an oppressive space with a ferocious glare, writhing silhouettes, and the roar. The glare came from a wall of plate glass that faced south, looking out over New York Harbor, the Statue of Liberty, Staten Island, and the Brooklyn and New Jersey shores. The writhing silhouettes were the arms and torsos of young men, few of them older than forty. They had their suit jackets off. They were moving about in an agitated manner and sweating early in the morning and shouting, which created the roar. It was the sound of well-educated young white men baying for money on the bond market.[10]

This was where men made money, where real men made real money, a supercharged, 1980s version of the heavy industry that had defined a previous generation of masculinity: blue collars and half-moons of perspiration seeping through the shirt, but the shirts are Brooks Brothers and the rivers in the background run with capital, not molten steel. The trading room Wolfe visited for his research was none other than that of Salomon Brothers, where you might find the biggest of all 'big swinging dicks', in the phrase of Lewis' 'Human Piranha'. These are icons of finance, fixed in our collective narrative imagination; they are part of the story of the market.

Writing, narrative and rhetoric have always been present in the development of finance; finance is a written as well as spoken domain, and financial markets are underpinned by styles of writing. Mundane financial objects such as banknotes, cheques, ledgers and contracts are written things. Even in the digital world, a vast infrastructure of written tallies supports the card or phone that we tap at the supermarket counter. Mortgage bonds are nothing more than writing, promises of future interest repayments from baskets of mortgages underpinned by contracts and legal documentation of bewildering complexity. These insights come from literary scholar Mary Poovey, who argues that from the 17th century onwards imaginative writing – and there was not, back then, a stark demarcation between fact and fiction – helped people to understand the new credit economy and the kinds of value that operated within it.[11] In the 17th century the abstractions of credit were problematic for a population that had always dealt in coinage, in specie. We have already seen the animosity directed at the stockjobbers, who preyed upon and destroyed all honest industry by dividing it into shares, turning productive material toil into something ethereal, fleeting and untrustworthy. The developing genre of fiction, suggests Poovey, helped readers to practise trust, tolerate deferral, evaluate character and believe in things that were immaterial, all essential skills for negotiating their new market world. A population trained to understand borrowing as a fundamentally social arrangement could not otherwise begin to understand how financial value could be held by texts. This kind of work built the foundation on which later skyscrapers of credit, from the slavers' notes to the collateralized debt obligations of 2008, could be erected.

Three hundred years ago, Daniel Defoe wrote *Robinson Crusoe*. I read it for the first time just a few months ago, and it is far from the tame story I knew from primary school: there's slavery and cannibalism, white supremacism and European-Christian expansionism. Crusoe is not keen on Catholics, but he has no time for them being eaten by heathens. He shoots everything – no sooner does an endangered beast lumber or roar into view than Crusoe has bagged its hide as a trophy, or, as the story progresses, a hat. He is an industrious citizen of the 17th century, an archetype of the petit bourgeoisie. He writes. He etches a calendar on a post and keeps books of accounts in a ledger scavenged from his shipwreck. Crusoe imposes the worldview of any good 17th-century Englishman on his tiny island dominion, where he eventually becomes king over a growing and hard-working population. His tools are the leger and the gun, the twin means of control that accompanied Britain and other European nations as they built their empires.

Crusoe is a writer within a novel, and Defoe was a central figure in an era sometimes called the 'Age of Projects'. A prolific author of fiction and non-fiction, he was one of the first to earn a living from his pen and he strove to shape the world as he did so. Valerie Hamilton and Martin Parker, both scholars of organizations, have drawn attention to the parallels between Defoe's fictions and the rash of corporations that emerged in the same period. 'The figure of Daniel Defoe', they write, 'inventor, businessman, writer, politician and secret agent, characterises the age. His first published work, *An Essay upon Projects* (1697) bottles this energy.'[12] Defoe defined a project as 'a vast undertaking, too big to be managed, and therefore likely to come to nothing.' Yet some do succeed. Take Phips' 1687 treasure hunt, the spark that set London's would-be shareholders aflame with desire, or Crusoe's task, the unlikely, implausible, but ultimately fruitful endeavour of turning brute nature into a well-disciplined, productive domain. Hamilton and Parker see the Bank of England as the queen of these projects, growing from the chatter of a few traders in Jonathan's Coffee House into a building of 'timeless rusticated stone', solid and substantial in the heart of the City of London.[13]

Poovey argues that Defoe followed his own extraordinary project, nothing less than the attempt to incite belief through print. 'In the realm of fiction', she writes,

> the negative connotations associated with invalid money were neutralised by the claim that imaginative writing did not have to refer to anything in the actual world; in the realm of economic theory, the fictive elements intrinsic to credit instruments were neutralised by the introduction of abstractions, which would claim simultaneously to be true and not to be referential.[14]

Or, more simply put, as writers like Defoe sought to establish a new genre by refusing to be held to account for the factual content of their stories, credit came along for the ride. Meanwhile, a growing cadre of financial journalists aimed 'to demystify the operations of the city and make even the arcane language of finance familiar to ordinary Britons helped make economic theory seem relevant to everyday life and, not incidentally, make investing in shares in acceptable thing to do with money.'[15] Walter Bagehot was the exemplar of these men, an early and influential editor of *The Economist* magazine. Last of all came the experts, economic theorists like Stanley Jevons, whose flights of marginalist fancy and economic scientism depended both on the existence of dispassionate, factual writing and the availability of abstraction, even the suspension of disbelief, tools assiduously cultivated by the novelists. The very existence of the economy, or 'finance', as a self-contained and self-referential entity is the result of enormous efforts in storytelling and narrative work.[16] Finance, then, is a story, and how it is told matters.

★★★

From the 1980s onwards, the great predators of the market have roamed as freely in the world of fiction as they have in Fernand Braudel's real-life 'anti-market'. They have one thing in common, these 'Masters of the Universe': they are all men. Think again of Pierce & Pierce's trading floor, those young men baying for money in the bond market. Literary scholar Leigh Claire La Berge argues that *The Bonfire of the Vanities*, published days before the 1980s bull market finally collapsed, helped to 'cement an aesthetic mode that captured the way a new financial class was beginning to identify itself and its economic object.'[17] The book's historical realism self-consciously mimics the great realist novels of an earlier era, of Dickens or Balzac: a new city, a new age, with all its vanities and perils, needing a new chronicler. Wolfe paints finance as complex, a world of leverage buyouts, bond yields and other such exotic, risky, dangerous creatures; a world accessible only to the 'big swinging dicks' who inhabited it, needing the intermediation of a white-suited literary giant to make it legible to the rest of us.

Wolfe makes clear the difficulties involved in representing an exclusive, elite financial world. And yet, says La Berge, he gained entry and reported carefully:

> *Bonfire* includes a careful cataloguing of the difference between styles of town cars, codes of cordiality and comportment on the bond trading floor, rules for private school kindergarten admission, and how to hold the Wall Street Journal in public space. … What those who had allowed Wolfe to observe them received as compensation was a conception of finance as complicated, difficult, hard to define, and reserved for wealthy white men.[18]

Wolfe made a pact with Wall Street. In return for the access he needed, he would take their performances of finance at face value. His prose is littered with exclamation marks, onomatopoeic grunts and groans:

> Wolfe records sensations of speed, sexual excitement, anxiety and pleasure. In this world of masculine sensation, finance finds its form. Men understand it. As he glares at his wife across the table, alternately planning a bond sale and justifying his affair to himself, Sherman thinks: 'Judy understood none of this, did she? No none of it'.[19]

Wolfe got his 'Masters of the Universe' slogan from Michael Lewis, and the two wink at each other in their texts, the great chroniclers of the excesses of 1980s finance capitalism. Two decades on, and Lewis finds another crisis in need of translation. His book *The Big Short* offers another production of finance as cliquey, gendered and complicated. The heroes who bring down those corrupt banks can see clearly only because of their outsider status. The film version of Lewis' *The Big Short*, directed by Adam McKay, is even more overt in its presentation of men as cool, rational and in command,

and women as distracting and dangerous. In one scene the leading short seller, determined to see the state of the USA's mortgage market for himself, interrogates a topless dancer as to the viability of her mortgage payments. By the end of their conversation she has stopped dancing, her voice cracked with panic, while our hero calls the office to strike a deal. 'There's a bubble', he says. Old conceptions of who should and should not participate in the market – shadows of gender, class and ethnicity – circulate under the surface of the narrative.[20]

Finance is not just screens and wires; it is also a cultural production, an attitude. Fiction therefore shades into fact, and finance self-consciously reproduces its tropes: meetings conducted in strip joints and clients entertained by prostitutes, foul-mouthed masculinity and speech littered with a repertoire of bodily metaphors involving penetration, or the steely disposition of the screen trader who pukes in the bin after taking a particularly bad loss and goes on 'scalping' – itself a typically agonistic, raced and gendered term – without further pause.[21] Take the macho hell-raising of *The Wolf of Wall Street*, where Jordan Belfort addresses his crew as warriors: 'It's up to each and every one of you, my highly trained Strattonites, my killers, my killers who will not take no for an answer. My fucking warriors, who will not hang up the phone, until their client either buys or fucking dies!'[22] Through narrative, financiers can conceive of themselves as hunters, the aboriginal inhabitants of the stock markets; after all, a common expression for those working on a commission basis is 'eat what you kill'.[23]

★★★

The historical relationship of the market and gender is more complex. The early English stock market offered opportunities to women, if only because no legislation or social conventions existed to prevent them participating in this novel activity. They were, it seems, successful market participants. This bothered 17th-century society and upset social mores. The market, with its wild and unpredictable nature, was associated with feminine passions, even hysteria. Speculative activity was somehow feminine, set against the masculine stolidness of land and property. Women bore the responsibility for the collapse of the South Sea Bubble and the ruin of many market participants – again, 'we have been ruined by whores'.[24] Defoe believed Lady Credit was important to the economy, regarding it as the duty of financial man to temper her passions. By the 1840s, the era of a frenzied speculation on railway shares, investment handbooks exhorted men to approach the market with an appropriately detached and diligent persona, breaking with hysterical speculation: he must show attention, vigilance, carefulness, uninterrupted study of companies and continual observation of events.[25] He who invests in the stocks of railways must be as much an engineer as the man designing those same tracks.

All this machismo is productive. Recent scholarship has also shown that discourses of masculinity play an important role in sustaining markets as they are. There is a deep relationship between the notions of freedom that circulate in contemporary political economy and those of masculinity: calculation, enterprise, risk-taking and ultimately risk management are fundamentally masculine conceptions. For many feminist critics, the idea that risk can be captured and traded, or squeezed out of the market altogether by careful management, is a kind of masculine hubris that ended up in the credit crisis. Leslie Salzinger has argued that the engine of financial activity depends on risk. This 'contrast between the performative, hysterical, ultimately feminized aspects of trading practice and culture and the abstract, rational masculine marketplace produces a sense … that the universe of risk they are producing can be relied upon to keep the neoliberal economy in dependable, productive balance.'[26] This is not empty theorising. Salzinger spent time watching traders at work. 'Many of the basic social relations on the desk', she writes, 'seem to be organized around "men behaving badly". Traders greet each other with punches and slaps, throw things at each other, slam phones down so hard that they break, play constant, sometimes cruel practical jokes on each other, receive and send dirty jokes online.'[27] Metaphors are bodily. They often involve penetration (if the trade goes well) and being penetrated (if it does not). All this excessive masculinity, she suggests, makes the markets function. Acts of trading are sustained by narratives of masculinity, and the honour code that underpins markets based on spoken deals is a distinctly masculine one. Meanwhile, as the traditionally feminine creature of the market is made masculine, so the traditionally masculine productive economy, now given over to female workers, is feminized. The feminization of industry makes its decline bearable: nowadays, real men make their money in the market.

Empirical evidence bears out these prejudices. Women working in finance are still paid less and offered fewer opportunities than men. Elisabeth Prügl catalogues just some of the issues:

> In the United States women accounted for only about 18 percent of corporate officers in the finance and insurance industries in 2008, and for 7.3 percent of chief financial officers in Fortune 500 companies. … In some of the United Kingdom's top finance companies, women received around 80 percent less performance-related pay than their male colleagues. … The three major Wall Street firms … all had paid out more than $100 million each between 1990 and 2006 to resolve sex discrimination suits. … In 2009 – according to a front-page story in Forbes Magazine – five female executives charged Citi with 'recession discrimination.' Apparently women accounted only for 12 percent of executives in their department, but they made up 45 percent of those laid off.[28]

Such norms are inculcated in financiers before they even get hired. The anthropologist Karen Ho documents the Wall Street recruitment process on the Princeton University campus. Over and over, she encountered the notion of 'smartness'. Potential recruits are constantly reminded that they are the smartest of the smart, in the most smart of universities, seeking to join an industry rammed with the smartest. Ho sees through any claim to intellectual distinction. Instead, it means something quite specific: 'such characteristics as being impeccable and smartly dressed, dashing appearance, mental and physical quickness, aggressiveness and vigour reference the upper-classness, maleness, whiteness and heteronormativity of ideal investment bankers … the specific elitism that is the key valence of smartness.'[29] It helps to have been educated at Harvard or Princeton, as Wall Street recruiters recognize fine distinctions even between elite US institutions. Doors are held wide for a Princetonian; a Yale student wanting to make it on Wall Street needs to be studying economics; at Penn State it has to be the Wharton School of Business. 'It is precisely these differentiations', she writes, 'between "always already smart" and "smart with qualifications," between unquestioned, generic and naturalized smartness and smartness that must be proved, that enact and solidify the hierarchies on which elitism is necessarily based.'[30]

The global financial crisis of 2008 upset these stereotypes. Clearly, the endeavour to manage risk was a failed one. Bankers were blamed for exactly the kind of behaviour that masculinity invokes: the risk-taking, the late nights, the excess of all kinds. Journalists and politicians started to wonder whether things might have been different if women had been in charge, if it had been 'Lehman Sisters' instead of Lehman Brothers. Prügl sees this as a myth, a kind of public morality play where some essential differences between men and women allow the reanimation of a kind of finance that had failed morally as well as economically. Woman, the Other to the financial buccaneer, can bring her virtues of caution and risk aversion – her 'civilizing and moderating influences' – to remedy all that is wrong with finance and find 'a happy ending in the gender diversification of the financial sector.'[31] But, worries Prügl, this might not be such a happy ending after all: a narrative that identifies these differing gender characteristics could equally become a justification for keeping women in second-class jobs in the sector. Indeed, films made since the financial crisis suggest this might be the case. *The Big Short* keeps women strictly side-lined, while *Margin Call* hints at the possibility of a female redeemer in the person of the only female character, the head of risk management who is first ignored and then scapegoated by the bank's senior management. But these films do not embrace excessive masculinity either – that is for the traders on the losing side.

What triumphs, suggest James Brassett and Frederic Heine, is a kind of misfit masculinity based around superhuman maths skills and an ability to see differently from the rest of the crowd.[32] Such skills reflect a finance now driven by science and numbers, but they do not come easily, at least in narrative terms – they are packaged as social awkwardness and often come with an origin story, a hinted-at behavioural condition or a personal tragedy. The films depict a masculinity that has come untethered from more traditional performances, that is uncertain and humbled in the face of the complexity of finance. As the bond markets and with them the global economy come tumbling down, men emerge in control once more – even if the performance is more anxious techie than predatory buccaneer.

8

Wires! Shocks! Sausages!

And so, after a detour through the spectacle of finance – the public theatre of prices, the rhetoric of financial maths, stories of bond-jamming 'big swinging dicks' and corporate-raiding buccaneers, anxious oddballs piloting arcane equations while calm women sooth their fevered brows – it is time to bring the 1980s to a close. There is no better way to do so than with another story, of a pantomime villain and larger-than-life character, Tom Wilmot, London's very own Wolf of Wall Street.

Wilmot became a household name in 1985 after publishing a bestselling introductory guide to the UK's over-the-counter markets. Trading OTC, as it is commonly known, simply means that the stock has not been admitted to any market but is traded by the broker's firm. In avoiding admission to a market, however, stocks bypass one of the biggest quality controls that protects investors.[1] Wilmot's firm went by the reassuring, stolid name of Harvard Securities. According to his book, Harvard acted in 'dual-capacity', dealing what it happily described as 'speculative share issues'. This fact is crucial. Harvard Securities not only sold stock to the newly propertied Sids of the mid-1980s, but also *made the market in those stocks*. In the last few chapters we have seen how prices contain the power relations of the context of which they are assembled, and how, in order to claim legitimacy, they must be made in some kind of daylight. Harvard was better informed, better capitalized and better staffed than those who purchased its shares, yet the broker itself was opaque, the spectacle of public proof very much absent from its dealings.[2]

The firm was founded in 1973 by a Canadian named Mortie Glickman; Wilmot refers to him in his book as 'Mr M.J. Glickman'. It later emerged that Mr M.J. Glickman had what journalists call a 'colourful background'. Working with a man named Irving Kott, he had set up a broker named Forget in Montréal. The company made a living employing high-pressure telephone sales to push stocks in dodgy Canadian companies onto European investors; much of the work was done through a Frankfurt-based operation, also set up by Kott and Glickman. The recipe was simple and involved buying a stake in the firm at a very low price and selling it on to investors at an inflated one. Forget was suspended by the Québec Securities Commission in March 1973 and promptly went out of business. Eventually, the Canadian authorities prosecuted Kott – but not Glickman – for fraud.[3]

Wilmot worked with Glickman, both as directors of Harvard Securities, from 1975 until the latter stepped down in 1985. We might speculate that he learned his trade during that first decade. 'Tom was the biggest rogue of the lot', one old market hand told me, 'and while Tom was dealing instructions to his dealers were, "Don't buy anything, you are only a seller".' Of course, a market with no buyers would look suspiciously quiet. Indeed, it would not by any meaningful definition be a market at all. The ingenious Wilmot had a solution. In his book, he boasts that Harvard Securities was taking the lead in making information on the OTC market more widely available, paying the *Evening Standard* and *Daily Telegraph* – among others – to carry lists of stock prices. But these 'prices' were, allegedly, not actual prices resulting from stock trades, but indicative 'basis prices' made – made up – by his own office. 'Just to convince people it was all right', said the jobber, 'he would put out his list of stocks, not many of them, 20 or 30 and he would move them up 1p a day, down 1p a day. And then he would move them 2p a day. … People thought that it was all right but in fact they had bought a load of rubbish.'

In the early days Harvard Securities sold lines of US stock that, due to the SEC rules, could not be disposed of at home. In the late 1970s it began promoting its own offerings. It was busy during the boom years of the 1980s and bought a succession of companies to the markets. Some of these, notably Hard Rock Cafe and Park Hall Leisure, moved on to the main markets and became household names. The press reported that Harvard Securities gained 20,000 new investors through the BT flotation in 1984, and Harvard claimed to already have 45,000 names in its database by that time. Inexperienced investors who had made safe gains on a reputable issue – whether a government privatization or a famous leisure name like Hard Rock Cafe – then became the targets of aggressive telephone sales that exploited goodwill from the initial successful dealings. At the peak of the boom, turnover reached £200 million.

Wilmot bought a salmon-pink turbo-charged Bentley. He ran through staff quickly. At one point he was changing secretaries once a week: a colleague, quoted in *The Times*, remarked acidly that Wilmot 'likes them to be pretty, to be a hostess and to do instantaneous work – it's a difficult job'. He moved into an eight-bedroom house, a 1930s affair designed by Bauhaus architect Walter Gropius. And anyone who had seen Wilmot arriving at the office in his spanking new pink limousine might have called the height of the boom, but once again Wilmot had an answer: the man who always told investors to be wary of a company if its chairman drove a Rolls simply pointed out that his machine was a Bentley.[4]

In 1984 Harvard Securities raised £2.1 million through a public offering, valuing the company at nearly £5 million, and listing its shares *on its own market*. The money was, he claimed, intended to develop the firm's market-making activities and create a war chest for investing in early-stage firms with promising prospects. This implied that the cash would be used for buying 'founder' shares at an early stage that could then be resold to investors at a huge profit, a legal if somewhat disreputable practice. The offer had the side effect of making Wilmot, who owned 37 per cent of the firm, a paper millionaire – a very secure one too, as his salesmen controlled the price of that paper. His investors did not do so well. Many of the companies Harvard Securities introduced simply went bust. Wilmot shrugged this off. 'From the onset', he said, 'we have told clients that for every 10 companies in which they invest, two or three would fail in business within a two-year to three-year period; three or four would perform reasonably well; while three or four should perform spectacularly.'[5]

Wealth is not everything. As we have seen, the world of stock exchanges is a closed one and Wilmot wanted to be on the inside. In 1986 Harvard Securities announced its intention to apply for Stock Exchange membership. Soon, however, the OTC practitioners committee, of which Harvard Securities was a prominent member, suggested that the licenced dealers would do better to launch their own regulated exchange. 'It is not', said Wilmot, 'in the interests of the industry for the Stock Exchange to control the OTC.'[6] These plans came to nothing, and, in April 1987, Mortie Glickman sold the remainder of his stake to David Wickins, a reputable businessman and founder of British Car Auction Group, in return for a £1 million investment. The deal fuelled speculation that Wilmot would step back from the company and that Wickins would become the new chairman; Wickins hoped to end the practice of cold calling customers and instead re-brand the firm as a specialist corporate financier focused on growing companies. These talks broke down in August 1987, the very peak of the long 1980s bull market. At the same time, the London Stock Exchange refused to accept Harvard Securities as a member and effectively blackballed Wilmot. Shut out by the financial establishment, Wilmot tried and failed to find a buyer for his own stake in the firm.

***

It is not hard to discern why Wilmot's aspiration to start his own exchange marked the very zenith of his fortunes. Things were changing quickly around him and the notion of what an exchange actually was, in terms of its role, functions and physical structures, was shifting by the day.

Automation had long been a preoccupation of stock exchange officials. Often, it had egalitarian underpinnings: if automation could reduce manpower, wrote one author, 'we might even reduce the costs to such an extent that small orders became profitable and the ideal of the Cloth Cap Investor at last became a reality.'[7] Fischer Black, the economist whose option pricing theory was then transforming the financial world, had dreamed of a fully automated securities market. His pamphlet on the topic was illustrated with a line drawing of an enormous machine straight out of B-movie science fiction, a riveted dustbin on stilts with enormous tentacles, like vacuum cleaner tubes, reaching down onto the desks of bankers and traders. It is hard to read the expressions of those occupying the desks, but they certainly are not joyful.[8] Thinking such as this was never entirely benevolent: it also had roots in the desire for effective supervision of market participants, whose dealings by handshake and conversation could be easily hidden. But we should be careful of reading the history of automation as a smooth transition, driven by visionary executives, from lumpy, inefficient bodies to sleek, efficient machines. In fact, bearing in mind the comfortable, profitable market positions held by senior players within the organization, why did automation happen at all?

The sociologist Juan Pablo Pardo-Guerra, who has written extensively on the topic, shows that the move to total automation happens almost accidentally.[9] It begins with the routine tasks of settlement and clearing; in London, the postwar years saw mechanical calculating devices, and then computers, introduced to streamline what had been a labour-intensive, time-consuming process. These early machines allowed a new kind of participant, the technologist, into the closed world of the London Stock Exchange. Calculators and computers demanded technical expertise, and the technologists who worked on them built their own quiet and often invisible networks of power within the organization. The members of the exchange (the brokers and market-makers) were used to treating back office workers as staff, secondary in status and in access. They treated the technologists the same way. Pardo-Guerra passes on a story about a member meeting the Exchange's new technical director – a senior appointment – in the lavatories of the 17th floor, a space reserved for members, and expressing his displeasure about sharing the facilities with 'the staff'. One can hardly blame the technologists for pushing on with changes until one day, the members woke up to find that they were no longer in charge.

In 1970 the London Stock Exchange introduced its Market Price Display Service (MPDS) to show middle prices on black-and-white television sets in offices throughout its newly constructed concrete tower block. The service was a manual-automatic hybrid that relied on Exchange representatives patrolling the trading floor, physically collecting prices. MPDS prices often differed from those made available by *The Financial Times* and Extel – rival data producers – so the Exchange banned these organizations from the trading floor, thereby creating a monopoly in the new and lucrative commercial market for data. This early analogue computer, with data carried in coaxial cables, was soon outdated. The London Stock Exchange implemented a database called EPIC (the Exchange Price Information Computer) able to hold a limited amount of price information for every single stock traded. Then, in 1978, it launched a new system named TOPIC (or, less snappily, Teletext Output of Price Information by Computer) based on the Post Office's teletext system. 'TOPIC', writes Pardo-Guerra, 'was not simply a scoping device, a way of seeing the market: it was, rather, a common platform, a standardized mechanism for displaying market information – from prices and company announcements, to charts and tailored analytics – and reacting to it from afar.'[10] As Pardo-Guerra points out, the crucial advantage of this system was that data could flow both ways – from the trader's terminal to the central hub and back. TOPIC made possible new modes of visualization and calculation. It was, in other words, creating a new market *place*: the screen.

On Monday 27 October 1986, London's markets finally went electronic. This was the 'Big Bang', at least the most visible aspect of it. The London Stock Exchange introduced a distributed, screen-based system called SEAQ, or Stock Exchange Automated Quotation, a mash-up of TOPIC and EPIC. Market-makers – who replaced jobbers and were able to deal for clients and on their own account – published 'two-way' (buy and sell) prices on the screens. The best prices for any security were highlighted by a yellow strip at the top of the screen, and a broker who wished to deal would call the market-maker on the telephone and strike a bargain. London had borrowed this distributed-trading model from NASDAQ: even the name showed a debt of gratitude, the Stock Exchange Automatic Quotation, echoing the National Association of Securities Dealers Automatic Quotation. The new system looked so like the US OTC market that the New York Stock Exchange put itself in a perilous political position by banning its members from trading on the London Stock Exchange, just as they were banned from NASDAQ. A week later New York retracted, a spokesman conceding that, 'If the British Parliament says it is an Exchange, that's good enough for the Big Board.'[11]

Those designing the new market had no wish to disrupt the old one. The system was built with continuity in mind and made it possible for people to trade on the Stock Exchange floor, just as they had always done. Many firms took leases to pitches on the new floor, refurbished and upgraded at the cost of several million pounds. But the jobbers knew that their world was changing, and that many would never set foot on the trading floor again. Friday 24 October, the last official day of spoken trading, was packed with wild festivities. Dealers chased a pantomime horse containing two clerks round the floor, and the *Spitting Image* puppet of Chancellor Nigel Lawson made an appearance. In all, says one historian, it was more a 'rowdy Irish wake' than the solemn, final day of a mighty institution.[12] Managers, expecting business as usual, were caught out: 'Within five minutes of Big Bang', said one, 'on Monday morning, it was clear to me that the floor was dead. I'm not bragging. I was the last person in the City to figure it out.'[13] But there was no reason to loiter on the floor, struggling to elicit a deal from a seething crowd of traders when you could survey the whole world of prices from the comfort of your desk. The crowds just moved to their offices upstairs. In January 1987 only a hundred people traded regularly on the floor – just a tenth of the crowd that had traded there a year previously – and *The Financial Times* was speculating that the new six-sided pitches might become a 'Hexagonal Wine Bar'. It closed three months later.[14]

Moving to screens did not mean abandoning all those social relationships that had sustained trade on the floor. Telephones connected traders and they spoke to each other frequently – more often than they did to their spouses, as one wryly pointed out. At the same time, screen-based trading had many advantages. Traders had always been required to deal at the offered price and were still obliged to do so; screen prices were 'firm prices'. But if the telephone was ringing, it was always possible to check the screen before answering. In fact, one of the great complaints about screen trading was that during sudden market movements dealers stopped picking up the phone. The trading floor had been designed to preclude informational advantages, with everyone immersed in the same noise and depending on the same communications. Now traders could have more screens on their desk, bringing in all kinds of information from the outside world; salespeople, analysts and other experts in the office could be easily within reach. In fact, the office knew the news *first* – the technology inverted the relationship between floor trader and clerk, between front office and back.

***

Screen-based markets are the 1980s' great legacy to finance. They made it possible to trade without any human help at all. In many ways, this was the dream of visionaries such as Fischer Black, using machines to cut costs and trim trading margins until a truly efficient, democratic market was achieved. According to a certain line of thinking, the proliferation of trades that machines bring creates liquidity and benefits all market participants. Others disagree. Computers react more quickly than people and without any sense of restraint. At the time of the Big Bang, computerized trading had nothing of the sophistication of modern algorithms. Robots followed a simple set of rules designed to launch sales if the market fell too quickly. Program trading, as this was called, came to the world's attention when global stock markets suffered their worst ever day of falls: 19 October 1987, Black Monday, just a year after Big Bang.

The warning signs came from New York. Shares began to slide on Wednesday 14 October. On Thursday the slippage worsened. Overpriced shares were knocked by fears of interest rate increases, and it is widely thought that program trades exacerbated the fall. When Wall Street sneezes, the saying goes, the rest of the world catches a cold, and one might have expected panic in London on Friday. But nothing happened, because on Thursday night, while New York's traders had been piling on the sell orders, South East England was hit by the most savage storm in a century. Eighteen people died as walls collapsed and trees were uprooted, falling through buildings and onto cars. The hurricane shredded power lines and blocked railways, wrecking the capital's infrastructure. London's financial markets never opened that morning. Many could not get to work, and those who did found power cuts and darkened screens. Even the Bank of England stopped dealing in government bonds. 'Commuting into work was positively eerie', writes Michael Lewis, whose *Liar's Poker* ends with the crash of 1987. 'The streets were empty, and shops normally open were boarded shut. A crowd huddled beneath the awning of Victoria station, going nowhere. The trains did not run. It looked like an ABC mini-series on nuclear winter, or perhaps a scene from the Tempest.'[15] The Stock Exchange did manage to get its screens running by lunchtime, showing a rudimentary service, but there was hardly anyone in the office to deal. Those who did were busy short-selling insurance companies as quickly as they could, or picking up stock in the young and hungry do-it-yourself retailer B&Q, which announced healthy sales of chainsaws and wheelbarrows and that its stores would be open all weekend – unheard of in 1987! The half-hearted trading session finished at roughly 2pm, just before the US markets opened.

So London was, for once, not paying much attention to the goings-on at Wall Street. On the other side of the Atlantic, things were not good at all. Friday 16 October was a bleak day for the US stock exchange: 343 million shares changed hands, more volume than any day previously, and the Dow Jones index fell by 4.6 per cent. Traders were worried about interest rates and the long-term economic output; more and more, they were just plain worried, for this had been the worst week that Wall Street had ever seen. Then came the weekend, a queasy quiet before Monday.

London opened before New York. Traders, shaken by Friday's events, both meteorological and financial, tried to pre-empt heavy selling by marking prices down even before the market had opened. To no avail. Phones rang and rang, traders panicked and computer screens struggled – the new electronic systems had never before been tested in battle, so to speak. The London Stock Exchange was obliged to post a 'fast market notice' on its price screens to show that screen prices might be wildly different from those actually available from a broker; the fundamental basis of screen-based dealing, that the screen's prices would be honoured, had been smashed by the sheer volume of sales. During the course of the day London's market lost 12 per cent of its value, roughly £50 billion worth of assets evaporating in a few hours.

John Jenkins' trading desk at Guinness Mahon, his new employer, had lost a fortune before trading had even begun. A market in meltdown was made even worse by electronic dealing that simply could not cope with the speed of the collapse. 'We were five million pounds down before we could even…' Jenkins says, 'we had crap computers in those days, they were slow, they would hang up, you would look at the screen and something would be 25p, or whatever the thing was, but in actual reality it was 12p, because our machinery that we had was slow, ineffective, total crap.' Many traders simply gave up answering their phones, much to the frustration of clients.

Newspapers used the words 'bloodbath', 'panic', 'meltdown', and even 'Armageddon'. Black Monday, 19 October 1987, smashed records for the largest single-day fall all over the world. Panic spread. The Australian Stock Exchange lost 20 per cent of its value in the first few minutes of trading and the Tokyo Stock Exchange fell 11 per cent. It was not just professional traders who were burned, but also the legions of newly minted private investors. In Oxford Street, the Debenhams department store contained a small investors' boutique run by the fledgling private client broker The Share Centre. *The Guardian* newspaper records a crowd of individuals seeking to rescue some value from their ruined portfolios, and the broker's total inability to transact in the market: '"Just do the deals," said Share Centre manager, Jackie Mitchell, a former filing clerk. "Can't do the bloody deals, and they won't answer the phone," came the voice down the intercom.'[16]

There is little honour in a collapsing market. The chaos gave traders an opportunity to get their own back on rivals, and suddenly being known as a sector's go-to guy did not help at all. 'We got annihilated', says Jenkins,

> Old scores were settled against us. They were! Because we had this big rep in our sector that we were bigger and better. Some bloody fool in the bank published that we had an 85% market share of all the leisure business. … You have got BZW on one side, you have got Smith Brothers, you have got Winterflood, you have got all of these other big market-makers, you can see their guv'nors turning round and going, 'Hang on a sec, these people, they have suddenly got 85% of the market share?' So they were out to get us. We got nailed, that first week. … They just sent brokers [to us]. They said, 'Oh no I don't have much business, go and see Jenkins he does all of the business.' We just got nailed.

For the rest of that week, markets seesawed. Small rallies in New York offered moments of hope, whether to big-time traders or the private investors of Oxford Street. Although the overall direction continued to be downwards, there was enough movement for nimble-footed traders to make some of their money back. Jenkins instructed his traders to stay the cheapest seller and unload stock into a rising market, buying it back as the market turned again. 'You just had to be incredibly light on your feet', he says, 'and we did that for … I don't know how many days.' It all seemed something of a bad dream: 'I have no memory of that week at all really … we tried to stay on the right end of it all of the way through. We made good money, we had some big days, some million-pound days. But they were coming off a £10 million loss.'

***

Stock markets are remarkably robust, their well-established organizational architectures sociologically anchored in years of history and practice. Black Monday and the weeks following it did not destroy the markets; Jenkins and his colleagues may have lost £10 million on Monday, but they were trading again on Tuesday and Wednesday, nimble, sure-footed, making money. Prices keep on being made, even if those making them do not care for the direction of travel.

Harvard Securities, on the other hand, was not robust. Nor was its price-making machinery. Investors suddenly began asking for their money back, and when it became clear that the broker who had sold shares was unwilling to buy them again, they wrote to the Department of Trade and Industry (DTI) and complained. Harvard laid off staff, and in February 1988 reported a loss of £2.5 million for the first quarter. Its auditors qualified the accounts: it was not clear, with the Financial Services Act looming, whether the business could continue in any form if it couldn't secure regulatory oversight. In the summer of 1987, a formal motion was raised in the House of Commons by the Labour MP for Workington, Dale Campbell-Savours, advising investors to pull out of Harvard Securities. Campbell-Savours was emerging as an unlikely champion of those investors who had been sold stock by the firm. He prodded the DTI to investigate and asked the shadow secretary for industry – a little known politician named Tony Blair – to take up the cause. Wilmot dismissed these allegations, saying that investors who had made a profit did not write to the DTI. Although there was an embarrassment of riches as far as potential misdemeanour was concerned, investigators focused on a film distributor called VTC; the dealers had sold £132,000 of stock by promising buyers exciting figures and a significant increase in profitability – while VTC itself had supplied accounts predicting a £1.1 million loss. Campbell-Savours also noted to the House that Harvard Securities' salesmen had been instructed to avoid repurchasing stock in distressed companies. It later emerged that dealers earned double commission for selling OTC stocks to investors but had their commission docked should they repurchase any from a client who wished to sell.[17]

In September 1988 Harvard Securities shut its doors, its final year's loss £7 million. An estimated £20 million of investors' money disappeared. Approximately 3,000 investors, many of whom had been sold Harvard Securities' own stock, had written to the DTI.

Wilmot moved on. You cannot keep a good man down, and City gossip columns gleefully followed the progress of his new firm, a sausage company. The pink Bentley doubled as the firm's van, sausages heaped on the back seat and a refrigerator jammed in the boot (cue the strapline: 'Wilmot's old banger'). When deliveries were too far away Wilmot delegated driving to his chauffeur, who also seemed to act as personal assistant, fielding calls from journalists. Perhaps this doubling up was a sign of straightened times. If so, it was the only one, and Wilmot was soon abroad and embroiled in a lengthy dispute with the taxman. Wilmot's son Christopher even joined the sausage business, leaving one commentator to speculate that he might learn some bad habits from his father. The commentator showed some prescience: in August 2011 Wilmot and his two sons were jailed for a total of 19 years for operating a 'boiler room' scam on an enormous scale. The scammers controlled 16 offices stretching across Europe – Christopher ran the IT operation from Slovakia, for example – and during five years of operation they relieved members of the public of some £27 million, £14 million of which was never seen again.[18]

Harvard Securities was not the only casualty of Black Monday. Many reputable firms also struggled. The crash made apparent organizational problems that had been hidden by the rising markets. Brian Winterflood, John Jenkins and Andrew Beeson were among those who sold their firms to foreign banks; all three described the subsequent years as among the unhappiest of their careers, as they suffered a change in culture from staid partnership to aggressive target-driven regimes. The newly merged firms rode out a year of boom but were found lacking by the long, slow bear market that followed Black Monday. Strategic mistakes, or the lack of strategy altogether, became apparent. 'The mistake we made…' Beeson says, 'when ANZ bought [the firm] they did not know what they were going to do with it. We assumed that an owner would have a plan. Come the crash of 1987 it was quite clear by then that they did not.' Despite selling their firms, the former partners remained burdened by responsibilities to employees, many of whom had worked for them for years. 'I formed up to the management of ANZ Bank', he continues,

> and said, 'Either you shrink this business to what it is really good at' – because despite the fact that we had these specializations it was still all things to all men – 'or we might buy the business back, or I'm leaving with five of my former partners and we are going to start again'. … Clearly having been a partner for 15 plus years, you know, you had a

> responsibility to quite a lot of people. Where of course Australians are wonderful people, but they don't like to be bowled out, if you know what I mean, and so they fired me.

Jenkins' canny trading may have recouped much of the losses of Black Monday, but he and all his colleagues and staff were soon out of work. Guinness Mahon was taken over by the Bank of Yokohama, which shut the trading activities down, saying they were too risky. The business his father had set up in 1960, and in which John Jenkins had worked for a quarter of a century, suddenly ceased to exist. 'I had to make everybody redundant', he says, 'people I had worked with for 25 years we had to make redundant. … Everybody hated that place in the end. We all hated every brick in it. They just made us sit there all day long, not allowed to do anything, touch anything, answer a phone, we just had to sit there.'

The brittle, greedy 1980s had come to a gloomy end. Journalists speculated that second-hand car lots would be brimming with Porches and BMWs looking for new homes. Britain would soon be at war in the Middle East, and Margaret Thatcher would be chauffeured away from Downing Street for the last time. Britain entered a prolonged economic downturn, lasting until the early 1990s. But from the ashes of the 1980s new markets rose, phoenix-like, to serve the boom of the next decade.

PART III

Opportunity Lost

9

Other People's Money

In August 1999 I was a 25-year-old stocks and shares journalist. I did not have a clue what I was doing. I like to think that makes me one of the good guys, an innocent swept up in the maelstrom of dotcom speculation. In truth it made me into a kind of collaborator, happy to be wined and dined and to repeat the lines that I was spun to a credulous and excited public. I was naive enough not to realize that regular lunches at London's finest restaurants do not come free; that there is always a reason, and that someone is always paying.

I was a young reporter at the newly formed *Shares Magazine*. I liked the job. I liked the deal it came with even more: being handed the first gin and tonic as the hour hand crept towards one; riding across London in the back of a black Mercedes, on the way to air my views in a television studio at Bloomberg or the Money Channel; the buzz of young colleagues and new technology and the sense that the world was changing for the better. I liked the fact that a mysterious woman called Bella, whom I never met, used to telephone me regularly for syndicated radio news bulletins that I was never up early enough to hear. Most of all, I liked the smell of money being made and believed that somehow, in a small way, some of it could be mine. A fellow scribe, equally well qualified, had landed the precious small companies correspondent job at a prestigious news outlet. In this, his first job after university, he would find himself speaking to a chief executive on one line, with a stream of callers trying to get him on another, his mobile ringing, thrown in a drawer. On one occasion he tipped a small firm and saw the shares rise 50 per cent, adding £11 million to its market capitalization. 'At the age of 24', he says, 'that was a big deal.' When you are 20-something and impoverished student days are a very real memory, it is a fine thing indeed to be a stocks and shares hack in the middle of a market boom.

Daniel Defoe wrote of 'projects' – start-ups, or entrepreneurial endeavours, we might call them – as 'vast undertakings, too big to be managed, therefore likely to come to nothing'. He could well have been describing the late 1990s, as the dream of the 'world wide web' finally arrived. These were years rich with 'the humour of invention', which produced 'new contrivances, engines, and projects to get money'.[1] We looked forward to the internet freeing us all and at the same time making us all rich (see how that one turned out). The technology was still rudimentary. If you wanted to 'go on the web' at home, you plugged a computer cable into the phone socket and listened to beeps and wheezes as the connection dialled up. But a wide-open and connected future beckoned and stock markets were banking those future profits right now. Every Sid and the occasional Sandra (by my reckoning, the ratio of male to female private investors was about 10 to 1), now recovered from the wounds of 1987, was piling into the market. Stocks were on the news and chatted about by taxi drivers; everyone hoped to get a piece of the next dotcom sensation.

Shares Magazine, or just plain *Shares*, had been set up early in 1999 to capitalize on some of that exuberance. It was fronted by Ross Greenwood, a cheerful, kind-hearted Australian, at the time taking a sabbatical in London. It was not an intellectually demanding publication. The cover of one of the early issues featured a newspaper small ad, bolded and circled in red pen: 'Earn £100,000 a year investing from home', the block print proclaimed. As hordes of punters, many with remarkably little financial literacy, strove to find their little piece of the dotcom magic, copies of the magazine flew off the shelves and the publishers, tough veterans of trade magazines and commercial advertising sales, rubbed their hands with glee. Their only problem was getting the staff. Not just competent staff, but anybody at all. The British economy was in overdrive, and young professionals hopped from job to job with abandon. I emerged blinking from a long stint in university libraries to find my friends racing around in cobra-striped hatchbacks, some of which even had six gears. Everyone I knew with any skills at all had a job and enough freelance work on the side to put down a deposit on their flat (property in 1999 was still almost affordable, even in London) with enough left over for purple emulsion and an IKEA coffee table. I attended an undemanding interview, after which, with a mixture of derring-do and desperation born of economic ambition and organizational crisis, *Shares Magazine* hired me.

Shares occupied a scruffy, overheated office in Southwark. Throughout history, Southwark has had a peculiar relationship with the City of London. It lies due south, across the river. It became the lawless no man's land on the City's doorstep, its ancient flint cathedral rising from among dens of squalor and iniquity. The City's prison, 'the Clink', was built there in Clink Lane. Brothels and gambling, prohibited in the City itself, were permitted. In 1999, it remained the City's poor relation, offering cheap space for those providing goods and services to their neighbours on the other side of the river. Borough Market, now famous as a gentrified foodie hangout, supplied fruit and vegetables to much of London. As you stepped out of the newly opened steel and glass underground station you stepped back in time: shouting porters, forklift trucks shifting huge crates of vegetables, the green paint of the Victorian ironwork overhead covered in a thick layer of soot and grime. Trains to Dover and Brighton rattled along overhead tracks banked up on redbrick arches, and rats feasted on the remains of fruit and vegetables pulped by the wheels of delivery vans and handcarts. Across the road, a pub called The Market Porter enjoyed special licencing privileges, and at eight in the morning the doors would be wide open, the voices of those just off shift carrying out on air rich with the smells of drink and fried food. The office was opposite the building where the heroes of Guy Richie's *Lock, Stock and Two Smoking Barrels* hid out, just around the corner from where Colin Firth and Hugh Grant crashed through a restaurant window, battling over Bridget Jones. It was a very long time ago.

My inability to spot what was new in this bizarre dotcom world, where 25-year-olds could move markets and people followed them with their life savings, was not surprising. Everything was new, and everything was madness: firms that had existed for weeks, with no products or sales, now worth millions; two-bit corporate finance outfits ranked more highly than industrial concerns. One mid-size broking and advisory firm, Durlacher – a newish outfit, although one that carried an esteemed City name – saw its market value climb enough for it to qualify for the FTSE 100. Tragically, by the time the quarterly reshuffle came around, the bottom had fallen out of the market and the broker's holdings in the internet start-ups it had brought to market were not worth as much as had previously been thought. (Durlacher later suffered the ultimate stock market indignity: it became a shell company, an empty carcass, valuable only because it maintained a quotation on the exchange.) Individuals also found themselves in possession of substantial paper fortunes: 'In January 2000', one small-time financier told me, 'one of my colleagues came to me and said, "I've just worked out what your options are worth." In January 2000, my personal options, according to my colleague, were worth substantial double figures of millions. I'm glad I didn't go out and spend it.'

As we have already seen, the social contract forged during the 1980s emphasized self-help and entrepreneurship. Share ownership had become part of economic citizenship, the essential activity of shoring up one's financial future. In this new worldview, the flourishing of the stock market was necessarily linked to that of the polity, and booming stock markets became a policy objective. In the early 1990s, the US Federal Reserve began to lower interest rates aggressively and pour money into the economy in order to boost the stock markets. This tactic was employed every time the markets stuttered, and became known as the 'Greenspan put'. With interest rates lower than inflation, anyone trying to save found themselves losing money – far better to borrow and invest! Cash poured into property and the financial markets.

The structural changes of the 1980s helped the flow of money. The Big Bang reforms had broken up the stock market cartels and made it possible for brokers to offer services they called 'execution only', communicating with customers by telephone and post, and charging small percentages to buy and sell shares as the clients wished. These brokers were quick to recognize the potential of the internet for their own business organization. In a competitive sector with wafer-thin margins, it offered the ability to cut costs to the bone and simultaneously reach a broad public. Economies of scale allowed US broking giants to expand quickly into the UK and elsewhere. These firms were soon selling more than stock: brokers swiftly realized that they could offer a crude simulacra of the marketplace as experienced by professional traders, turning the whole business of private investing into a sophisticated leisure pursuit for the tech-savvy investor.

It was the same for financial media. Before the 1980s British financial journalism had been the preserve of *The Financial Times*, which published a daily list of closing prices and some company news, and a few specialist publications such as the august *Investors' Chronicle*. Information flowed through personal contacts and private channels, and by the time it got into the papers it was – quite literally – yesterday's news. Growing private ownership of shares led to an explosion of publications and broadcast media. *Shares Magazine* was just one such example, a brand-new, nationwide, weekly publication launched to an audience that had not existed a few years previously. Market news became an accepted component of news broadcasting, and business channels thrived. The celebrity financial pundit arrived on our television screens. Ross Greenwood was one such. His fame was nothing compared to that of Maria Bartiromo, the news anchor who, in a predictably gendered put-down of a clever and dynamic journalist, became known as CNBC's 'Money Honey'. (Bartiromo now works for Fox News and has trademarked 'Money Honey' for future ventures – when life gives you lemons, I suppose.) The whole thing became a self-reinforcing cultural circuit, paid for by the torrents of private investors' money that flooded through the brokers' portals.[2]

***

Even the exchanges that traded these stocks were new. We saw in Chapter 6 how the Jenkins family established a small jobbing firm in London, specializing in dog tracks and holiday camps; how John Jenkins grew to be senior partner; how the firm made £1 million in five minutes of trading when the British Telecom issue came out; and how it was sold to Guinness Mahon and thence a Japanese investment bank. In the bear market that followed the crash of 1987 the trading desk was closed and Jenkins found himself unemployed, bruised and battered by a difficult period in a toxic working environment. But he had not just traded dog tracks. Trading 'over the counter' he had also developed a specialist expertise in the London Stock Exchange's little-known Rule 163.[3]

The rule, which later became Rule 535, and then Rule 4.2, allowed members to conduct occasional trades in companies not listed on the London Stock Exchange. Trades had to be conducted on a 'matched bargain' basis. This meant that the jobbing firm had to line up a buyer and a seller and 'put through' the trade, taking a commission of one and a quarter per cent on each side. Each bargain had to be reported to the Stock Exchange and was noted and approved by the listings department. It was clearly not meant to support a volume operation. S. Jenkins & Son Ltd already traded like this: jobbers in the smallest stocks could not rely on a steady flow of buy and sell orders so were reluctant to hold stock on their books, tying up capital, possibly for years. Instead, they would build up lists of potential buyers and sellers, and only when they could make a match would they trade.

By the early 1990s Jenkins was twiddling his thumbs and missing his old trading days. He fancied starting a new firm but his application to the London Stock Exchange was twice turned down. He was on the verge of giving up when he discovered that Paul Brown, his former 'blue button', had been made redundant. Brown remembers the conversation: 'John said, "I can't pay you a lot of money but it's a start-up, we'll get an office, just you and me, and we'll give it a go. " So I said, "Yeah, fine."' The third submission was accepted by the London Stock Exchange, and on 11 February 1991, Jenkins and Brown set up J.P. Jenkins Ltd with a mandate to trade 'over the counter' under the Exchange rules.

There followed a period Jenkins remembers as one of the happiest in his working life. J.P. Jenkins occupied a small office above the Our Price music store in Finsbury Square. A friendly Dutchman on the floor above would come down to their office mid-afternoon bearing a bottle of gin. It was just 'two guys and a sofa', low-tech trading with pen, paper and phone. 'John had this old computer', says Brown, 'so he brought it in, so it sat on the desk, but we never used it. We just had it there for show … it was a sofa and a computer that didn't work. It did absolutely nothing. I mean it did nothing. It just sat there.' Business was about making lists and matching, and the firm was soon known for the catchphrase 'I'll take a note'. They never said 'no'; they just made a note. They had a good name, and they did well.

In 1992 the firm moved to Moor House in Moorgate. There was a separate room for the back office. A typewritten catalogue of stocks includes some well-established entities such as Rangers and Liverpool football clubs, National Parking Corporation (NCP), breweries such as Daniel Thwaites and Shepherd Neame, Yates' Wine Lodges, and even Weetabix. Alongside these were the stocks of smaller, high-risk, or less frequently traded entities: Pan Andean Resources, Dart Valley Light Railway and Ecclesiastical Insurance, to name three at random. Trading business grew steadily and the firm was profitable; Jenkins' horizons were not much bigger – no 'delusions of grandeur', as he put it. But no man is an island, even the smallest market-maker, and the tendrils of automation soon began to wind their way into the comfortable life of these traders.

Ironically, Jenkins was always an early adopter of technology. Even before the Big Bang swept terminals into London, he had travelled to the USA, visiting a broking firm named Herzog Heine Geduld, and watched the traders dealing on the computer-based NASDAQ. He returned one of the few believers. 'It was coming, scary, but people did not believe it, people honestly did not believe', says John.

> I'd come back and I would say, 'I have sat with a trader in the room with NASDAQ, there is no market floor, I have sat with these guys in a room, sitting there with a computer terminal and they are doing their trades and this, that and the other.' You could see even my own lot think, 'That is not going to happen here is it, you know, it is just not going to happen.'

His firm soon got rid of the broken computer and installed its own bespoke system to replace pen and paper. But the important part of story was unfolding outside of Jenkins' office.

Alongside SEAQ, the Exchange set up a 'non-SEAQ board'. It was just another set of teletext screens, a home for Rule 163 stocks. It published rudimentary data and historic trades. In the process it made the firm's profits visible. 'It used to piss people off', says John's son Jonathan, "because you'd get someone saying, "I bought them off you at nine and it prints on there you bought them at six." It showed everybody exactly what we were doing.' Nonetheless, it was the marketplace for these stocks, and at some point in the early 1990s, when the London Stock Exchange threatened to discontinue the board, J.P. Jenkins took over its operation. Jenkins then struck a deal with Reuters – following a chance conversation with a salesman – and alongside the non-SEAQ board the firm created Newstrack, a rudimentary news service for the small companies that it traded. This displayed prices, trading volume and a limited amount of company information over the Reuters network. A rudimentary connectivity between the market-makers and Newstrack meant that that if the price moved, the market capitalization would also move. Firms released final and interim results through the pages, published dividends and were encouraged to make trading announcements. In other words, Newstrack consciously mimicked the London Stock Exchange's Regulatory News Service (RNS). J.P. Jenkins realized that there was money to be made here and started charging firms to use the service; it had inadvertently stumbled into the business of data provision, a new and growing revenue sector for stock exchanges.

Suddenly J.P. Jenkins was operating something that looked very like a small-scale exchange. It offered a venue where smaller companies could have their shares bought and sold, and where they could attain some of the publicity and regulatory kudos that comes with a public listing. J.P. Jenkins was making a tidy profit from its market-making and starting to make inroads into the data sales sector. All of this under the London Stock Exchange's regulatory banner! Exchanges are themselves businesses and they operate in a competitive market for exchange services. The London Stock Exchange soon started to feel uncomfortable with this arrangement, so much so that it gave in to political pressure on another front and set in motion a process to launch its own market for growth stocks.[4] That really is another story, and I will come back to it in Chapter 14.

What matters here is that in 1995 the London Stock Exchange closed both its Rule 163 reporting *and* the non-SEAQ board. It was an overtly defensive measure, but it was too late. Many of the companies traded by Jenkins did not want to go to the Exchange's new venue. They petitioned Jenkins, who – naturally – was keen to keep his business going. Now *he* was confronted by another problem, the loss of his public venue, of his market*place*. He had no option but to build his own space onto his existing data infrastructure. He called it OFEX (for 'off exchange'). Bolted onto the exiting Newstrack service, running through Reuters' wires, OFEX was technically a trading facility, existing in the regulatory space of 'don't know why not ... we've got no rule that says you can't', as one executive put it. But taken as a whole, the assemblage – the wires, the screens, the trading mechanisms and networks of corporate financiers – could be seen as a capital market. On the basis of 'walks like a duck, talks like a duck' (the same executive), it really was a stock exchange. OFEX, specializing in the stocks of start-ups and small companies, was ready and waiting for the dotcom boom.

***

OFEX's entry requirements were light and application was straightforward: a London Stock Exchange member firm, or a member of a recognized professional body such as a qualified accountant, could apply on a company's behalf. It needed to present an application form, a questionnaire and some directors' declarations, together with a non-refundable application fee of £250 plus VAT. Entrepreneurial corporate financiers soon saw the opportunity and began to use OFEX as a place to raise funds for new businesses. The first public offer of securities on OFEX was Syence Skin Care, which raised £250,000. Jenkins reportedly told John Bridges, the adviser responsible, that he 'scared the hell' out of OFEX's management, who had never envisaged that a company would raise money on the market.

It was not even clear that this was strictly legal, and OFEX was not really ready for such traffic. Unpleasant scandals rocked the young market. The most infamous was Skynet, a firm that offered satellite-operated tracking devices for cars. Having listed at 27p, the stock climbed to 275p, valuing the company – despite an absence of sales, or even a viable product – at £30 million. Following outrage from investors, board resignations, demands from the tax office and the landlord, and finally an auditor's declaration of insolvency, the shares were suspended in January 1998 at 4p. The reputational damage of Skynet's demise was compounded by a rescue plan from Tom Wilmot, proprietor of the salmon-pink Bentley.

In response, OFEX began to evolve the structure and organization that befitted a capital market. J.P. Jenkins moved to tighten standards and began to promote the market in a more systematic way. It supplied price and company data to resellers such as Bloomberg and Reuters, launching itself into the cultural circuit of late-1990s finance capitalism. *The Financial Times* and the *London Evening Standard* carried closing prices of some of the more important shares. By 1999 a redeveloped website allowed private investors to access content that had previously been distributed via Newstrack, such as company fundamentals and announcements. In what OFEX described as 'a turning point in the battle to get up-to-the-minute OFEX information freely accessible', the site provided data in real time in a format accessible to private investors. Today's easy access to markets detracts from the fact that this was a big deal – everyday punters could, in theory, participate in the market on the same terms as professional investors. Jenkins established a selection panel to screen firms that wished to join the market and emphasized compliance structures to the point of 'seeming paranoid', as Emma Jenkins put it. In 1998 OFEX changed from being a badge for a trading operation to a self-standing market, its business model based on charging listing fees to companies and providing market information. J.P. Jenkins remained market-maker, a lucrative monopoly in a heady bull market. As the millennium drew to a close, its traders could not deal fast enough. A story circulated that they had put a bucket in the corner of the dealing room so they did not even have to dash to the lavatory; the more prosaic truth was that they wedged the fire doors open so that those essential trips could be done as swiftly as possible. By November 1999, John Jenkins, by now chairman of a substantial group of companies, found himself back answering the phone in the trading room.

At the centre of all this excitement was the dotcom stock, its novelty sparking an old-fashioned speculative boom. The 18th century had the South Sea Bubble, and the 19th a mania for railway shares. There was, before the First World War, a craze for rubber, and after the Second, a short-lived boom in the shares of dog tracks. By 1999, the investing public was in a frenzy for the next bit of dotcom, as the internet promised to radically reshape the way we did business. It did, of course, like the railways; as was the case with the railways, the real economic gains were eventually captured by large corporations, not by the punters that funded the infrastructure. At the time all that mattered was that shares kept going up and new issues on OFEX became seen as a sure-fire way of making money. They offered retail investors a chance to join the dotcom party at the beginning, as opposed to buying already inflated stock in the secondary market. Market euphoria fired up the ambitions of the meekest firms. One financier said,

> I knew people who walked into financial advisers and merchant banks and so forth with a business plan and said, 'We'd like a million quid please to see if we can prove the point,' only to discover that two days later they had a fully blown prospectus and they were raising at least 25 million.

OFEX became a reliable venue for raising money, often for very speculative ventures: a firm called printpotato.com, set to revolutionize t-shirt printing via the internet, or, if my memory serves me well, balls.com, the 'one-stop shop online' for anything ball-related. The domain name is now an enthusiast's blog on sports balls. How could it not be? There was 'E-male order', setting out to capture what was, in 1999, still called the 'pink pound'. The crucial device for all these fundraisings was the prospectus, a 60-page A4 booklet jammed with legal boilerplate. The financiers assembling them did not have a legal protocol to follow so they repurposed the offer documents of more senior exchanges. Offer rules were based on *caveat emptor* – buyer beware – so however imaginative the offer might be, it need only be displayed in the prospectus and buyers were expected to discriminate accordingly. Investors, often with only rudimentary financial literacy, would send off for a prospectus and digest these legal complexities before putting up their money. On the back page, a tear-off slip invited anyone inclined to send in a cheque. 'Occasionally', said one advisor, 'you would get somebody calling up saying, "I have just sent in a £1,000 cheque for whatever it was, but when are you going to cash the cheque?" "I will probably go to the bank later today", I would reply. "Oh, I will not get paid until the end of the month."'

How did the public find out about these exciting new offers? That is where we, the media circus, came in. Young, hungry journalists and public relations (PR) firms formed an interface between the company raising millions to fill a warehouse with tennis balls and the investors who hoped to be a part of the brave new dotcom world. The PR executives operated a simple formula, described by one as 'If I take you [journalists] out and get you pissed a lot you'll write about my company'. As recent graduates, we were ideal candidates: we may not have known much about stock analysis, but we were true experts on free booze. Yet there was more nuance to this strategy than first appeared. The rule was to keep the journalists at lunch until late in the afternoon so they had no time to do any research and, cushioned by a warm cloud of claret and sirloin, would write the story as it had been passed to them. There was a fine line between good-natured inebriation and incapacity, so it was the task of the host to send the journalist back to the office while they could still write; 4.30 pm was widely held to be the ideal breaking-up time, leaving the hack foggy-eyed at the screen rewording press releases for a deadline. Regional reporters would be entertained at 'ARCE lunches' – that's Association of Regional City Editors – each given topped-and-tailed press releases with a regional anecdote or focus, and the issues would receive coverage all over the UK. The cost of all this hospitality fell on the future investors, although I remember one story about a firm that went bust at the mere thought of the restaurant bill, leaving the PR man to pick up the damage and the tab. This same man, a ruby-faced, genial version of Monty Python's Mr Creosote, passed away just a few years ago in his grand residence in the south of France, until his late 80s a living reprimand to all things health and diet-related.

The formula worked. The extraordinary demand for stock threatened to overwhelm the small finance firms: 'There was one particular day', Bridges told me,

> when I personally fielded over 300 phone calls. My receptionist logged 275 phone calls that she couldn't put through to me, because I was on the phone … they were almost always all the same, 'Did I get a piece in your last float, can you put me down for the next one?'… On a Sunday, phones rang all day long, people in the hope of getting somebody on the line that they could give money to.

Many advisory firms made a great deal of money in a short space of time. It had become customary to issue warrants (a form of stock option that allowed the holder to purchase stock for a nominal price) as delayed payment for advisory services, and firms found themselves suddenly sitting on enormous paper gains. Like independent record labels, small advisory firms only really needed a single success to enjoy a comfortable life hereafter.

Not everyone agreed that dotcoms were worth what was claimed. Daniel Beunza and Raghu Garud document a very public spat between two Wall Street analysts.[5] These equity analysts provide research, supposedly impartially, to their employers' clients as a means of stimulating trading commissions. The spat concerned a strange new company called Amazon. Jonathan Cohen, a well-regarded analyst at Merrill Lynch, argued that Amazon should be valued as a bookseller and forecast $50 a share based on a generous $1 billion of revenue. Henry Blodget, an unknown newcomer at a Canadian bank, called Amazon an 'Internet company' – some other kind of thing – and predicted $400 a share. Investors slugged it out until, as the writers put it, 'the episode finally resolved itself in Blodget's favour. The stock exceeded the $400 price target in three weeks, and Blodget entered Institutional Investor's All-Star team.' There is a double epitaph here. Blodget became Merrill's star tech analyst but was completely discredited when regulators discovered that he had been selling his audience duds. He had publicly rated one, excite@home, as a 'short-term accumulate' while telling colleagues that it was 'such a piece of crap'. He was fined heavily by the regulator and his Wall Street career was over. As far as Amazon was concerned, however, Blodget was right. Amazon really was some other kind of thing, and its current share price makes his target seem entirely insignificant.

In dotcom London, the role of super-aggressive tech analyst went to one Dru Edmonstone of not-quite-FTSE 100 dotcom powerhouse Durlacher. When I returned to academia I thought I had heard the last of him, but in a story that amused and delighted the editors of serious news outlets, Edmonstone – a distant cousin of the Duchess of Cornwall – was, in 2018, found guilty of fraud. He had, *inter alia*, claimed various welfare payments under the names of his sister, of an employee of his father, Sir Archibald Edmonstone, the 83-year-old 7th baronet of Duntreath, and of *Fight Club*'s Tyler Durden. He had masqueraded as a doctor to sell refreshments to walkers passing through his family's 6,000-acre estate in Scotland. The Sheriff presiding said Edmonstone had 'a long history of manipulative behaviour and sociopathic behaviour'.[6]

Such were ideal personality traits, it seemed, for the venal dotcom world. It was always 'other people's money' or 'OPM', as the wide boys termed it: it paid for the fees, it paid for the lunches, it paid the executives' salaries until cash ran out. It bumped up the price of shares so promoters could sell them at a profit or cash out their warrants. Sharp operators set up deals where they not only raised money for the company but also sold investors shares that they had previously issued to themselves, usually 'in return' for the concept or their management efforts. The result of these so-called founder or vendor shares was a straight transfer of funds from investors to promoters, with no benefit to the investee firm. I remember one such, also with aristocratic connections, where the promoters cleared £1 million in this manner; in a *caveat emptor* market, putting the arrangement in the prospectus made it legal. If those other people could not read the prospectus, the more fool them.

10

Fear and Loathing on Wall Street

Boom time never lasts. By the spring of 2001 selling had started in earnest. The law of gravity applies to speculative financial investments as much as it does to apples. The fledgling market OFEX gave back most of its profits and found its new infrastructure – a telephone system installed to cope with the volume, for example – coupled with its capital market business structure, an expensive proposition. Oddly, I don't remember the drama of the dotcom collapse. There was a bad week in April 2001, with heavy selling on Wall Street, but the pundits were sanguine, commenting that it was simply the froth being blown off the market. Diane Coyle, then economics editor at the *Independent*, described it as a 'slow puncture' in the dotcom bubble.[1] This turned out to be a prescient description as short-term losses segued into a short but sharp recession, a period of deep gloom that in the autumn turned to existential dread. On 11 September I was marooned in London by a train strike, and the milling crowds of people, the general sense of panic and the live stream of unutterable images from New York gave a far more end-of-the-world feeling than even the heavy falls on NASDAQ. So, too, did the films of tanks rolling into Iraq and the sense of despair that pervaded all things economic as once-mighty firms – some of the globe's largest corporations – turned out to be fraudulent (Enron and WorldCom) and negligent (Arthur Andersen). These I remember much more than the falls of April 2000.

During those frenzied months working at *Shares Magazine* and elsewhere, I developed a fascination with private investors. Professional finance holds that private investors are 'dumb'. Academic finance researchers are barely less scathing, although they prefer the term 'noise traders'. Werner De Bondt, one eminent scholar, laments 'the failure of many people to infer basic investment principles from years of experience', as if one might magically infer portfolio management theory from a few shaky bets on Tesco or Carillion.[2] There are plenty of studies showing the kind of things they do wrong. They trade too often, incurring excessive trading fees. They are overconfident, staking too much on risky firms, and are then unwilling to cut their losses, because selling means owning up to failure. They are prone to buying stocks of firms that have been in the news (and are therefore overpriced), that they work for (an unwise lack of diversification), or firms located near where they live. These are all psychological biases well documented in the literature, and built on the findings of two experimental psychologists, Daniel Kahneman and Amos Tversky, who, in 1974, published an article in the prestigious journal *Science*. It showed, on the basis of solid laboratory evidence, that human brains were so programmed as to systematically and consistently miscalculate chance. The authors called these biases heuristics.[3]

Kahneman and Tversky's work has been enormously influential in economics. The ambitious young graduate students of the mid-1970s who took their insights and built them into research programmes are now among the most senior members of the economics profession. We have been treated to a slew of popular books, each full of examples of the strange and wonderful way that we think about things. Michael Lewis himself has written a biography of Kahneman and Tversky; Dan Ariely, Richard Thaler, George Akerlov, Robert Shiller, Kahneman himself, and many others are well known outside the academy. They have influenced policy and practice, with governments embracing the behavioural tactic of 'nudging' to get what they want in scenarios from traffic calming to pandemic management. The behavioural perspective has become the default explanation for stock market boom and bust. Alan Greenspan famously referred to the 'irrational exuberance' of the dotcom era: people just got carried away! *The Big Short* (the film) includes a cameo from Richard Thaler and Selena Gomez, billed, respectively, as 'President of the American Economic Association and father of behavioural economics' and 'international pop star'. Thaler's monologue highlights the 'hot hand' aspect of the fiasco – the sense that property had been going up for so long, and people had been making so much money from it, that observers thought it would just carry on going. The crash was just a matter of our innate behavioural biases.

I cannot be alone in feeling that these explanations are a little sparse. As our excursions through the history of finance have shown, we have bodies, are enmeshed in practices and routines, and are embedded in webs of social relationships. Fund managers buying into dotcom would have done so in the knowledge that the penalty for being wrong, with everyone else, would certainly be lower than the penalty for being individually wrong, and that being individually right would incur their colleagues' displeasure as well.[4] Much of the narrative drama in films like *The Big Short* and *Margin Call* comes from the difficulties the hero-outsiders encounter simply on account of being right. It seems to me that the more pressing question is elsewhere: how do people manage to be rational in the market *at all*, even if they do not quite carry it off? Commentators complain about the irrational greed and fear that fuelled the credit crisis, but the more extraordinary aspect of the disaster was that you could buy financial instruments that reflected, and I am being precise here, the future revenue streams of wagers on the future revenue streams of wagers on the repayment of mortgages on houses half-built in another part of the globe. Now that *is* interesting.

***

All scientific activity is dependent on previous advances in techniques buried in the everyday equipment of the laboratory. Every machine unnoticed in the laboratory itself contains an entire history of laboratory work and technological advances folded into its programmes and circuitry. Finance works like this as well. Traders sit at their screens, scanning numbers that have already been parsed and processed by numerous socio-technical systems. They will run additional calculations, send messages, have conversations with colleagues and counterparties. They buy and sell. Their decision-making seeps out across networks of society and technology, drawing on other networks now nested into their calculative machinery. The construction of financial fact and trading decision is intimately linked.

Let us take an example. We hear a great deal about hedge funds. It is rarely flattering. They have done this, or that, betted against the pound, raided our pensions, or funded a political party to achieve nefarious aims. The language we use gives it away: the hedge fund is a thing, a composite, a single market agent; in the jargon of social science, an 'agencement' or 'socio-technical assemblage'. A fascinating study by Ian Hardie and Donald MacKenzie treats the hedge fund as exactly that.[5] These piratical, globally domineering organizations turn out to be rather small. The one Hardie and MacKenzie examine has just five employees, including the 'sometime intern'. They sit around a large central desk, occupying a trading room in some small, non-descript offices in a desirable part of central London – hedge funds prefer Mayfair and St James' to the City. The sociologists spent a week in the trading room watching what was going on and reported that much of the day was spent in complete silence: the whirring of fans, or the tapping of keyboards broken only by the occasional cryptic exchange about the valuation of bonds or a telephone call to place an order, several million here, several million there. The room is an epicentre of information gathering, with the three trading partners' specialized knowledge paired with bespoke calculators, often built in that room, in making sense of the deluge of conversations that pours in through email and newswire. 'If human beings had unlimited powers of information processing, calculation and memory', write Hardie and MacKenzie, 'a single unaided human could perhaps turn the information flowing into the room into an optimal trading portfolio. Since human capacities are limited, as Herbert Simon emphasized long ago, the necessary tasks are distributed across technical systems and multiple human beings: what goes on in the trading room is indeed distributed cognition.'[6] Hardie and MacKenzie show how conversations between the three partners and their counterparties elsewhere converge on eventual trading strategies, wrapping together the output of their tools and calculators. The hedge fund is a computational 'agencement', combining the social and the technical to manipulate market information.

This hedge fund seems very small, at least in terms of its physical presence and organizational structure. Yet it can wield financial firepower so substantial that, when hedge funds gather, governments tremble. Like any contemporary knowledge business, the hedge fund can only exist in a network of outsourcing relationships with firms that can offer competitive advantages in their own fields, be that cost-efficient manufacturing or, in this case, clerical services. It delegates the painstaking business of settlement to an organization in Dublin that itself employs hundreds of workers in Mumbai double-checking trades and smoothing problems while the London market sleeps. The pull-down menus of the trading system, leased from another provider, are the front end of this settlement operation, the visible tip of a computational and administrative iceberg. The fund's deals are conducted by a 'prime broker', an international investment bank that transfers the money necessary to make a trade on the fund's behalf. The bank effectively underwrites each trade, and this tiny Mayfair office now enjoys the credit rating of a global investment bank. Hedge funds are themselves allowed to borrow, and when this is coupled with the bank's creditworthiness, the combination is formidable.

As the hedge fund shows, in a market where information is ubiquitous and overwhelming, calculation is both a problem and an opportunity. Processing so much information is beyond the capacity of the individual human agent and, in an echo of the efficient market hypothesis, if everyone has all market information, it no longer confers an advantage. Advantages must derive from processes of interpretation, and these must be faster, more accurate and more imaginative or sophisticated. In another classic study, Daniel Beunza and David Stark explore how traders in a bank's dealing room try to discover arbitrage opportunities in the extraordinary complexities of market information.[7] Arbitrage is the pursuit of risk-free profit: if you can buy goods from Sally at one pound and sell them to Simon for two, doing so at the very same moment and without the possibility that the goods might break or be stolen in transit, or that Simon might not want them when they get there, that is an arbitrage. Entrepreneurs in the productive economy earn their profit because true arbitrage almost never exists in the real world. In financial markets, the mere possibility of arbitrage keeps prices the same in New York and London. But Beunza and Stark suggest that arbitrage opportunities can be found if traders are clever enough. Sophisticated calculation and hedging strategies allow the individual properties underlying financial instruments to be traded: a trade in pure risk, for example, or in a portfolio of non-aviation firms' indirect exposure to aviation, or a mispricing across a chain of obliquely linked bonds. Arcane mathematics and massive, distributed computation arrangements can illuminate arbitrage opportunities invisible to the naked eye. Beunza and Stark find the physical layout of the trading room organized to maximize social fluidity, interaction and the transfer and overlap of ideas. Calculation happens on the screens, across the desks and between the desks: it is distributed throughout the trading room. This is how professionals see and think in the market.

★★★

Non-professionals do not think like this. For many, being an investor is part of being an economic citizen. When researching investment clubs in the USA, sociologist Brooke Harrington heard justifications stressing the moral obligation to be in the markets. 'Where else are we going to put our money? In the mattress?' said one.[8] Investing is a means of stating one's place in the world, a narrative performance as well as an economic one. Harrington writes that 'When individuals buy a stock … they are also buying a story. And in buying the story of the company, they are buying a story about themselves: the great investment decision becomes a core element in the autobiography of the modern American.'[9] In Taiwan, where private investing has become almost ubiquitous in recent years, the activity is shot through with social relationships: people doing each other favours, people using investment to demonstrate their superior situation, investing to gain access to social situations and groups. When I interviewed investors in the UK I heard stories of self-development, of getting back at the man, of one day trading from a beach in paradise rather than a bedroom in the Midlands. Investment is a particular performance of oneself. They make pilgrimages to fairs and shows that offer a noisy simulacrum of being in the market: screens everywhere, lectures, debates, exciting products and risky services. In the case of noise traders – as the scholars call private investors – it seems that the noise is the bit that matters.[10]

Private investors are consumers of investments, with consumption choices reflecting their self-image: Harrington witnessed groups deciding not to buy stock in Harley-Davidson motorcycles and La-Z-Boy (a manufacturer of lounge furniture) because of the cultural connotations of the products they sold.[11] But they are also consumers of investment services. At the most basic level, this insight explains the way that investment services are sold to them, as exciting, or risky, or complicated. It is an echo of the Tom Wolfe and Michael Lewis-style narratives of finance, mass-produced for the commodity market, the investment shows acting a carnivalesque version of the great trading rooms of the 1980s.

What exactly do they consume, these non-professional investors? The sociologist Karin Knorr Cetina characterizes the market as 'everything, how loudly he's screaming … what the central banks are doing … what the Malaysian prime minister is saying, it's everything – everything all the time'.[12] The market is experienced by professionals as an extraordinary barrage of information, which they wrestle into profitable submission with their workbenches and algorithms. Non-professionals buy a commodified, simplified version of this world. It comes with everything: its own rules and understandings of market function, information sources and the requisite tools for making sense of these. Most non-professional investors do not have MBAs and do not know how markets 'should' be understood. Instead, they choose the method that feels right to them. For most private investors, choosing investments is in the main part a choice of what kind of investor to be – which of many competing investment service packages to adopt – and that is a consumer choice. We all know how to be consumers. Once entangled in a particular kind of investment practice, individuals distribute calculation across the network organized by the investment service provider. Their choices spread across a calculative network within which everything hangs together, reasonably and rationally, even if it sometimes looks bizarre from the outside.

A couple of examples will help here. Some investors specialize in the shares of smaller companies, or 'growth stocks', the latter an ironic name, as many will do anything but grow.[13] These are often cheap and are also known as 'penny shares'. There is a long tradition of snake oil surrounding penny shares (think Harvard Securities). In thin (illiquid) markets, small company shares can move around a great deal, netting their owners valuable paper profits, profits that disappear as soon as the owner tries to cash them in. Most small company investors are smarter than this. They are heirs to another investing tradition, one that can be traced back at least to the 1940s, when investment guru Benjamin Graham published his book *The Intelligent Investor*. This is 'value' or 'fundamental' investing, its greatest exponent being Warren Buffet. Graham argued that investors should pursue value, buying stocks when the market price of the shares is less than the parcel of assets each share represents. These days Graham's approach is more problematic. Asset values can contain all sorts of intangibles such as capitalized brands and 'goodwill'. Growth company investors, however, do not look for value that has already shown up on the balance sheet; their endeavour is to find unrecognized future possibility. They believe that the costs of researching growth stocks are such that the 'big boys' – whoever they may be – are unable to spot opportunities, but the nimble individual can. It is all about rolling up your sleeves and working hard, getting to know the companies you are investing in.

This 'growth company' discourse offers a narrative account of how the market works and how you should act when facing it. The discourse is embedded in the tools and devices that growth company investors use to navigate the market – the tip sheet that proclaims its delight in getting into an opportunity ahead of the 'big guys', or the pundit who explains that there is value to be found if you are prepared to do the work. In practice, however, much of the work is done elsewhere. The tip sheet renders company financials down to single figure indicators like the 'PEG', 'price-earnings-growth'. Popularized by investment guru Jim Slater it is easy to understand: less than one means buy. Slater's catchphrase was 'elephants can't jump', and I have heard it in a dozen different formulations. Investors would tell me that small companies are a great place to make money – or would be if they could only get their formula right.

Inevitably this is framed in an antagonistic relationship with the 'big guys'. One investor described his practice as a way of 'outsmarting the large brokers, finding good opportunities that are likely to do really, really well but nobody knows about them, because nobody investigates them.' And, he says, 'It's really satisfying.' Or, as one pundit says, 'I love banking big stock market gains – especially if it's on the blindside of other investors. Seven years ago I quit my high-flying career in the Square Mile to join a newsletter called. …'[14] Investors I interviewed during the bull market of 2006–07 were hoping for 30 per cent annual returns, all at the expense of these 'big guys' – but not entirely, because the whole practice depends on the possibility that sooner or later a big guy, or at least other small investors, will spot the value as well, and the stock will be hauled up to its rightful price, taking the plucky prospector with it. It is a kind of delayed efficient market hypothesis – the market will be efficient, but only after I have got there first.

Another popular kind of investing practice is that of charting, or technical analysis. This, too, claims a rich investing heritage, dating back to the arrival of the ticker tape and linear time in the markets. In essence, the practice aims to predict future prices from the pattern of previous ones. From the point of view of economic theory, this is madness. The main factor affecting stock prices is news, and news is by its very nature unpredictable. Consider the spring of 2020, and a global rout of shares by a virus that a few weeks before we did not know existed. No chart could have predicted this. For the behavioural economist, there is a little more sense in the method. If we know that people herd, and that they are irrational and over-emotional, we may expect prices to overreact, to have some momentum, as the jargon goes. It makes sense to chase the trend, and research shows there are small, short-term profits to be made by doing so.[15]

Chasing trends does not really capture the chartist's endeavour, which is based on an almost theological claim about the nature of the market. He (invariably) has signed up to a view of the market predicated not on randomness but on underlying order. The noisy mess of prices is nothing less than a code that can be deciphered using Fibonacci numbers or Elliott waves. Through elaborate retrospective testing he seeks to discover the perfect pattern of indicators. He peers at long-term moving averages crossing short-term moving averages, or plots clouds of stock prices lying beneath a share's graph and supporting it or hanging above, weighing it down. This is the Holy Grail of charting – to be able to fit a curve so perfectly to historical data that it will be able to predict the future. The only problem, as social scientists know, is a methodological one; the more precisely a curve fits historical data, the less its predictive power.

Even this does not really capture the chartist experience, because the actual practice of being a chartist involves paying for some expensive software, configuring the computer and leaving it running overnight. Just like those tip sheets, the computer takes away the burden of the difficult computational problem, sifting through the market to find profitable investment opportunities. 'Elliott', one chartist told me,

> is a wave structure, a simple wave structure which is basically a series of impulse waves followed by a series of retracement waves, and the impulse is broken into a series of five simple waves upwards, and then you have two retracement waves, and then a series of 'a', 'b' and 'c' waves … a series of five simple waves up followed by three simple waves down. And when you see a movement such as the share price or a commodity price in the stock market you'll very often see the series of five smaller impulse waves up followed by two retracement waves, an 'a', a 'b' and a 'c'. …

But, at the end of the day, all you do is pay some money and run some software. A few clicks of the mouse and it is done.[16]

Non-professional investors can sound irrational, noisy or 'dumb'. From the point of view of MBA finance, they may be. But they are not just investors; they are consumers as well. They consume an entire market ontology – a vision of how the markets actually are – linked to an account of how one should behave in them, which is linked to or inscribed into the devices they buy to distribute their calculation across the marketplace. We all know how to consume, and as consumers we buy things that reflect our preferences and enact how we understand ourselves, the hardworking, plucky underdog or the tech-savvy market savant.

★★★

Investing is a lonely and stressful business. In my work on investors in the bull market of the mid-2000s I wrote that they engaged in a kind of confessional ritual, meeting online and in person to trade war stories, commiserate and share reflections on their often woeful performance. Since then, some things have changed, but strangely, many things have not. The credit crisis of 2008 shattered the fragile covenant between Middle America and Wall

Street, just as the arrival of the smartphone made access to the markets even easier. I had noted, 10 years earlier, the arrival of exotic financial offerings such as 'contracts for difference', spread-betting and options trading. These have now become mainstream among private investors. A new kind of market participant has appeared, younger, technologically sophisticated and seemingly prepared to take huge risks. Where participation in the stock market had previously been conceived as prudent, seeking steady returns for the long term, these traders prefer to gamble everything. Pundits have speculated that this attitude is a response to rising inequality and the destruction of traditional pathways to long-term prosperity over the last two decades: saddled with debt, often student debt, faced with uncertain employment in gig work industries, with property prices sky-high, these youngsters have little to lose. Hanging out in online fora they make big plays and celebrate their losses (private investors still lose most of the time) with gifs and memes and guffaws, a steady stream of investment chatter, online fist-bumps and schoolboy jokes about masturbation. (Among the things that have not changed is the gender distribution of private investors, although the accompanying attitude seems to have greatly worsened.) Technology firms were quick to supply the necessary infrastructure – outfits like Robinhood offering rapid, and supposedly low-cost or even free brokerage via mobile phones, while at the same time cannily suggesting that they were part of a general uprising against corrupt bankers who had stolen the future of Middle America.

All of this hit the headlines in the spring of 2020 when WallStreetBets, the Reddit community that played host to many of these investors, staged a popular uprising against big finance. Users, led by Keith Gill (who posted on Reddit as RoaringKitty, formerly DeepFuckingValue) noticed that a hedge fund called Melvin Capital had heavily shorted (sold shares on margin in the expectation of falling prices) a high street retailer called GameStop. Gill shared a stock-picking video from Mike Burry, the real-life contrarian investor made famous by Lewis in *The Big Short*. Perhaps GameStop had a nostalgic appeal for these investors who may have spent teenage years browsing its shelves. By whatever chance, Gill's view caught the Reddit imagination. Word spreads quickly online, and the investors piled in, whooping and posting gifs about their parents' foreclosed mortgage. Elon Musk tweeted a cryptic single word of support. A short seller's exposure is limitless, and within days, Melvin had lost half of its $13 billion capital fund. Some traders became very rich, although many suffered from the decision of Robinhood to temporarily bar trading in the stocks; Melvin, Robinhood and others were eventually investigated by US Congress where they denied collusion and claimed regulatory responsibility to supervise the market. Gill was given a grilling too, and in his statement he invoked the creed of the growth company investor seeking value through solitary graft: 'the tedious work of digging through a company's financials and focusing on its real long-term value, not prevailing market sentiment or headlines.'[17]

There is a lot going on here. It is clear that private investors, mobilizing collectively, wield real market power – although rival hedge funds were quick enough to join the fray at Melvin's expense, and GameStop is a relatively small corporation with a smaller market capitalization. There is also a question of fact. In our postmodern age, rival versions of expertise spread quickly online, and the cultures of WallStreetBets are exemplary. Battles over scientific fact are won by the strength of networks (the number of scientists, the density of data, the elaborateness of instrumentation – happily, all a proxy for accuracy) enrolled into each one; in the case of GameStop we see amateur researchers taking the lead in determining the proper prices for a stock, accompanied by professional investors and larger funds. Expertise need not be restricted to professional traders. GameStop did go to the moon as the gifs predicted, although it soon enough fell most of the way back. Yet it is far from certain that the GameStop affair represents the profound change in market structure that some commentators hoped.

Interviewing investors I frequently heard a version of the same story: that investing offered an end to the daily grind, that it could be done from the beach in the Caribbean, that it offered freedom and self-direction. If only, investors would say, I can get my formula right. Capital has a habit of feeding on critique, and this narrative was institutionalized into the marketing of the new generation tech-brokers: 'It played into an emo version of the "bullshit jobs" narrative: your job is pointless. Stop working for the man and become the Man by seamlessly buying tiny slices of companies', says writer Brett Scott.[18] But the day traders are often not even in the market, and these apps are a modern-day version of the Chicago bucket shops. Traders are consumers, another source of profit for the financial services industry, even on the free-to-trade apps they favoured. Before the crash investors could be described as 'docile bodies' of neoliberalism, their hopes, efforts and savings rendered into yet another revenue stream for finance capital. Despite the noisy celebrations over the demise of a hedge fund, this has not changed at all. The confessional ritual has evolved into an entire online culture but it serves the same purpose, celebrating loss and disciplining economic subjects for the future. Scott puts it well, when he says that investment service firms 'pen the day traders into closed ecosystems where they can fight each other, while retail firms harvest them for fees and interest before laying off the residual risk into the actual markets.' The heterodox expertise of the day-traders is powerless against the cold, random universe of the financial markets. The rule of other people's money still holds good. 'Here's the thing', Gill told Congress, 'I've had a bit of experience and even I barely understand these matters. It's alarming how little we know about the inner workings of the market.'[19]

11

The Burden of Empire

One morning in March 2000 I received a telephone call from a retired but very well connected journalist. He had some information and wondered whether I would like to follow it up. It concerned a South African mining outfit called Petra Diamonds Ltd, then traded on the London Stock Exchange's junior market AIM (Alternative Investment Market). He had got wind of a big deal heading towards Petra, but didn't know what it was; he suspected that the chief executive, Adonis Pouroulis, was seeking to take the company private – to remove it from the stock exchange – against stockholders' wishes. (This was certainly not the case. On 31 March 2020 Pouroulis finally stepped down from the firm he had founded 23 years previously.) I spent two days telephoning everyone whose number I could get hold of and eventually reached Pouroulis himself. He listened to my questions, thought for a moment, and said, 'You'd better come for breakfast.'

Breakfast was at The Cadogan hotel in Chelsea, famous as the place where Oscar Wilde had been arrested in 1895 on charges of gross indecency. John Betjeman even wrote a ballad about it: 'Mr Woilde, we 'ave come for tew take yew/Where felons and criminals dwell/We must ask yew tew leave with us quoietly/For this is the Cadogan Hotel,' sing the Cockney policemen. As you might expect from the place that Wilde chose to hang out with his louche pals, it was impossibly elegant. When I arrived at the breakfast table there were several men gathered, all suited: Pouroulis, his deputy Geoffrey White, and a lawyer called David Price. My memory is a bit hazy, 20 years later, but I think that was his name. There was also the firm's head of security – strange – and even more strangely, a man who appeared to be connected to the Zimbabwean army. I am convinced that there were two others present who did not do much talking or breakfasting either. Pouroulis explained the proposed deal. Petra Diamonds was to become the vehicle for a reverse takeover – a kind of merger where the incoming company swallows up the host, keeping its name and, crucially, stock exchange listing. The incomer was called Oryx Diamonds, a firm registered in the Cayman Islands and run from Oman. Oryx's business was operating a diamond concession in the Democratic Republic of Congo (DRC). As even I knew, the DRC was a troubled country, with a history of destructive civil war, repressive government and a reputation for 'blood diamonds' mined by forced labour and used to fund conflict.

I remember Pouroulis stirring honey into his coffee as he set out the specifics. The concession was worth $1 billion – $1 billion of diamonds waiting to be taken from one of the poorest, most violent and most corrupt countries on earth. Forty per cent of profits would go to Oryx (or Petra). Forty per cent would go to Osleg, a company linked to the Zimbabwean army, which was charged with providing 'security' on this immense mining operation. The Zimbabwean army was already in the area – Robert Mugabe had sent 11,000 troops to the DRC to support Laurent Kabila's government. The remaining 20 per cent would go to Comiex-Congo-Operation Sovereign Legitimacy, a company that David Price (the lawyer) vigorously denied being President Kabila's slush fund.[1] These details became clearer over the coming weeks when the prospectus was published, but it was immediately obvious that there was a great deal of money at stake here, and that it was not going to go to the people who you might want to get it. It was also, more slowly, becoming apparent to me, right then, over breakfast, that I was sitting with a group of truly scary individuals. I was habituated to market spivs and wide boys and the occasional East End loan shark, but these were of a different order. When one of them, I don't remember who, asked me in a conversational manner what kind of a story I thought I might write, I replied that I would write a simple and informative news story. And that's what I did, just a column's worth. As an excuse I offer the fact that this person's voice maintained the kind of casual menace that you can only deploy if you have entire battalions of an African army, two dictators and $1 billion of undiscovered diamonds at your disposal. These were, you might say, some very heavy dudes.

In June 2000, Oryx hit the front pages. The offer documents were released in mid-May, and trading restarted in Petra's shares, previously suspended on rumours of a deal. The firm indicated that it was not planning to raise money upfront but might soon be asking shareholders for contributions to exploration costs. All those diamonds still needed geographical surveys and preliminary digs before they could materialize on a balance sheet. Details became clearer. The concession had previously been owned by a state-owned diamond producer but was now owned by Zimbabwean-registered Oryx Zimcom Ltd. Osleg was described as being controlled by the Zimbabwean government. Reports circulated that the venture would 'reimburse Zimbabwe for its assistance to the DRC government in its war against rebel forces', and that Comiex, the 20 per cent stakeholder, was controlled by the DRC's national army.[2] As the June listing date approached, Geoffrey White argued that the venture had a social mission to provide jobs and stability, 'a semblance of normalcy in the region'.[3] Newspaper stories hardened. 'In a move of astonishing disdain, greed and ruthlessness,' wrote *The Sunday Herald*, 'President Robert Mugabe, who has demanded that Britain compensate whites whose farms he is confiscating in Zimbabwe, plans to raise money on the London Stock Exchange this week to enable him to exploit Congolese diamond mines captured by his national army.'[4] The Foreign Office was said to be exerting pressure behind the scenes, and Grant Thornton, the giant accountancy firm, wrote to Oryx to say that it would no longer act as its adviser. The London Stock Exchange made it clear that it would not be welcome. Petra remained defiant, a spokesman saying: 'There are companies on the London Stock Exchange who are selling jets to dictatorships and whose guns are being used to arm children – why should a legitimate mining operation be blocked?'[5] Still, this was a deal too far for the City.

***

Why, in March 2000, as the dotcom world began to unravel, had a collection of African businesses come to an exclusive London hotel to promote a business deal that spanned Sub-Saharan Africa? To answer, we will have to deal with two things: the recent history of London's junior markets, introducing London Stock Exchange's junior market AIM, and a much longer tradition of colonial relations in London's markets.

In 1981 the London Stock Exchange, finding itself out of step with the new entrepreneurial zeitgeist, accused on all sides as a brake on British productivity and determined to 'ingratiate itself with the new Conservative government', set up its own 'junior' market.[6] A junior market is one with lighter listing rules aimed at smaller, earlier-stage businesses. The Exchange called it the 'Unlisted Securities Market', or USM. It was much easier to get on to than the Official List and was perfectly timed for the mid-1980s bull market.[7] Sir Nicholas Goodison, businessman and chairman of the Stock Exchange from 1976 to 1986, described the introduction of the market as 'a very important event in Britain's commercial history … [the USM] greatly helped the progress of the British economy in terms of products, services, and jobs … this new market did a lot to alter attitudes to risk among investors who, during the 1960s and 1970s, had become averse to risk.'[8] Goodison captures the Exchange's preferred narrative and one that resonated with the spirit of the time: a Britain transformed from a risk-averse, socialist backwater to a vibrant engine of commerce, risk-taking and entrepreneurial.[9]

Brian Winterflood, the young jobber whose partner had advised him to 'mind his fucking eye' trading with the firm's money, was by now a partner of Bisgood Bishop, one of the larger firms. He recognized the USM opportunity for what it was and, despite a lukewarm response from his colleagues, determined that his firm would offer prices in every single USM stock. This was a stroke of genius. The Old House's exchange trading floor was organized by sector, with markets in South African stocks, say, physically separate from those in the leisure or pharmaceutical industries. Winterflood realized that brokers had no desire to trail round the house trying to find buyers for these strange little USM shares; they would rather come straight to him where they knew that they would get a price. Soon his firm's pitch was a 'wall of stocks' and his nickname 'Mr USM'. It could be risky, but market-making on the USM was a profitable business. 'Winterflood,' said one financier, 'made a fortune because his bid-offer spreads were embarrassing ... you could drive an 18-wheel truck through them.' Market-makers could avoid the worst of the risk by trying not to hold stock. In the pithy words of one trader, 'You did not have to put your cock in the custard' unless you really wanted to.

The crash of 1987 eventually caught up with the USM. The boom years that had made it an easy venue to raise money had ended: in 1992 only two companies had joined the market from a peak of 103 new arrivals in 1988. A Stock Exchange consultation, published in December 1992, conceded that 'the quality and attractiveness of the USM has deteriorated in the eyes of companies and investors.'[10] The sentiment was shared by many in the City, who felt that the USM had a 'spotty reputation'. New European regulations lightened the requirements of the Official List and eroded the USM's offering. For these reasons, so the story goes, the London Stock Exchange decided to close its junior market, with an unnamed official joking in a speech, 'it is often said that you cannot have too much of a good thing, but to have two, almost identical, markets in one exchange is going too far.'[11]

This is not quite the whole story. In practice, the USM was just an appendix, an afterthought, a small set of rules heavily cross-referenced to the Official List rulebook, making the continuation of its very existence a tedious administrative chore. The burden was carried by the Exchange's Listings Department, which existed as an almost entirely separate entity from the rest of the Exchange. Its office contained market-sensitive information and was secured by coded door locks. It had a reputation for bureaucratic stolidity and unparalleled expertise in the regulatory aspects of market administration, but it was disconnected from the commercial side of the Exchange, by then a business in its own right. Fed up with the administrative burden maintaining this failing market, the Listing Department decided to shut it down. 'They weren't commercial,' said Giles Vardey, a senior manager at the Exchange,

> I remember the management meeting, and the Head of Listing came into the room and said, 'We've been looking at the USM ... there's really no point in maintaining a separate section. What we'll do is bang the whole thing together. Yeah, and we're going to write to the companies and say they've got a year to either comply with the main

market rules or basically they can piss off.' And, of course, there was an absolute maelstrom.

The USM had powerful supporters. There was Winterflood, who had cornered the market-making business; Andrew Beeson, by now senior partner of Beeson Gregory, a successful small company stockbroker; and 'Ronnie' (Sir Ronald) Cohen, a leading venture capitalist, who depended on the USM as a mechanism for getting his money out of successful investments. They shouted about UK PLC, and how important it was, and by implication, how important they were and how they should be allowed to carry on doing what they were doing. Cohen argued that without a means of exit, financial contributions to the venture capital sector would shrink, and an important part of the entrepreneurial engine of UK PLC would grind to a halt. Winterflood, who was at the time in the process of selling his recently founded Winterflood Securities to Close Brothers for £15 million, campaigned most forcibly. The three formed a 'ginger group', in Winterflood's words, to lobby politicians and the London Stock Exchange on behalf of UK PLC. This group became the City Group for Smaller Companies (Cisco), later the Quoted Companies Alliance, or QCA). CISCO argued that there was an underlying demand for a junior market, that the Exchange was reacting too hastily to a long and deep recession, and that better economic times were coming. Its April 1993 newsletter contained a long plan for a three-tier equity market, and even hinted that Cisco would be prepared to support a new market beyond the purview of the London Stock Exchange if necessary. Indeed, Cohen spent much effort trying to set up a pan-European market.[12]

Those managers at the Exchange who faced the financial community after the closure of the USM remember a deep anger among brokers and investment managers in the City and across the regions. There was a concern that a uniquely British small company equity culture would wither away, and that the Exchange was out of step with the zeitgeist of a nation trying hard to recover from recession. By March 1993 Nigel Atkinson, head of the London Stock Exchange's Listing Department, had begun to give ground. The Exchange agreed to extend the USM's life by several months and set up a working party to consider a new market. It was unusually vulnerable at the time. In March 1993 it had been forced to scrap its Taurus paperless settlement system, a vast fiasco of an IT project that embarrassed it in front of the City, cost the Exchange £75 million and the community as a whole several times that amount, and eventually caused the Exchange to lose its settlement function entirely. Chief executive Peter Rawlins resigned. The media did not spare its barbs: Rawlins, reported the *Independent*, 'was a frustrated thespian whose early search for fame took him as far as an appearance on Bruce Forsyth's *Generation Game* [a Saturday night light entertainment show].'[13]

But the London Stock Exchange was still a venerable institution, and it did not cave in to pressure at once. It denied the fundamental claim that it was prejudicing the entrepreneurial dynamism of the UK. 'I totally refute suggestions that ... the Exchange is somehow stifling entrepreneurs,' said Atkinson. The real impetus came from John Jenkins and his thriving venture in Moorgate, now developing into a full-scale capital market under the Exchange's regulatory aegis. The Exchange was forced to act. The new market that emerged in place of the USM was designed to put a stop to the competition and entrench the London Stock Exchange as a dynamic contributor to UK PLC. It was called AIM.

The story of AIM's development is fascinating, and I will come back to it in Chapter 14. Launched in 1995 it swiftly succeeded in its ambition to become an economic engine for the now thriving UK PLC. In the late 1990s, the Exchange's decision to fast-track local technology heroes such as lastminute.com on to the main board saved AIM as the dotcom fire sale pummelled prices elsewhere. By the middle of 2001, AIM was claiming to have attracted 800 companies and raised £7 billion since its launch, pointing to a failure rate of a 'more than respectable 3 per cent'.[14] In the aftermath of the dotcom boom, the City as a whole looked overseas for new business, and AIM's focus began to move away from the entrepreneurial flourishing of UK PLC. This was in keeping with the spirit of globalization sweeping through the world's economy, but there was also an immediate, pragmatic motivation for this change. Throughout the autumn of 2000 the London Stock Exchange had been fighting a hostile takeover bid from the Swedish stock market operator OMX. The third and final defence document, published on 19 October, set out the Exchange's vision for building the business. As part of this Don Cruickshank, the Exchange's chairman, explicitly promised to develop AIM as an international market.[15]

London already had expertise in the exploration and oil and gas sectors, having supported the development of the North Sea fields, and this could easily be repurposed to serve the international mining community. Thanks to the new Sarbanes-Oxley legislation in the USA, introduced in 2002 in the wake of the Enron and WorldCom scandals, London was now a more friendly place to list in regulatory terms, especially as AIM had managed to opt out of European stock exchange regulation. Most importantly, London had investors with money who were willing to sink it into commodities exploration firms. AIM rapidly imported the mining-focused equity culture of the Australian financial community. Said one broker: 'I went off to Australia for six weeks. I made a point of visiting brokers, and all they could talk about was mining. Mining, mining, mining. And up to a point I had shunned mining, because I always regarded it as being so problematic, why get involved? But you couldn't ignore it.'

Why this sudden interest in mining? Once again the markets were being shaped by the forces of globalization. The first decade of this century saw a massive expansion in demand for commodities. China's vast economic expansion led other nations, the so-called BRICS, in an insatiable demand for building materials, energy sources and the other raw materials of industrial production, such as copper, tin and aluminium.[16] Rapid development of technological infrastructure and the invention of the smartphone required an unprecedented volume of rare minerals, much of which came from countries like the DRC. By 2001, observers were already worrying about the destructive effects of this extraordinary demand in Africa,[17] and by 2008 commodity prices had become a source of concern for policymakers worldwide. Crude oil prices increased from $25 a barrel to $70 a barrel in the five years from 2002, as China's consumption increased by 50 per cent to 7.6 billion barrels a day over the same period.[18] The world needed more commodities, and at $70 a barrel, it was worth looking for them. AIM rose to the challenge. But the truth is that the financing of exploration by London's markets is nothing new. From the days of the East India Company and the Royal African Company, London's markets have a long and dark association with the nation's colonialist endeavours.

★★★

Railway shares boomed in Britain in the 1830s and 1840s. The boom transcended class and gender divides and spread the idea of share ownership across the nation as investors backed local railway companies. A network of local exchanges sprung up, financing these new companies. Railways needed cash up front, and this would take years to repay; the exchanges offered a means for investors to enjoy a return and reclaim their capital as needed by selling the stock to others. By 1853, investors had provided a staggering £194 million in capital for the railways and had become familiar with the practice of funding industry.[19] London, at the centre of a network of exchanges, could now draw on a deep well of capital. Improving communications connected London with bourses in Europe and, by the late 19th century, provided an efficient link to the exchanges in the USA as well.

At the same time, Britain's commercial links with its colonies and overseas settlements strengthened. 'After their early colonisation,' writes Bernard Attard, 'globalisation provided them with opportunities for long-term growth as suppliers of raw materials, minerals and food. But the creation of export capacity required enormous investment in railways and other forms of social overhead capital.'[20] London, commercial centre of the Empire, was well fitted to provide this, and soon cemented its position as the Empire's financial centre as well: by 1913 60 per cent of the nominal capital of securities quoted in London was attached to overseas projects.[21]

As Attard and others have pointed out, London's money came with strings attached. The British public demanded that the overseas borrowers conformed to a particular expectation of organizational standards and structures, if they were to finance overseas projects, and the London Stock Exchange became the instrument that imposed such discipline. As investment was often channelled through overseas governments, the Exchange's mandate over who could obtain funds, and who could not, became a kind of soft power shaping the development of whole nations. It has been argued that India built railways rather than cheaper, cleaner canals largely to suit the expectations of the British investing public. The Exchange refused to accept further issues from governments of nations where firms had defaulted on dividends, effectively requiring those governments to guarantee, or at least enforce, British terms. New issues could only reach sources of capital in London and the regions through the London Stock Exchange's member firms (the brokers), and these refused to act without their customary quarter per cent commission. An increasing concentration of brokers into specialized syndicates and then single firms left national governments beholden to individual Exchange members. One such, R. Nivison & Co, eventually monopolized the underwriting of Australian, Canadian and South African loans. It is extraordinary to think that the capital expenditure projects of these three vast nations depended on the whims of the senior partner, Nivison himself.[22]

At times, the terms demanded by British investors were simply usurious. India's railways were funded by British investors, while the Indian government guaranteed a 5 per cent return for 99 years. Moreover, unprofitable contracts could be returned after two decades and the Indian taxpayer – via the government – would fully reimburse stockholders. Each year until the 1960s, writes anthropologist Laura Bear,

> Indian government tax revenue was paid to holders of East India Peninsula Railway, Great India Peninsula Railway, Eastern Bengal Railway, East Indian Railway, South Indian Railway and Scinde, Punjab and Delhi Railway Company shares. This produced more than a century of accumulation in the United Kingdom from the original contracts of the 1840s.[23]

The sheer scale of this expropriation was identified even in the 19th century, when the mathematician Dadabhai Naoroji's 'The poverty of India' quantified the capital drain from railway repayments at £66 million per annum – in 1876! British investors, via the London Stock Exchange and the efforts of a railway entrepreneur, Rowland Macdonald Stephenson, the East India Company and the British government in India had clinched a deal that 'converted socio-political inequalities and evaluations of racial capacity into secure capital flows and financial trading'.[24]

The first decade of the 20th century witnessed another boom in overseas assets, this one driven by the bicycle, the car and an insatiable demand for rubber. From 1903 to 1912, some 260 companies floated in London to develop rubber production. Investors were attracted by promised perpetual dividends of between 10 per cent and 25 per cent.[25] The mantle of funding rubber production was taken up by the Shanghai Stock Exchange, a London Stock Exchange-lookalike set up in 1904 by a group of expatriate European businessmen. The historian W.A. Thomas describes the process:

> The route for bringing in a state to the market was well tried. A group or syndicate would buy up an estate of new-planted trees, or even plant up an estate, then sell the property to a newly formed company, accepting either cash or vendors' shares in payment. The capital for this transfer would then be raised from the market by a prospectus offer. In the enthusiasm to sell estates ... [he adds tactfully] promoters were prepared to mislead investors.[26]

Prospectuses were advertised in the local press and widely distributed, with offers quickly oversubscribed. It is striking how similar was this process to that of listing dotcom stocks: a prospectus promoted in the press, excited punters and a complicated deal between market and the listing firm. In Shanghai, too, the vendors' shares worked into the deals offered investors' funds a direct passage to promoters' pockets, and an inquiry that followed the rubber boom heavily criticized the exchange for allowing such practices.

These stocks tended to be small denomination, so small gains seemed disproportionately exciting, and the Shanghai Stock Exchange operated a quarterly settlement, which meant that shares could be bought on credit for almost three months. An investor hoping to benefit from a rising market could buy stock and sell it again before the settlement period closed, never parting with capital and simply taking the profit. The reckless enthusiasm of individual investors foreshadows the dotcom years. The *North China Herald* reported that 'all the small Smiths in town ran amuck … for five weeks brokers had their clothes almost torn off their backs for excited plungers who desired to buy shares forward at three or four hundred percent premium'.[27] Where the rubber boom differed from the dotcom bull market was in the underlying economics of the plantations. 'Even the humblest investor,' writes Thomas, 'could see the appeal of the business where the cost of production was reckoned to be one shilling and sixpence per pound, and the market price of raw rubber stood at 12 shillings per pound.'[28]

The rubber came from Malaya, then under British rule. The British had introduced industrialized farming and developed a plantation system based around huge estates. This demanded intensive capital and labour, both imported from elsewhere in the Empire. Capital came from London and Shanghai; labour came from India. Workers, usually young men, agreed to travel to Malaya where they would work for a fixed period to pay off their travel costs. On the plantation they found themselves trapped by wages too low to settle these debts and an inability to speak the language or move beyond the boundaries of the plantation. Wages were tied to the fluctuations of the rubber prices, further shielding plantation corporations from risk by shifting it onto workers. Large plantations might house 1,000 workers, often recruited and managed by gangmasters called *kangai*. From 1844 to 1910 a quarter of a million indentured labourers came to the plantations, and from 1910–20, 50,000–80,000 came each year in *kangai* schemes. 'For Indian workers on the Malayan frontier,' writes Amarjit Kaur, 'the plantation became the boundary of existence, where they were trapped in an unending cycle of dependency and poverty.'[29] It was slavery in all but name.

In answer, then, to the question of how rubber could be produced at an eighth of its selling cost, we see exploitative labour and industrialized destruction of the environment. As with the Indian railways, the Malayan plantations offered a means of converting social and economic inequality into durable revenue streams. As with the railways, the exploitation and dispossession necessary to bring these revenues into being were hidden from stockholders through the mechanisms of public offer, prospectus and the circulation of stock. Instead, railways and industrial farming could be presented as civilizing, modernizing innovations offered by a generous Empire. London, with its bountiful well of capital, stood at the centre of a web of colonial power relations and prejudices, and these calcified into long-term revenue streams, the monetization of deep unfairness. Yet this is little different from the patterns of capital and power we see today, whether in outsourced manufacture of fashion and technology, or the dreams of the wild frontier that the mining promoters inhabit.

12

Extractive Industries

In the early 2000s, a raft of prospectors and promoters dusted down their maps and permits and came to the market in London. Geographical resources must be proven. This is an expensive process, and it brings together many of the attributes of stock markets that we have discussed so far: the brute materiality of diamond core drilling, with tubes of rock sent to the laboratory for analysis; international capital flows, environmental concerns and rights of ownership; the labour practices that might eventually be involved in excavating the minerals; and, last of all, stories of the future – of wealth and possibility – and the past – of national identity and colonial relations.

There is a division of labour in mining exploration. Large firms, with the capital required to set up mining operations, attend to the business of digging materials out of the ground. It is a huge, international business, dominated by a handful of giant corporations, and run from global centres of commerce. Mining firms do not like funding exploration, however; at its earliest stages exploration is simply too risky, with the chance of success of any single location less than a single per cent. Here, junior firms step forward, each with a cluster of licences and the local knowledge of a prospector. The firms seek to raise money from shareholders, to be spent on seismic mapping and exploratory drilling. At the beginning there is nothing more than a story, perhaps backed up by the geologist's past record, or that of the promoter. These stories must invoke possibilities of future riches in order to persuade shareholders to part with their money: they are the imagined futures on which much economic activity depends.[1] The unknown reserve slowly gathers shape and form on the exploration company's balance sheet. Each successful round of drilling is rapidly reported to shareholders in the hope or generating enough speculative excitement to finance the next round of analysis, and so on, until eventually the whole can be bought out by a giant, cash-rich corporation, and those brave, early shareholders get their rewards.

In Chapter 10 we met private investors doggedly seeking hidden value, hoping that their hard work would turn up riches overlooked by the big players. Many investors are motivated by the exploration story, but give it another name. 'Fundamental analysis', for these investors, does not reference the net assets of the firm's accounting statement but rather the speculative assets tied into its stories: how many billion barrels of oil the shareholder fervently believes his chosen exploration company has under the lease, waiting to be proven up. Exploration financing depends on this kind of speculative imagination, where fundamental analysis is more a fundamentalism of belief than a look at the underlying financial considerations (the 'fundamentals') of a firm. Yet, as the previous chapter showed, such considerations may not be entirely speculative; they may also be anchored in the cold rationality of unequal power relations, of the kind that permitted the production of rubber at a fraction of its selling price. Political scientist Paul Gilbert has shown that such colonialist imaginings persist into present-day resource financing. Resource finds are evaluated on the basis of their future cash flows, calculated as today's 'net present value'. This figure is as social as it is scientific, as it contains the community's collected estimates of the political and economic viability of the deposit. Is there a danger, perhaps, of political instability – or worse still, the dreaded 'resource nationalism', when a nation seeks to demand a larger share of royalties from a mine so inconveniently (for the permit holder) located within its borders? Scientific observations, the judgement of geologists and assayers, combine with the financial community's understanding of the political tractability of a nation. All of this comes together in the 'discount rate', the percentage by which future revenues must be discounted to take account of inflation, opportunity cost and risk. Among all this laboratory testing and robust analysis of reserves, the choice of discount rate – often the deciding factor over the viability of a find – stands out as a moment of pure speculation. 'The discount rate,' write Gilbert, 'ought to be understood as a technology of the imagination, one that is particularly good at prompting analysts, investors and miners to conjure up images of relative opportunity in the "first world", Canada or the Congo [sic].'[2] The discount rate is another financial fact, laboriously constructed. Layers of power, politics and even prejudice are sedimented into its folds. And yet, as is the case with all financial facts, the circumstances of its production are soon forgotten, naturalized into the number as it circulates through the markets. Postcolonial might, asymmetries of capital, technology and calculative power are all endlessly and invisibly reproduced through a single percentage point.

As the young journalist involved in covering the mining sector for *Shares Magazine* I was partly culpable. We had all sorts: geologists moonlighting as promoters while claiming to be, as one used to say, 'horny-handed sons of toil'; a former boxer and a well-connected ex-cricketer; the Texan driller who opined at his crowded AGM that 'my oil well is just like a woman – it has mood swings,' (pauses) 'sorry ma'am' (to a female investor in the front row); the softly spoken gentlemen of The Cadogan hotel. Gilbert notes that firms are often introduced by way of the physical or sporting prowess of their promoter, narrative figures reminiscent of colonial era anthropologists. I remember meeting one, chairman of a small company quoted on OFEX. He was a genial and tweedy character, educated at Harrow and Oxford, the son of a distinguished parliamentarian. He was raising money from private investors to buy a dredger and exploration permits from an outfit in Brazil, run by a man called Harry. Harry put his name on the company, and probably on the dredger too, which shows what a big deal he was. There was little in the way of documentation available for investors; all they had to go on was an eight-page report produced by a corporate finance adviser who himself sat on the board. The dredger was going to look for diamonds deposited in the rivers in a remote and bandit-infested part of Brazil. The promoter spun me yarns about guns and cowboys, precious stones and huge snakes. The one that stuck in my mind concerned a labourer swallowed by an anaconda; his fellow miners had to wait until he was completely past the snake's head before they could lop it off and extract him. The firm soon enough discovered a serious problem with its contractor and cut its links with Harry. It kept the dredger, but shareholders did not keep their money.

When I started to learn about mining, everyone was talking about Bre-X, a monumental fraud perpetrated just a couple of years before. (When Gilbert did his fieldwork, 15 years later, they were still talking about it.) The final reason that London's AIM came to prominence in the late 1990s is that Bre-X utterly destroyed the reputation of Toronto as a hub for exploration finance. The story is well worked over now, an exhausted seam, and has been given a more scholarly treatment by the anthropologist Anna Tsing; the short version is that, in 1994 a small Canadian exploration company discovered, at Busang in Indonesia, what appeared to be the largest gold deposit in the world; that a speculative fever broke out, drawing in the savings of many North American small investors; that by late 1996, Bre-X was capitalized at £6 billion; that on 19 March 1997, the Indonesian geologist in charge of the site fell 800 feet from a helicopter into the jungle, where his body was consumed by hogs before it could be recovered and identified (but not his Rolex, which somehow remained on the helicopter); and that, when the independent assayers finally arrived at the mine, they found no evidence of gold in the cores, none whatsoever, and determined that what gold the samples did contain had come from a river, not a rock. For all the excitement, the noise, the conspiracy stories, there was nothing. For Tsing, however, the absence of gold is almost immaterial to the whole affair. What matters is the spectacle:

> Bre-X was always a performance, a drama, a conjuring trick, an illusion, regardless of whether real gold or only dreams of gold ever existed at Busang. Journalists compared Busang, with its lines of false

> drilling samples, to a Hollywood set. But it was not just Busang; it was the whole investment process. No one would ever have invested in Bre-X if it had not created a performance, a dramatic exposition of the possibilities of gold.[3]

The dotcom excitement that had engulfed London in the late 1990s may have deflated, but it had soon enough been replaced by another moment of spectacle and speculation. This one was driven not by visions of technological utopia, but by the mingling of exotic stories of wilderness and exploration with more prosaic accounts of nations rising into prosperity among belching chimneys and gaping furnaces, all hungry for oil and metal and concrete. As with the dotcom boom, the markets became places where this excitement was acted out, places where Sid and Sandra could get their hands on a little bit of gold without having to soil them. The markets were shaped by global forces, and the hierarchies of capital and politics reproduced themselves within them. We inhabited an inlet in this sea of global money, these private investors and I; the gentlemen breakfasting at The Cadogan hotel hinted at what lay further out from shore.

★★★

'Frontier culture,' writes Tsing, 'is a conjuring act because it creates the wild and spreading regionality of its imagination. It conjures a self-conscious translocalism, committed to the obliteration of local places.'[4] The conversion of local specificity into extractable and pliable forms is a central characteristic of contemporary finance. Mining is not the only extractive industry. While the dreams of North America's private investors were being set ablaze by tales of gold at Busang, the corporate banking departments of Wall Street were preoccupied by another problem.

Gillian Tett begins her account of the 2008 credit crisis with a retreat for J.P. Morgan executives who were, among the usual boys behaving badly antics, imagining new ways of arranging loans to large corporations, reliable borrowers wishing to extend their debt.[5] Constrained by new regulations, the bankers sought to shift risk from their balance sheets so they could conduct more business. They constructed tranches of corporate debt that were organized and paid out in the same way as the mortgage bonds pioneered by Salomon in the 1980s. Any defaults were soaked up by the junior tranches. The bankers could not know which bonds would default, but they did know the probability of default across the whole, so the tranches could be designed in such a way that it would skim the risk from the whole pot. These tranches of risk earned more interest and were bought by specialists, while the mezzanine level was sold to more conservative investors. The super-safe senior level was so safe, and therefore offered such low returns, that it was not worth selling. The issuers held on to the bonds, effectively shifting them off their books by means of insurance; insurers thought this was money for nothing, as all risk short of global calamity was held elsewhere. Their premia were low, but the bonds were huge, so this was a profitable affair for all concerned.

These CDOs, or collateralized debt obligations as they should properly be known, were initially successful but were badly hit by the dotcom collapse, with its WorldCom and Enron scandals. Fraud, scandal and collapse of some of the globe's largest corporations were not what the bankers' models predicted. Mortgage bonds, however, continued to thrive in a steadily rising housing market, with interest rates held artificially low by Alan Greenspan. A new practice arose in corporate debt offices. They began to use mortgage bonds as the underlying material for CDOs. What made this so attractive was the fact that the high-paying, risky, junior tranches from a number of *mortgage-backed* bonds (asset-backed securities, or ABS) could be scrabbled together into a *debt-based* CDO that would pay out at much lower rates. Indeed, following a logic identical to that of the mortgage bonds, the riskier the underlying tranche, the larger the spread (the difference between income and payout, valid for the life of the bond), the bigger the gains to be made on the deal.

Again, issuers took to insuring the super-senior (safest) layer with giants like AIG, which thought it good business and offered premiums for just 15 basis points (0.15 per cent) of the whole. Insurance is the final step in the concretization of this value, a legal guarantee that even in the event of catastrophic failure, the bond remains worth what it is worth. It is not clear, notes Donald MacKenzie in a fascinating aside, that the insurers could ever have afforded to pay in the event of an economic cataclysm severe enough to trigger collapse of the safest tranches, nor whether anyone expected them to do so. The whole thing was a pantomime that allowed the traders to book their profits up front and draw their bonuses accordingly.[6]

Like the other tools of finance we have encountered, these bonds were epistemic engines. They depended on various assumptions to make the un-knowable concrete and tractable. One such was the idea of correlation, or the extent to which defaults are linked and dependent on one another. MacKenzie found that measures of correlation for debt-based bonds settled at around 0.3. That was a most conservative assumption: if one-third of US blue-chip business simultaneously defaulted on its debt, there would have been an economic Armageddon. It was also adopted for the modelling of ABS-CDOs, but a flaw in this logic seemingly eluded the great minds of Wall Street. Quite apart from the fact that the factors likely to cause default are unlikely to happen in isolation – the economic collapse of a neighbourhood, or the closure of a large local factory, or a general bursting of an unsustainable property bubble – there is a much more significant structural problem with these knowledge-making machines. All these bonds are devices for creating future certainty, and the future certainty created by the mortgage bonds is that all of the defaults, *wherever* and *whenever* they might arise, will end up in one place: the risky, lower tranches. For this reason, if you take a bundle of those low, risky tranches you will be holding not some, but *all* of the defaults on the property market, and a relatively tiny movement in the underlying portfolio will completely destroy the value of the bond. Safety in this arrangement, when applied to the higher tranches, comes from diversification, but the first round of bonds has used it all up. An ABS-CDO is by construction un-diversified. With the exception of a few sceptical hedge fund managers, nobody seems to have figured this out. One celebrity trader, Howie Hubler, made the basic error of confusing mortgage bonds with CDOs made from mortgage bonds, and wound up with a $9 billion loss on his deal. (Again, you cannot keep a good man down: Hubler left Morgan Stanley soon afterwards with a $10 million pay-off and started a firm to help homeowners overburdened by debt.) MacKenzie suggests that the problem lies in the organization of the banks, with large departments that did not talk to each other re-duplicating a process and therefore destroying its benefits. AIG could not have known, or it would not have insured the super-senior tranches and suddenly found itself needing $182.5 billion in taxpayers' funds to meet its obligations. The matter was worsened by the invention of 'synthetic CDOs'. Despite the best efforts of brokers across the USA to make expensive loans to those least able to afford them – and again, predatory lending was directed at the poor, at migrants, at the black and Latino communities – there simply were not enough bad loans to satisfy Wall Street's deal machine. A synthetic CDO copied an existing CDO, with the payments in generated not by mortgages but by premia paid by those willing to bet against the market. The arrangement is almost perverse: not only are the future earnings of those borrowers minted as revenue streams again and again, but the very mechanism that should in theory be bringing the market into balance is being manipulated to amplify the excesses.

I began this book with the slave ship Zong. Social theorists Zenia Kish and Justin Leroy propose that the Zong Massacre is a

> cautionary tale of how moral outrage at instances of overt racial violence can obscure the more subtle and persistent relationship between race and finance … the fact that England's financial development over the previous half century was predicated not only on compelling African bodies to work but also on innovating ever more creative ways of extracting value from those bodies.[7]

Here, argue Kish and Leroy, modern finance offers an uncomfortable parallel: the future labour of homeowners, tied to exorbitant interest payments, shackled for decades to the bond holder, and yet, at the same time, obscured, distanced and sanitized. Future labour becomes the collateral for loans, the basis for ever-more elaborate extraction. Twentieth-century rubber plantations, or the vast factories and warehouses of the present, gig-working drivers and meal deliverers, these are all of a piece. Finance is an industry of extraction, and stock exchanges are its fulcrum.

***

A story cannot be all villains. There are heroes and visionaries too, the well intentioned, those whose principles sometimes lead them to failure. Finance is often darkly comic, but it is sometimes tragic as well.

One company that was using AIM as its founders had intended – as a launch pad for entrepreneurial Britain – was OFEX.[8] Hit hard by the dotcom boom, OFEX had retrenched and set out to restore its reputation. It wanted to look like a regulated stock market. From July 2000 the market was included within the insider dealing legislation, and in December 2001 it became a Prescribed Market under the Financial Services and Markets Act (FSMA). In 2002 it secured exemptions from stamp duty in line with the privileges available to a recognized investment exchange (RIE). These exemptions and inclusions were the result of extensive lobbying by the firm and were ratified by the House of Lords. On 1 December 2001 OFEX finally became a market in the eyes of the law. External changes were matched by an internal reorganization. On 4 January 2002, the market was moved into a new vehicle, OFEX PLC, which absorbed the Newstrack operation. There was now a parent company, SJ&S (named after the original family firm) with two subsidiaries, the market-maker J.P. Jenkins Ltd and OFEX PLC. Jonathan and Emma Jenkins became joint managing directors of the latter. No longer operating a trading facility, J.P. Jenkins could target advisory revenues too. John Jenkins and Barry Hocken, having witnessed the 'very comfortable living' being made by corporate advisers bringing firms to market in the late 1990s, established their own advisory boutique called Gateway Securities. Advisory and market-making operations became physically separated from the market as they moved out of the existing offices and into Fenchurch Street.

Yet this reorganization had an unintended consequence. As the firm sought to *look* more like a stock exchange, it had to make its living as a stock exchange, and so it became vulnerable to a downturn in trading and listing numbers. During 2002 just 29 companies joined the market, and OFEX booked a pre-tax loss of £662,000. There was no reason why it could not do what any other ambitious young company might do in the circumstances – seek a listing on a junior exchange and raise money from shareholders. But which one? As a small and still risky endeavour, although one with much potential, OFEX was the perfect 'OFEX company'. Instead, on February 18 2003, OFEX announced that it would list on AIM and raise up to £2 million at a valuation of £4.5 million. The decision was contentious. AIM was, in many ways, a rival to OFEX, although it served a different constituency. OFEX PLC was too small for AIM, and not raising enough money, and for the operator of a small company market to contract the services of another looked odd. In fact, the move was a technical, regulatory decision hinging on the perceived competence of any firm to supervise itself as a listee on the market that it ran, while a clearly related company continued to be the sole market-maker in its stock. Simply put, OFEX would have put itself in an identical position to Harvard Securities two decades earlier, and its management was keen to avoid that outcome. Said one executive:

> We got a lot of crap from that [decision], and we couldn't turn round and go, 'Look, the only reason we did it is because the FSA [the UK's financial regulator] said we would. We think AIM is entirely the wrong place to be, for where we are and what we do. We should be on OFEX. We're a classic OFEX company.'

In April 2003 the offer got away, but only just, with £1.45 million raised rather than the expected £2 million. The market moved out of the family group and on to AIM as OFEX PLC. August 2003 saw Teather & Greenwood join as the first new market-maker, and in November, Winterflood Securities also agreed to make markets in OFEX stocks, subject to the installation of a new quote-driven trading system. By July 2004 OFEX would claim that four firms – Jenkins, Winterflood, Teather & Greenwood and Hoodless Brennan – would join as market-makers, and that each security would benefit from two-way quotes from at least two market-makers. According to the press, the prospect of institutional investment seemed even closer. Rumours began to circulate that OFEX was getting ready to take on AIM: 'In November, I said OFEX was flexing its muscles to challenge AIM, the Stock Exchange's junior market. Now it is gathering the financial ammunition to strengthen its assault', said veteran pundit Derek Pain, writing in the *Independent*.[9] Journalists suggested that the multiple market-maker system, combined with the availability of institutional funds, made OFEX look an ever-more attractive destination for listing companies, especially as EU regulation threatened to drive up the costs of an AIM listing. Listed companies did not seem convinced. In 2003 OFEX offered to waive the listing fees of companies moving from AIM, and few, if any, took up the offer. Cynics might note that corporate advisers to AIM companies charged far higher fees than they could to a firm listed on OFEX: perhaps their advice was not entirely without self-interest.

Still the company burned through cash, booking a full-year loss of roughly half a million pounds as it continued to work on its regulatory status. So OFEX decided to go the whole way, to raise a big chunk of capital and win accreditation as an RIE, a move that would put it on an equivalent legal footing with the venerable London Stock Exchange. It was going to shake off the vestiges of its reputation as a family firm and head for the bright lights of mainstream finance capital. 'We were going to become an RIE,' says Jonathan Jenkins,

> so we were going to raise £5 million. Dad was sort of retiring and stepping back, Simon was coming in as CEO, I was stepping back into the background a bit. We raised £5 million to do it and that was what we were doing. I have the press release, I mean, we were *that close*.

In the last week of September 2004, disaster struck. The funding was to be announced on Wednesday alongside the results. Jenkins was at Bloomberg's London office in Finsbury Square, addressing a group of retail investors. 'I can remember standing on the platform,' he says, 'on Monday night, saying: watch this space, there is some interesting news to come out and I think OFEX is going to go from strength to strength.'

While Jenkins was speaking, his phone began to vibrate in his pocket. It was only later, after the last investor had drifted away, that he listened to the message. It was from OFEX's business development officer, a man of a Gallic temperament given to moments of triumph and despair, and his voice was thick with tears. The cornerstone investor, a City individual of huge stature whose presence had helped recruit the others, had pulled out. It could have been that the investor had never actually committed any funds. No one seems to have checked that he intended to do so. Now £2 million of the needed £5 million was left unaccounted for. Whatever the truth, without this investor there was no new money.

It did not take Jenkins long to think through the implications. As chief executive of a quoted public company he was still going to have to report its results. A stock exchange is a fragile thing. Like a bank, it depends on confidence to stay in existence. Investors tend to be much less keen to risk their hard-earned money by trading on a market soon to go out of business. Firms are unlikely to go through the arduous and expensive process of securing a quotation if the exchange itself looks precarious. And regulators have a tedious habit of setting demanding capital requirements, which means you cannot just tighten your belt and hold on for dear life – the favoured strategy of the small company in trouble – if you happen to be boss of a stock exchange. Things can come unravelled very quickly, and on Wednesday they did.

Media reports spread word of the disaster, often with undisguised glee. 'Shares in OFEX dive as it fights imminent collapse', crowed *The Times*, 'OFEX, founded by John Jenkins and controlled by his family, said it had only enough money to remain solvent for another nine weeks. The announcement precipitated a 54 per cent plunge in OFEX's shares', adding maliciously, 'It is understood that the revelation of OFEX's dire financial position took the company's senior management by surprise.' Elsewhere, *The Times* spoke of 'grim news' for a firm that 'did not do itself any favours when it decided to list its own shares on AIM'.[10]

The marginally more sympathetic *Independent* reported that 'an emergency fund-raising put together by the company's broker, Numis, collapsed at the last minute, forcing the OFEX to admit spiralling losses and a looming cash crunch.'[11] 'Emergency fundraising', while full of journalistic vigour, puts OFEX in the crisis ward even before the funding collapsed.

John, meanwhile, was stuck in China. Confident that everything was in hand, Jenkins – still chairman and a substantial shareholder in the company – had taken a trip on a group visa that prevented him from returning early. Over the next few days he was marooned on the other side of the world, unable to help as his company was 'rescued'. At one point he dialled in for a meeting with the firm's broker, now in charge of arranging the emergency placing. The meeting began, as meetings do, with some pleasantries. 'So, John, how's the Great Wall of China?' asked a young wag from the brokerage. 'It's a fucking wall! Now what have you done to my company?' yelled Jenkins in reply, some way from his usual self.

Jonathan Jenkins and his sister Emma, joint chief executives of the market, sorted matters out as best they could. The jackals were seen off. The original investors, bar one, came together and, on Friday 8 October, they refinanced the business to the tune of £3.15 million. But the terms were much harsher, and although OFEX was saved, it was the end of the road for the Jenkins family. Jonathan Jenkins stepped down, embarrassed by his announcement and hurt by the vicious press comment, and Emma resigned alongside him. There were no golden executive pay-outs. John remained as chairman for a few more weeks until a replacement could be found. The family's stake was diluted from 55 per cent to 12 per cent, and several hundred thousand pounds worth of loans that Jenkins had made to the firm had to be written off.

The new bid still had to be ratified by shareholders at the end of October, and on Friday 29 October, a group called Shield tabled a rival bid. It offered stock and cash, conditional on the Jenkins family remaining at the helm. Mindful of their obligations to their customers, to all who depended on the market, and to the market itself, Jonathan and Emma rejected Shield's offer – and with it the family's future in the firm. It was with understandable bitterness that Jonathan Jenkins commented to the press, 'We've fought so hard to get this market back on its feet and now I won't be a part of its future.' But what really rankled, more than anything else, was the lack of acknowledgement for what the family had done to date, and for the sacrifices they had made in the end.

'I don't think we ever got acknowledged,' says Jonathan,

All the noise was, oh look, they have fucked up, they have run out of money and everything else like that. Actually we got let down … then we did what we thought was the right thing. Our severance pay was pathetic, but we did what we thought was right. It was the way that Emma and I were brought up, and Dad. We should do what is right for the marketplace.

PART IV

Financial Futures

13

Finance Takes Flight

The Frankenstein story – the monster that bursts out of the laboratory and pursues its creator – is firmly embedded in our collective imagination. The novelist Robert Harris gives it a spin in the *Fear Index*, published in 2011. His monster is an artificially intelligent trading algorithm launched by a Geneva-based hedge fund. It is fantastically, malevolently intelligent, able to penetrate secret files and to discover the worst imaginings of its designer, to conduct a reign of terror through purchase orders and contracts. As its creator attempts to burn down the servers that house it, the algorithm uploads itself into the digital netherworld where it roams free, doing as its code instructs: feeding on fear for financial profit.

Harris' fictional financial cataclysm echoes a real one that took place on 6 May 2010. Where the collapse of the late 1980s was strung out across several days, this one was wrapped up in an afternoon. A wobble in the US markets, and then a spectacular tumble: the Dow Jones losing 998.5 points in 36 minutes, a trillion dollars of capital evaporating in 5 minutes. This was the 'Flash Crash'. There was no panic, no shrieking or shouting. The whole affair was conducted algorithmically, as high-speed trading machines performed the electronic equivalent of yelling 'Sell! Sell!', unloading stock to each other at ever-falling prices. Algorithms do not panic, but they do form expectations, and they do so in thousandths of a second, creating a self-fulfilling cyber-crash. Circuit-breakers – automatic cut-outs designed to stop the market self-destructing – halted trading. When trading restarted, prices climbed quickly back to the morning's levels. Although individual traders may have made or lost fortunes (we don't know – and Harris deftly weaves fiction into the gap), very few ripples spread into the wider economy.

An initial investigation found that a large sell order had triggered the flash. There was a veiled reference to a problem with the timing of data feeds, a technical, structural problem. But international law enforcement officers turned up in London to arrest a man the media soon dubbed the 'Hound of Hounslow'. This was Navinder Singh Sarao, a solitary London trader with unusual personality traits who built an engine to 'spoof' the Chicago algorithms and made millions trading from his bedroom. US regulators became convinced that his activities had sparked off the crash. Sarao was extradited to the USA to face justice. The judge, expecting a criminal mastermind, saw instead a 41-year-old man with autism who still lived with his parents. Sarao may have made $70 million, mostly from legitimate trading, but much of his money seems to have ended up in the hands of fraudsters and questionable entrepreneurs. The only thing he purchased was a second-hand VW car, which he was too nervous to drive. The judge laid down a lenient sentence of a year of house arrest, even if Sarao had threatened to cut off the thumbs of a market administrator.

We can think through the changes that have swept through financial markets in different ways. They are a technological project driven by the endeavours of engineers. The result has been a wholesale transformation in the materiality of markets. To physically step into the place of a 21st-century market is to step into a warehouse of humming and chattering servers. Like the traders of old, they jostle for space around a central exchange, but this space is measured out in fibre-optic cables and milliseconds. We can also think of these transformations in terms of a wholesale shift in our understanding of how exchanges should work. The metaphor that underpins them has moved from one of the market as a fundamentally social entity to one of the market as a computational device, where efficiency becomes of paramount importance. The market ceases to be a concrete thing in a specific place and becomes a distributed network located nowhere and everywhere: Wall Street, Chicago and Houndslow.[1] This, in turn, reflects longer term shifts in our understanding of the economy. From Ludwig von Mises and Friedrich Hayek onwards we have grown accustomed to thinking of the economy as a vast, disembedded computational device as opposed to a specific set of social and material situations. The efficient market hypothesis, the claim that all available information is incorporated into a price, maps these ideas onto financial markets. In theoretical terms, the market is the ultimate cloud-based computer. In real life, the market has begun to look like this as well.

The change in technology has been matched by a change in culture. Hounslow, for those who do not know London, is an unremarkable borough to the west of the city: suburbs, offices, few tourist attractions. Although the pun may have been too tempting to avoid, it tells us something. In the place of the champagne and cocaine-fuelled high life of Jordan Belfort we have a super-trader in an upstairs bedroom clad in a hoodie and jeans. In a US cultural register, he would have worked from his mom's basement, or perhaps the family garage. The Hound is just one manifestation of the cultural shift that has shaped financial markets over the last two decades. Hoodie and baseball cap are squeezing out shirt and tie, techno wizard replacing Princeton-educated 'Master of the Universe'. Markets populated by algorithms scarcely understood by their creators raise all kinds of new problems, such as transaction speeds that test natural laws. They bring us unfamiliar characters, whether fictional physicists based in Geneva and leveraging their experience of quantum mechanics into monstrous artificial intelligence or autistic coders living with their parents.

We can, if we wish, map other ideas onto these transformations. The economic historian Fernand Braudel saw the flowering of finance capital as being 'a sign of autumn' for every capitalist era. Money seeks ways of moving more quickly, more freely, more flexibly in pursuit of returns. As in earlier historical episodes, it passes into the realm of financial speculation, an 'increasingly feverish search for new kinds of profits available in financial transactions,' writes Fredric Jameson, where 'capital itself becomes free-floating, it separates from the concrete context of its productive geography.'[2] Yet, as we have seen, the flights of Jameson's free-floating, alienated capital must be supported by a mundane, material architecture; flash crashes happen somewhere, and must follow rules, even if these are set by the boundaries of theoretical physics.

We saw in Chapter 9 how, in London, the process of exchange automation began with settlement and clearing, letting the machines do tedious, routine work. Treated at first like second-class citizens, the engineers built a series of systems that incrementally advanced the automation of trading until, on the day of the Big Bang, 6 October 1986, the London Stock Exchange opened in a fully electronic form. We saw how this change took many by surprise, not least the Exchange's own managers, but the engineers' institutional advancement did not, at this point, upset the money-making hierarchies of the Exchange. A different kind of challenge came from outside the Exchange. By the mid-1990s, as Juan Pablo Pardo-Guerra shows, an industry had sprung up in the provision of computerized infrastructures that could be bought almost off-the-shelf by anyone with the desire to set up a new exchange. These systems emphasized a new kind of trading infrastructure – the order book – a mechanism quite different from the long-established market-maker system. 'Within this sprawling ecology,' writes Pardo-Guerra, 'there was increasing recognition of the dominant design ... electronic order books that allowed for the direct interaction of instructions from investors without the intervention of humans to coordinate transactions.'[3]

Three engineers, Peter Bennett, Michael Waller-Bridge and Stephen Wilson, had spent years at the London Stock Exchange trying to set up a pan-European order book system. Blocked in this endeavour they set out on their own. They called their start-up system Tradepoint, and lodged it symbolically outside of the City, in the architect Lord (then Richard) Rogers' building in Thames Wharf, also home to the renowned River Cafe, the first of London's new generation of stripped-down palaces of gastronomy. All of this was a performance, even if the restaurant did help bring visitors to the office and allow them to make their case on home territory. It was a performance of difference, of outside status, of the power of technology to break up cliques and upset the existing order. One part of this performance was the 'computer room'. This ordinary room, equipped with a huge ventilation duct and mains cable, out of bounds apart from the sign on the door, helped to convince visitors that the market was backed by sufficiently massive technology. In fact, the computer system was quite moderate, enhanced by the programming skills of a colleague called Ian McLelland, who customized a software package bought off the shelf from the Vancouver Stock Exchange. As for the upsetting of the existing order, that was a performance as well. Tradepoint brought to bear an impressively deep network of social relationships with existing players, including making an agreement with the London Clearing House and inviting its boss, Sir Michael Jenkins, on to the Tradepoint board.

There was, as Pardo-Guerra points out, a moral imperative to the Tradepoint offering: 'by allowing competition beyond the control of the LSE's [London Stock Exchange's] market-makers, their electronic order book would narrow spreads, driving down costs for end investors.'[4] Order books are electronic auctions conducted without the assistance of jobbers or market-makers. The order books, and the practices that came to be associated with them, notably anonymity, were attractive to overseas investors, derivatives trades and hedge funds.[5] It was a venue for early robot traders, market participants 'represented by installed boxes literally sporting flashing lights'.[6] Tradepoint never amassed the volume of orders necessary to be a commercial success, but it did, in Pardo-Guerra's words, change 'the language of what was possible and permissible.'[7] Although an attempt in 1995 to forcibly introduce an order-driven system led to a members' rebellion and the sacking of chief executive Michael Lawrence, order-driven trading was now inevitable, and in October 1997 the London Stock Exchange introduced its new system, SETS. Order books began to diffuse through the institution from the most senior markets downwards.[8]

Electronic order books are the material manifestation of the move away from thinking of a stock exchange as an institution rooted in geographic and social place to seeing it as a distributed network of information processing. In this aesthetic – that of the engineer, not the financier – speed, efficiency and structural elegance are the things that matter, and they become the next battleground in the struggle for institutional dominance.

★★★

We left OFEX in dire straits, with the Jenkins family expelled from the firm following a failed fundraising. Into this void of leadership stepped Simon Brickles, a former barrister who had been instrumental in setting up the constitution of AIM and who had later become head of the market. He had left the London Stock Exchange in 2003, frustrated by an increasing emphasis on order books and its move away from his vision of a market with light-touch regulation. Brickles sensed that the way out of OFEX's predicament was a headlong charge, not away from the Exchange, but towards it.[9]

His shareholders agreed. The market-makers who had supported the rescue fundraising to become major shareholders in OFEX were chafing at the high fees imposed by the London Stock Exchange – still effectively a monopoly, but now a demutualized and revenue-focused global corporation – for settlement and transaction. The European MiFID (Markets in Financial Instruments Directive) regulations, expected in 2007, sought to open up competition between markets, but there was no possibility of competition unless a vehicle to challenge the Exchange could be found. Brickles therefore began to expand the market's offering. The company announced a £2.5 million fundraising to pay for an expansion in the number of securities traded, stating 'the company intends to markedly broaden its existing trading services to encompass an extended range of securities. The enlarged trading service will allow brokers and investors flexibility in selecting their execution venue'.[10] In other words, the junior market was to be positioned as a direct competitor to the London Stock Exchange, especially to AIM. On 10 November 2005, *The Times* reported a private meeting at the offices of mid-tier broker Charles Stanley:

> Present at the meeting were representatives from Stanley and dealers such as Seymour Pierce, Peel Hunt and Winterflood Securities, which has led the opposition to the LSE. Some brokers are upset at the extension of the LSE's SETS part-electronic trading platform to various small-cap and AIM stocks, for which they claim it is unsuitable.[11]

That unhappiness is more than a disagreement about infrastructure; it is a battle over the rights and privileges to make money in the markets.

On 30 November 2005, after a period of intensive work, the PLUS service (as it was now called) was launched. It enabled brokers to trade any stock on the Official List, 'everything from Vodafone, down to the smallest FTSE All-Share.' But it was not yet a fully-fledged stock exchange and another funding followed, pegged to the ambition of achieving a licence as a recognized investment exchange (RIE). According to the offer document, the firm, currently focused 'on providing cost-effective quote and trading services dovetailed to the needs of small and mid-cap companies … is seeking to expand into offering services to meet the quotation and trading needs of larger companies and the UK institutional community.' In February 2007 the offer, heavily oversubscribed, valued the company at £43 million.

Central to the whole endeavour was PLUS' trading system. It had to be fast. Tradelect, the London Stock Exchange's new £40 million system, went live on 18 June 2007, cutting order processing time to 10 milliseconds and greatly reducing trading costs. PLUS ordered a platform from the Scandinavian firm OMX, but that was just the start: it needed to connect to market-makers, brokers, data vendors and the internal surveillance system. It had to be robust. It was, as Brickles said, 'a huge spider's web, and if any one of those bits of the spider's web doesn't connect you cannot launch the market.' July 2007 saw the granting of the RIE licence, and the OMX X-Stream platform launched in November, just as MiFID came into force. Both took up quantities of management time and were finished in time for the November deadline: 'No mean feat. We were running pretty hard,' said one of the executives. But, as Tradepoint's founders had clearly understood, starting a market is not just a technological project. PLUS' concentration on the material infrastructure perhaps distracted attention from the social and discursive labour involved in setting up a new exchange. Indeed, many in the smaller company community felt that PLUS was no longer seriously committed to its original constituency. They levelled the same critique that PLUS had been making against the London Stock Exchange: a steady drift upstream towards bigger companies and more lucrative business. John French, the businessman who chaired the advisory panel, described the task of maintaining a focused market for smaller company shares as 'pushing water uphill' in the face of scant interest from institutional investors and the market's own management.

Any doubts over the market's direction of travel – from smaller company nursery to discount trading and trade reporting venue – would have been settled by the Turquoise affair, a significant and 'traumatic' distraction for management in the autumn of 2007. Turquoise was a plan for a dark pool, a lightly regulated trading venue, that would offer anonymity and low fees. Like PLUS' move to compete with the London Stock Exchange's small-cap markets, Turquoise sprung from the fact that in the mid-2000s, according to one financier, 'people hated the LSE,' then run by Clara Furse, 'it was … vicious.' Turquoise had formidable backers, a number of senior executives of global investment banks, 'big swinging dicks, big players, nothing to do with small company investing but big players … [who] got it into their heads, probably rightly, that the LSE was taking too much of the pot in trading terms.' Although it had first been mentioned in the press in April 2007 it had not made much progress, earning itself the sobriquet 'Project Tortoise'. These executives needed infrastructure and expertise in market operation, and, on 6 October 2007, the *Daily Telegraph* 'revealed' that PLUS was negotiating the terms of a 'takeover' with Turquoise, while the *Independent* announced a 'merger'. PLUS shares were suspended. But nothing happened. By 19 October talks were over, and Turquoise was reported as looking for a deal with Cinnober, a Swedish technology firm.

Still no progress was made and eventually the whole thing was quietly absorbed by the London Stock Exchange, now run by the shrewd and politically aware Xavier Rolet.

The London Stock Exchange went on to block PLUS' trading access to AIM stocks, a strategic blow that thwarted the young contender's ambition. Fees were cut and the market-makers drifted back to the Exchange. The story of PLUS tails off in 2009 following a pyrrhic legal victory over the Exchange. Strategies, regulations and courtrooms, so vital in the evolution of markets up to this point, have by now become the exception. In the brave new world of markets, battles for domination are played out through technological systems. PLUS' chief executive was a lawyer by training, not an engineer, and the willingness of the small exchange to take to law rather than fight with the resources of speed and technological elegance showed a certain innocence of the new cyborg world. Elsewhere, the 'market in markets' longed for by regulators materialized in the wires of market systems and the code that flowed through them.

***

In the USA, markets followed a similar trajectory of technological development. Throughout the 1970s and 1980s ongoing institutional bricolage had led to the electronic NASDAQ system, where brokers displayed prices and dealt with each other by phone. Although the network spanned the USA, it encoded existing patterns of dominance and buttressed the power of the New York Stock Exchange and NASDAQ's broker-dealers. These latter colluded, at least by habit and practice, to offer prices in even-eights only, keeping the commission to a quarter of a dollar per trade.[12] At around the same time, the New York Stock Exchange was mired in its own scandals, including the payment of $139 million – a number so big it demanded a euphemism – to CEO Richard Grasso as a 'compensation package'. The scene is right for a coup, or at the very least, a market culture war. Just as Tradepoint had set itself up as a self-consciously outside challenger to the London Stock Exchange, so, in the USA, a new generation of code-writing techno-libertarians started to play in the markets. Their innovations cracked open the long-established monopolies of NASDAQ and the New York Stock Exchange.

Once again this is a story of technology, innovation and aesthetics, and again, it has humble beginnings. The NASDAQ-automated system housed a sub-market called the small order execution system, or SOES, designed for retail traders. After the crash of 1987, when market-makers had simply stopped processing orders, regulators made it compulsory for brokers to publish quotations and honour them. The unexpected consequence of this instruction was that SOES now provided a facility for outsiders to day-trade smaller sums in the NASDAQ markets: youngsters in t-shirts and jeans and baseball caps staring at screens and hoping to catch out the brokers with a speedy click here or there. Traders congregated in the offices of firms like Datek with its headquarters in Broad Street, just around the corner from Wall Street. These youngsters became known as 'SOES bandits', revelling in their outsider status as they needled the established players in ways that transgressed the etiquette of trading. Tensions often flared. MacKenzie and Pardo-Guerra report an episode where a member of staff of a NASDAQ broker-dealer located at 43 Broad Street, infuriated at being 'SOES-ed' by Datek's traders, crossed to no 50 and barged into Datek's trading room, screaming 'You did it again, I'll fucking *kill* you!' He leapt at one of the Datek traders, so a more senior trader picked up a letter opener and stabbed him forcibly, fortunately only in the shoulder. This trading was all-in, on the edge – 'No one blinked when a chalk-faced guy doubled over a garbage pail and puked violently, never leaving his seat and trading right through the puke.'[13]

At Datek, a young engineer called Josh Levine began to build hardware and software hacks that avoided more longhand operations, for example allowing quick keystrokes, or jacking the printer feed from a NASDAQ terminal directly into a computer. These eventually became a slick trading system in their own right, faster, sharper, leaner than anything NASDAQ could provide. A crucial step forward came when Levine realized that he could cut out the expensive NASDAQ dealers altogether by allowing Datek traders to exchange stock between themselves. This required a matching engine, and Levine built one. He called it Island. It had low fees and even offered rebates to those posting sell orders. Levine built systems that worked elegantly from an engineering viewpoint, completely rethinking the organization of algorithm and exchange, pursuing a programmer's aesthetic that valued speed and efficiency above all else. Trade time dropped from two seconds to two-thousandths of a second. Island's engine was so quick that users realized the distance between their own server and the central machine mattered, and the practice of 'co-locating' servers in the exchange building – for a fee – appeared.

The offices in Broad Street maintained the flavour of the high-tech start-up – t-shirts, hoodies, junk food and eccentricities – but soon enough, as MacKenzie and Pardo-Guerra put it, Island became a continent. By 2005, through a series of acquisitions, it had become part of NASDAQ and transformed the giant exchange from the inside out, rebuilding NASDAQ's technological infrastructure along the Island model. Other programmers moved from Island to exchanges elsewhere and spread the technology as they went. This technological upheaval transformed not just the exchanges, but also their customers. It wasn't long before the robots arrived, the real-world equivalents of Harris' fearsome algorithm. Program trading, where algorithms made suggestions to brokers, had been around since the mid-1980s. It had taken some of the blame for Black Monday in 1987, but the programs still depended on humans to get the orders transacted. Levine's Island was perfectly suited for entirely automated trading, even down to the hacker-libertarian politics.

In another study MacKenzie tells the story of one such firm, based in Charleston, Carolina, set up by academic statisticians who had previously built a model to predict the outcomes of horse races and thought the methodology would transfer to the stock market. At its peak the firm came to be one of the leading tech firms in the county.[14]

What MacKenzie shows, however, is that for all the barefoot, t-shirt, take-on-the-world hacker aesthetic, the firm only really flourished when it discovered pockets of systematic advantage that were already being exploited by human actors. So, for example, the programmers learned about the SOES bandits and built an algorithm that mimicked what these humans were doing, looking out for tell-tale signs of big movements in the markets. Then it was a question of machine competing against human, a simple race where the ones outcompeted were not the incumbent NASDAQ brokers but the human bandits in Broad Street. Trading at that speed needed a matching engine capable of managing the order flow and the algorithm plugged straight into Island's, sometimes breaching the order limit of a million trades per day. It was trading figures like these that forced NASDAQ to buy Island, inviting the algorithms into the mainstream. Once trading becomes a race then everyone must run, and some 90 per cent of global stock trade is now conducted algorithmically.[15]

One of the ironies of high-speed trading is that, just as the market has slipped into the cloud, so designers have had to pay attention to where trading actually happens. High frequency trading, or HFT as it is known, has foregrounded the brute material from which markets are made, and this material is political. Automated markets are housed in heavily guarded warehouses outside major cities, New Jersey in the USA or Slough in the UK. As the market is literally made in these places, the speed with which prices travel back to the trading algorithms is crucial. Co-location has become a taken-for-granted of HFT, with firms paying to locate their boxes as close to the Exchange's engine as possible. Links between exchanges also matter. Michael Lewis' book *Flash Boys* is held together by the story of an extraordinary construction project, the building in secret of a fibre-optic link between New York and Chicago, drilling through the Appalachian Mountains. Fibre-optic cables had already been laid along the railway track. The railway bends and twists through the mountains. The few milliseconds that could be saved by travelling in a straight line made the difference between being able to make a profit trading in the markets and never being able to do so: the investors who funded the line could hold traders to ransom. But the speed of light through glass is only two-thirds of the speed of light through the air, so rivals have installed chains of microwave dishes as close to the geodesic as possible. It is faster on a clear day, but slower in the rain, and the line of sight is sometimes blocked by the tidal pull on Lake Michigan. We are literally at the limits of physics and yet, as MacKenzie points out, this is an economic arms race of the classic kind, with huge and wasteful rents being paid just so players can stay in the game. Even the players can see this: in the middle of describing how engineers have worked day and night to shave 5 to 10 nanoseconds from the processing time of specialized chips, one of MacKenzie's interviewees pauses to reflect that all that training, all that expertise could have done something else … something different.[16]

Although we might like to think of algorithmic trading as possessing the diabolic intelligence conjured up by Harris, to the extent that algorithms have autonomy, they turn out not to be so intelligent after all. Indeed, writes the sociologist Kristian Bondo Hansen, algorithms often over-learn, making causal associations where there are plainly none. They must be taught to be good scientists, employing Occam's razor and the principle of parsimonious explanation.[17] Success is more a case of the early bird catching the worm, where the early bird is measured in power consumption, heat dissipation and metres of fibre-optic cable. This has, in turn, thrown up serious questions about the fairness of HFT. Michael Lewis argued that we – pension-holding, long-term investing citizens – are being scalped by these traders. Part of the difficulty is that algorithms are programmed to spot predictable trades and large buy and sell orders are by their nature predictable, despite the best efforts of brokers to hide them through their own high-speed slicing and dicing. Meanwhile machine learning and huge datasets have started to undo the formal anonymity of electronic exchanges as the most predatory algorithms learn to recognize and outmanoeuvre their more docile cousins.

Even if we do accept the necessity of HFT there are questions about how much the interaction order that we take for granted in everyday life, such as queuing, or telling the truth, should transfer into the world of algorithms. In the broadest of terms, should algorithms have a culture? The sociologist Christian Borch thinks so. He has argued that an algorithmic culture is needed to prevent a massive, destructive flash crash (small ones happen regularly). He writes about a group of firms working to introduce a better 'moral culture' in algorithms: 'they strive to eliminate any negative effects their algorithms may have on markets, and they have developed an ethos built on ensuring market integrity in every respect … these firms expend massive, ongoing efforts to comprehend how and why their algorithms behave the way they do, alone and together with other algorithms.'[18] The problem with wanting to impose a culture on algorithms is that they have one already. Algorithms contain the decisions of their makers, of the cultures and practices that form them. The engineer's aesthetic, the junk food wrappers and Star Trek posters signal another elite discourse, as gendered and riddled with privilege as the stock market monopolies it set out to break apart. Algorithmic culture is a dark mirror of our own.

Might we, in the end, concede to Braudel and Jameson, seeing finance as the autumn of capital engaged in an ever-more feverish hunt for profits? In the case of these cyborg markets we come close: a finance set free from the productive economy, unchained to circle the globe in a heated but ultimately futile pursuit of margin. Except, finance was never shackled to the productive economy, and has always feverishly pursued profits. In fact, capital seems ever more tethered, tied to chips and fibres, to bunkers full of computer servers in the suburbs of New York, Chicago, London or Frankfurt. It is still wrong, even now, to paint capital as monolithic and coordinated. Cyborg stock exchanges are, like all the others we have encountered in this book, the outcome of a series of struggles between established players and new ones, struggles over who can grab the lion's share. What we have is simply more of the same, abstracted to the speed of light. This simple observation begs the most important question of all: what could we do differently?

14

The Temples of Capitalism

I wrote in the opening pages of this book that critiques of finance, from both friend and foe, often hinge on the claim that finance has lost its way. Finance is *for* something, they argue, and it is no longer doing it. One long-established tradition of thinking about stock markets sees them as engines of enterprise and the foundation of industry. These ideas are popular with policymakers, investors and the exchanges themselves; so much better to have a purpose than to be simply accidental, the product of happenstance and opportunism. We have seen the builders of markets draw on those narratives over and again. They are untrue, we now know, but the veracity of these ideas often matters less than how they shape the world. If people believe them, they will act accordingly, seeking a purer, better, more focused market.

We saw, in Chapter 11, how the sudden closure of the London Stock Exchange's Unlisted Securities Market (USM) provoked howls of protest and intense pressure to offer an alternative, much of it couched in discourses of a newly entrepreneurial Britain. The country was, they claimed, bursting with entrepreneurial zeal, held in check only by lack of capital. Michael Lawrence, the incoming chief executive, clutched the lifeline that he had been thrown by campaigners touting the interests of UK PLC. This, he claimed, was exactly what the Exchange was for: growing Britain as a nation of entrepreneurs, not just in London but across the English regions, in Scotland and Northern Ireland, places devastated by the rapid de-industrialization of the late 1980s. He saw, too, an opportunity to fill the void left by the closure of regional stock exchange offices in the 1970s and 1980s. 'These smaller companies,' he would say, 'these earlier-stage companies are not going to be walking about the City of London, you know, they're going to be in the UK regions.' Received wisdom held that local investors preferred local businesses: 'One of the things I heard and learnt when I first came on with the role,' says Theresa Wallis, who led the AIM team and became the first head of the market, 'was … investors, when it comes to small companies they'd rather invest close to home where they can go and visit the companies and they look them in the eye and all that sort of thing.' There was money in the regions, too.[1]

The vision of all this lonely money and all these needy businesses would have set even the most lackadaisical of financial middlemen trembling, and so began the slow process of talking this new market into being. Lawrence recognized that a new approach to listing would be vital, and that, in the conservative institutional culture of the London Stock Exchange, this would require an entirely new team. He put Wallis, then a young and little-known executive, in charge of a working party with a brief to think about listing in a completely new way. A pivotal figure in this history, Wallis' efforts have never been fully recognized, although it is clear she displayed a remarkable energy and competence in making the market happen. She had been instructed to 'walk through walls,' said one interviewee, 'and she did'. Another described her as an 'incredible leader, a team player, politically aware … phenomenal … it was a blessing to be working with her.'

Wallis was a believer. She was, she says, 'inspired by the ability to [do] anything that can help the UK economy and can help … helping smaller companies grow, helping the UK economy.' She was generous in her retelling of AIM's beginnings, emphasizing how much support the working group received from the rest of the Exchange; she remembers colleagues with deep expertise in listing practices and regulations and the minutiae of running an exchange, while her own team fizzed with excitement and a real commitment towards helping the British economy. Wallis and two colleagues sketching on a flip-chart came up with the 'Alternative Investment Market' name, while Lawrence suggested the abbreviation that became the market's branding. At the same time, the new market could make use of the London Stock Exchange's expertise, infrastructure and prestige. 'The Stock Exchange,' says Simon Brickles, at that point one of Wallis' team, 'knew how to operate markets, it had got the facilities, it had got the people, it had got the resources, and it had got the prestige. … AIM could have its separate values, its own separate rules, its own separate problems, opportunities and so on and that was Michael Lawrence's vision.' Ironically, John Jenkins' over-the-counter business, the competitor that had grown from within the Exchange and eventually goaded it to action, served as the model for the new market. 'Here was a group of companies,' says Andrew Buchanan, a small company-focused fund manager, 'in which there seemed to be some perfectly reasonable trading activity but no obvious mechanism. And yet the lack of a mechanism didn't seem to inhibit the liquidity in the stock. So what was the problem?' Within the Exchange, Wallis' team had arrived at the same conclusion, proposing that they would re-regulate the over-the-counter exemption (Rule 4.2, or 535.2, as it now was) to an acceptable level, keeping not only the baby but quite a lot of the bathwater as well.

A stock exchange is a bundle of wires and screens. As the PLUS founders perhaps failed to recognize, it is also a community of trust, shared expectations and commitment to certain norms. The London Stock Exchange already possessed the screens; the team set about building the community through an extended and iterative conversation with future participants. The new market had to be *talked* into being. Martin Hughes, a young executive on secondment to the team from Scottish Enterprise with the responsibility of promoting the market north of the border, describes the process as 'knowledge building, consensus building, to inform an emergent model … all about the market, getting to understand it, and that engagement. … You could tell that it was understood why it was important … there was never anyone who was not willing to engage properly, and think about it.' Consultation documents, responses from the community, follow-up telephone calls, meetings or conversations over dinner, held to a steady pace by the Exchange's somewhat pedantic and bureaucratic routines, slowly wove a market from threads of narrative and conversation. As a place of collective trust, recognition and expectation, the market was performed, acted out, spoken into being by the narratives and conversations that underpinned it. These, in turn, were held together by a shared commitment to the wonderful institution of UK PLC.

One problem concerned the kind of companies that might be listed on this new market, and who would take responsibility for them. An onerous admission process handled by the London Stock Exchange's Listing Department seemed out of step with the UK PLC narrative and the entrepreneurial aspirations that it embodied. How could the companies of the future raise funds with some worried regulator peering over the shoulders of potential investors? Again, the new market took the success of Rule 4.2 as a model. It would be a market based on *caveat emptor*, buyer beware. 'Private investors,' says Wallis, 'investors who are buying on Rule 4.2 don't seem to mind – it's very much a *caveat emptor* market – don't seem to mind that it's not regulated. They know what they're going in for. Maybe this is going to be the solution, [if] we build a market around what was Rule 535.2 dealing.' Here we begin to see the story changing: it is no longer simply about UK PLC, but also about freedom of choice and the appropriate role of regulation in a capital market. For the free market enthusiast, the role of regulation is not to protect consumers but to allow them to protect themselves through freedom of choice: 'I don't think [heavy regulation] is the business of a Stock Exchange,' says Simon Brickles, 'we should be the high temple of capitalism, we should allow as much choice and freedom as compatible with a reasonable level of investor protection.'

Originally, one of the guiding principles of this new market was ease of access for companies, which, in practice, meant low costs. As most of the costs of listing on a stock market come from fees paid to advisers, it was sensible to suggest that firms did not need them. In particular, they might not need a sponsor, an expensive corporate finance adviser whose role it was to scrutinize the firm in the run-up to its public listing. There were squeals from the community: just imagine those poor, unprotected investors! Sotto voce: just imagine those rich fat fees! Most of the investors were institutions that knew their business well and would have been happy to do without advisers whose fees they eventually would pay. Their voices were outnumbered as the consultation results came in. Wallis' team hatched an ingenious compromise, proposing that each firm would employ a nominated adviser, or NOMAD, with certain guaranteed professional qualifications and experience. These NOMADs would police the companies on the market, ensuring full disclosure and certain basic probity, but without needing the Exchange to take on responsibility of oversight.

But who would guard the guards? This 'reputational market'[2] would work like the floor of the Old House. Everyone knew everyone else and if a firm gained a reputation for sharp practice it would find future opportunities rapidly shrinking. Investors sold substandard merchandise have long memories. This was scarcely a decade after the closure of the London Stock Exchange's trading floor, and the new market harnessed the close social networks that persisted in the City, many from before the Big Bang. It relied on, in Brickles' words, 'the tools and instruments of a club': blackballing and (mostly private) censure. Only in real cases of malfeasance would the Exchange offer a public reprimand. As one former director of the London Stock Exchange put it,

> When you run a stock exchange … you have two rulebooks. One is the written rulebook and the other is the unwritten rulebook. When it came to AIM, there was a network underneath which says, that company, don't touch it. And so an awful lot of this stuff was unwritten, unrecorded. … Can't discuss it publicly, deny all knowledge.

But clubs are never quite as strict as they claim to be. 'It was always implicit,' says the same director, 'we would shoot one a year *pour encourager les autres*. … I think the Stock Exchange didn't do that. They were too obsessed with the marketing, getting companies on.' It all became frightfully cosy. By the late 1990s Theresa Wallis had slipped quietly away from the market she created, and away from the Exchange as a whole. Perhaps it was too comfortable for her liking as well.

AIM was a remarkably original conception, especially in an age where stock exchanges are shaped by the efficient market hypothesis. Where contemporary stock markets – Fama markets, we could call them – have been purged of social connections, AIM positively encourages them. One can argue that the NOMAD-based structure fulfils the requirements of a liquid and informationally efficient market, operating like a market for goods organized by the producers that know and keep an eye on each other.[3] Finance scholars describe the NOMAD system as 'private sector regulation' and there have been long debates about whether it works or not.[4] But there is no denying that AIM has been a success in practical terms. Hundreds of companies have joined the market and raised funds through it. The combined capitalization of the market is roughly a hundred billion pounds sterling. Its model has been adopted worldwide, especially since the NASDAQ model fell out of favour in the post-dotcom world. It seems, however, that certain activities fall beyond the purview of this supervision. Jeremy Anbleyth-Evans and Paul Gilbert catalogue instances of what they regard as failures of regulation, including a string of scandals involving tax and offshore jurisdictions, environment and human rights abuses.[5] They note some transactions where the directors of resource explorations firms benefited from selling land and assets to shareholders at inflated prices, via offshore trusts. Even the site at the heart of the blocked Oryx deal seems to have found its way onto AIM. In its way, AIM really is a high temple of capitalism. In a *caveat emptor* market, almost anything goes, so long as it is written in the offer document.

***

NOMADs are market intermediaries. In the business school conception, the intermediary is not a rent-seeking gatekeeper but an essential market actor, who is rewarded for bringing new markets into being. It seems odd, then, that many imaginative schemes to develop financial intermediaries have come to nothing. One such endeavour formed the basis of my very first real encounter with the world of investing. It was the brainchild of a man named … well, let's just call him Sixtus.

The son of an esteemed civil servant, Sixtus grew up in the days when esteemed civil servants could afford a rambling pile in near the Thames, a flat in a smart part of town and still have small change left over to push several children through Eton. Oxford followed. But being possessed of a maverick bent, Sixtus eschewed a job in the City and instead, in 1969, headed for graduate study at Harvard Business School. He returned to the UK in 1971 and after an unhappy year consulting for Hanson – Sixtus knew by then he was a 'doer', not an 'adviser' – he determined to start a business.

'The problem,' he says,

> was that not only did I have no idea of what business to start, but that I also had no money. … Also I had no track record of any kind, being then only nine months into my first job, and that not a success, so that the prospects of persuading someone to back me did not seem bright. On the other hand, I had little to lose by trying.[6]

Only an Old Etonian would muster this level of sangfroid in the face of such appalling odds. On the other hand, being an Old Etonian does seem to shorten the odds considerably. Sixtus wrote a business plan to set up a chain of US-style hamburger joints in the provinces. He raised some half a million in today's money, tapping a friend made at Harvard, another friend from back home, and a few risk-friendly investors recruited via a small ad in the *Daily Telegraph*. He set up his own outfit in a former truckers' cafe in Bristol, mopping floors, making milkshakes and flipping burgers. By 1977, he had three restaurants, 50 staff and a manager. He sold the restaurants in the early 1980s, just before the golden arches arrived in Britain and did to Sixtus' burger joints what they had done to just about every other burger bar in the USA. He even made his investors a profit – more than many would-be entrepreneurs, me included, ever managed.

Then, in 1978, Sixtus did something truly maverick. In the same era that that the UK government was waking up to the galvanizing potential of small company investment and converting the sleepy government venture capital house ICFC into the dynamic behemoth 3i, and Sir Ronald Cohen was importing US-style venture capital through his legendary Apax Partners, Sixtus launched a magazine. It featured profiles of small companies seeking to raise equity investment. He would charge subscribers £350 a year, charge the companies for a write-up, and take a percentage of any investment completed by means of an article in the magazine. His thought honed by his time at Harvard, Sixtus sought to put together the pent-up demand for investment and for investment opportunity by a means more elegant than small ads in national newspapers. He would become an intermediary: a broker of information.

The magazine was never more than moderately successful. It had black-and-white photos and a small circulation, and was sustained by successive investors whose own business school training inclined them to see its potential and overlook its profit and loss account. Sixtus would invite his employees to the crumbling mansion, which he now occupied, and persuade them to play croquet. Anyone mistaking him for a harmless eccentric in a threadbare white school shirt and knee-high socks would soon be caught out by the competitive malice with which he wielded his mallet, sending opponents' balls hurtling into the flowerbeds at the slightest opportunity.

I joined the magazine in the summer of 1998, fresh from a Master's degree. Now two decades old and still only moderately successful, it occupied two small office suites in a science park outside the city. The room in which I worked was small and filled by boxes containing unsold copies of Sixtus' self-published book. There were three of us in that office, while Sixtus and his assistant had a room adjacent, from which he ran his newly launched investment funds. It was a hot summer, and the first thing a new employee noticed was the smell. A sewage farm lay on the other side of the science park, and when the wind blew in the wrong direction, as it did most afternoons, a heavy, foetid pall would settle on the office. You could brave the lack of air conditioning and close the window, but there lurked a Scylla to the sewage farm's Charybdis. Sixtus, forged in an earlier time, belonged to a class that regarded personal hygiene as the surest sign of the petit bourgeoisie. An office legend held that many years previously the staff had drawn straws as to who would tell Sixtus that his musk was making their lives a misery. The short straw fell to one of the firm's few female employees. She hesitated for a while, planning her strategy, and eventually sidled up to the boss: 'Sixtus,' she said, 'I must say, you're smelling very manly today.' 'Thank you very much', he replied. And that was that.

Despite his eccentricities and his absurd, frontiersman, do-it-yourself sufficiency, Sixtus did, in his way, contribute something to British business. He had imported another concept beside hamburgers – informal venture capital. Its practitioners, happily known as 'business angels', are prepared to put up moderate sums in return for a share of the ownership of a firm. These angels have been glamorized as the Dragons in the BBC's reality TV show *Dragons' Den*, but the principle is much the same as it was when Sixtus first brought it into town: a tough negotiation, a stake, a partnership.

The magazine claimed a few successes. There was an engineer who had invented a gadget to be fitted at the bottom of grain silos, a vibrating cone that kept the contents flowing, and whose firm grew large and profitable. More usually, a succession of peculiar would-be entrepreneurs came through the door. I worked alongside a man named Charles, a gentle, cultured, former investment banker. At home Charles had three small children, a grand piano and a picture of his father shaking hands with the Pope. We would sit, listen to eccentric pitches and decide whether to help them or not. Our decision invariably hinged on whether the would-be entrepreneurs were prepared to write a cheque for £275. Many were not, but perhaps they were assessing us as well.

My first write-up involved a tough North Sea diver with a project to expand a hard-hat diving operation. It was not funded. I remember a high-end pickle company. I never saw the pickles on the supermarket shelves and I was not impressed by the firm's do-it-yourself marketing posters featuring stock photos of the Andes draped in gherkins. There was the ageing Harvard MBA who complained the course had gone soft and not enough people committed suicide these days, and the property spiv who moaned about having to eat his own shoe leather in lean years. He refused to write the cheque before hopping into an enormous Jaguar. Charles and I used to peer down into the car park after meetings, and it was amazing how many penurious entrepreneurs still had much nicer cars than we did. Then there was the neuro-linguistically programmed former bond trader, a tall and unfeasibly energetic young American who claimed to have been a presidential adviser and waved his arms like a windmill as he pitched to us. His project involved a life-size cardboard cut-out of a policeman. He was accompanied by a sidekick who had been in the South African Special Forces and stood glowering in the corner throughout. They didn't write a cheque either, although the bond trader was courteous enough to telephone the next day and tell us why not: he thought we were crap.

***

On America's western seaboard, technology entrepreneurs have turned this angel investing into a kind of financial alchemy. It works like this. I start a firm and persuade you to invest. You propose to take a 33 per cent stake in the firm – Sixtus' rule of thumb said one-third for the management, one-third for the idea and one-third for the money. I believe I need £500,000. You are an easy negotiator, and I get my way. You pay the money into the firm, and it issues new shares in return. The firm is now worth £1.5 million: if things are worth what the market says, and we did a deal at that level, who is to claim otherwise? (A technical aside: there many well-established practices of financial valuation that might suggest otherwise, but these are based on profits; any stock promoter worth their name will avoid profits for exactly this reason.) My stake is worth £1 million, and I am now a millionaire, on paper at least. I spend my funds on promotion and expansion. It all goes well, and a year later my prototype does what it is supposed to do. Now I need to scale up production, and the first step on this path is going to cost £5 million. Let us say for the sake of easy numbers that an investor putting in serious money is going to demand 50 per cent of the firm (I am sure we could negotiate a much better deal), valuing the whole at £10 million. You and I have seen our percentage holdings diluted by half, so now I have just one-third of the firm, and you one-sixth. But my third is worth £3.3 million, and you are holding £1.65 million. The process can run on for as long as we can sustain momentum. The larger our firm becomes, and the more diffuse the shareholders we recruit, the more bargaining power we have. We must just keep looking into the future.

Perhaps we will become a unicorn, privately listed with a valuation of more than $1 billion. Wikipedia attributes the first use of 'unicorn' in this sense to venture capitalist Aileen Lee.[7] In November 2013 Lee could point to 39 of these billion-dollar start-ups; of the quarter-trillion total value, almost half came from Facebook. Now there are over 1,000, and neologisms such as 'hectacorn' ($100 billion) are needed to cope with them.[8] Such extraordinary valuations can only be made sense of in the light of the narratives of complete transformation that accompany them – what Susi Geiger, an expert on the organizing of markets, calls the 'eschatological narratives' of Silicon Valley.[9] While we may not believe these stories of the economic end game, we act as if we do: anyone with a pension fund, an insurance policy or a few shares tucked into a saving scheme is wedded to these narratives, because they are the helium that has kept our markets floating upwards for a decade.

The Silicon Valley model never made it to our office. The problem the magazine faced was that most of the businesses, even the good ones, were simply the wrong kind for equity investment. They did not imagine an end of uncertainty and societal transformation put into place by a new, unstoppable technology, or a 'cybernetic frontier where digital artisans discover their individual self-fulfilment in either the electronic agora', as the theorists Richard Barbrook and Andy Cameron memorably wrote.[10] They offered safer North Sea divers and tastier pickles. In their own small ways, these businesses could have made the world a better place: incremental improvements, not transformational ones, certainly, but none the worse for that.

I say the businesses were of the wrong kind for equity investment, but what if investors did not demand a unicorn be born from every single venture? What if the subjects were not businesses at all, but a diverse range of start-up ventures delivering social good? In all the chaos and complexity of financial history one thing does stand out. Stock exchanges are good at raising money. The venerable London Stock Exchange began life as a bridge between a needy exchequer and the bulging purses of London's merchants. Stock markets have raised money for canals and railways, rubber plantations, mineral exploitation, dog tracks, dotcoms and many other things; the corporate bond markets have linked lenders and borrowers, funding corporations, governments and even mortgages. Not one of these episodes has been blameless, but there does seem to be a common theme: rounding up cash seems to be the markets' single superpower. Would it be possible to turn this remarkable ability in another direction? Could some kind of equity exchange work here: a modern version of Sixtus' magazine, a well-intentioned, lowly temple of capitalism?

I doubt it.

There is already a long tradition of collective subscription schemes for helping the common good, but the internet has transformed them, allowing crowds of 'investors' to be targeted cheaply and at a distance. The synthesis of Dickens' Mrs Jellaby and technological utopia takes the form of 'crowdfunding', a 'step in the world's progress towards a globalized society promoting cultural and geographical diversification, towards pacification and education of all people, towards economic stability and equality, in our efforts to close distances and bridge gaps,' as one introduction to the topic gushes.[11] Alongside product-based crowdfunding arrangements, of which Kickstarter (a rewards-based platform) is the most famous, new kinds of civic crowdfunding have arrived on the scene. In the UK, one such arrangement, called community shares, offers a tightly regulated way of allowing the community to buy or sustain local assets. Yet there are questions as to whether these arrangements, well intentioned as they are, can be truly participatory: they require capital, technological sophistication and a certain degree of economic skill before you can participate. Barbrook and Cameron fret that the longed-for electronic agora may rather become 'a hi-tech version of the plantation economy of the Old South.'[12] Crowdfunding, others worry, replicates existing economic practices of financialization within a new and enticing, cultural regime.[13]

That I am even wondering how finance might help us shows, in fact, how the regime of finance has taken over our lives. Collective subscription schemes flourish in the absence of effective public services, often at times when such things cannot even be imagined. Mrs Jellaby is lampooned for neglecting her family, not for advocating a low-regulation small-state polity – Victorian Britain took *that* for granted. Using stock markets for social ends would simply subject yet more people to the logics of business schools, to the calculus of economic return, forcing those least able to look after themselves to shoulder the risk for their own development and personal transformations. We have endured a decade-and-a-half of shrinking national and local government, linked to the massive costs of bailing out the financial sector in 2008. The excesses of finance are the root of these problems – we should be careful about allowing it to take credit for fixing these as well.

The stock market enthusiast will argue that the examples in this chapter show how carefully designed and curated, fit-for-purpose markets could supply certain ends. They could rediscover social purpose, providing capital for small firms, with a focus on green technology perhaps, or local production and reskilling, and they could do so on terms not prejudicial to those who invest and are invested in. They would say that a middleman does not have to be a scalper dining on other people's money. They might even say that there is a role here for the sociologist of markets, tempering the abstractions of economics and the worst excesses of theory; market designers versed in the social as well as the economic.

Perhaps. We can hope, and many in the financial industry do. But the evidence does not persuade me. Our journey through the history of finance has shown that it is extractive through and through. It is a redistributive industry that works the wrong way, passing money upwards rather than down. The contemporary stock exchange is the engine of a three-decade-long social shift that has concentrated power and money in the hands of a tiny few, giving us a broken infrastructure and a society in a crisis, while a rentier class benefits from ever-increasing stock options and dividends. The global picture is one of climate emergency, famine and war. Our brief history shows that whatever finance sets its sights on is eventually consumed, and that the heroes rarely win through. It is spectacular, destructive and violent; stock exchanges were made with guns and chains as well as wires and ledgers.

Moreover, if I have shown anything it is that finance is not competent to be left in charge. It is haphazard, chaotic and fragmented. Its history is one of happenstance and chance, the summing up of generations of personal ambition; as Winterflood's schoolteacher so cannily observed, you go to where money is made in order to make money. Let us not believe the fairy tale in which finance cloaks itself. It will never have a higher purpose. There are other ways of doing, thinking and organizing. We have enough stock exchanges already, enough high temples to capital. The best kind of stock exchange to build is no stock exchange at all.

Epilogue: The Market Replies

Stock Exchange:	All right, all right! I can see you, Roscoe, I can see you getting ready to bash me to pieces. … Let me get up, let's talk for a moment like civilized people. … Yes, that's better, let me dust myself down and get myself straight. All this critique, it's wearing on a person. And does it get you anywhere? I don't think so. I mean, so what if I'm all about the spectacle? What's wrong with a little excitement, really? How was I to know that poor bloke was going to fall out of his helicopter?
Philip:	I thought you knew everything?
Exchange:	I know this much. Give me time, I can make something of critique. Metabolize it, says Eve Chiapello. I like the sound of that – delicious, tasty critique. I'll eat everything soon enough.[1]
Philip:	That's what I'm worried about. That's why I've gone for a different style, something a little bit gonzo.
Exchange:	What do you think? Have you had a good time? I've a quotation from old Dr Thompson just here. 'It had been a bad trip … fast and wild in some moments, slow and dirty in others, but on balance it looked like a bummer. On my way back to San Francisco, I tried to compose a fitting epitaph. I wanted something original, but there was no escaping the echo of Mistah Kurtz' final words from the *Heart of Darkness*: "The horror! The horror!… Exterminate all the brutes!"'[2]
Philip:	That's a good idea!
Exchange:	Exterminate me, ha! All those cities of steel and glass, those skyscrapers where the action happens on the 41st floor and you're on the pavement outside, with

your 'The end is nigh' placard. You are ridiculous, don't you know? While I – I – am the unstoppable, incredible calculating machine of the market. The most super super-computer ever made.

Philip: Yes, okay, I know. But I think it's something worthwhile, this gonzo, all the same. Sociologist Jesse Wozniak calls for 'gonzo sociology', an 'immersive, reflexive methodology which eschews rigidity and formulaic design in favour of innovative and imaginative research on places and peoples ignored by the academy'.[3]

Exchange: Pah, words, words, words. … Besides, I'm hardly ignored by the academy. I have whole schools about me.

Philip: Gonzo academic is never going to be that gonzo. It's a reaction against the 'staid practices of the field', as Wozniak puts it. Finance theory, come on. … I think we business school types can permit ourselves a certain licence – an element of reflection, of the personal, a struggle to find a voice that speaks more widely than the dry prose of the academic journal. So I have written about breakfast in The Cadogan hotel with the global heavies, about Sixtus' croquet and business angels, about how one family's world changed and reflected the shape of London's markets across three generations, and how my own experiences took me briefly into their world.

Exchange: What kind of a dilletante are you? Shouldn't you be concentrating on getting in all the best journals? It's a dog-eat-dog world out there. Stop messing around before someone eats you. Think of the rankings. I do – they make me tingle. They are the things I'm made of, rankings and Gaussian copula and net-present values. You couldn't imagine me if you tried.

Philip: That's exactly my point! We did imagine you! The stories we tell make the world! I've had enough of this dog-eat-dog, win by any way possible stuff. I'm not sure I even know the answers anyway. Perhaps Dr Thompson was right. 'Exterminate the brutes' may be a fitting epitaph.

Exchange: Okay, okay. Let me try and persuade you. Mark it all down as a bad trip. Fast and wild in some moments, slow and dirty in others, but on balance, a bummer – what then? Burn it all down? Tempting, except for your jobs and hospitals and schools, the food on the shelves in your supermarkets. When the government saved the banks, it wasn't just because they were worried about their cronies. You were looking at the end of the world. No cash, no medicines, no bread. You can't do without me.

Philip: Now you are just blustering. …

Exchange: I can do other things as well. You can have as many versions of me as you want. It doesn't all have to be 'big, bad finance', full of spivs and price gougers like that Shkreli guy. I never liked him. I've all sorts of people working for me. We can do things.

Philip: Such as?

Exchange: Let me give you an example. Every day, when you have finished preparing a meal, you carefully wash out the various bits of plastic packaging, cardboard and steel tins and put them in the recycling bin. Once a month – and yes, I know, if it wasn't for my 2008 antics it would be more often – the local authority picks up the materials and takes them away. You hope that they are sorted and sent to places where they can be turned into new bottles, or jumpers or tins or tyres. But for that to happen, they must move through a market for recyclable materials. Even there, you need me. Well, actually, it's my mate Steve who does the bins. But anyway. The contents of your bin become commodities and Steve sends them towards those who will pay for raw materials to make other things. It's a bulky and dirty commodity, like Chicago in the old days. Steve did that too, he's always scraping the shit off his boots, excuse my French. Let me tell you, he is in disarray. There is oversupply, while bottle manufacturers can't get hold of enough stock of plastic to recycle. Prices fluctuate wildly, so businesses can't plan or invest in new capacity. Trading is done over-the-counter. They all know each other and they just ring each other up! It's basically stone age.

Philip: That means the market is opaque and informationally problematic? Asymmetries of information lead to low prices that drive out all but the worst sellers. Not good. Jordan Howell, a professor of sustainable business at Rowan University, says the market is dysfunctional.

Exchange: That's right. He is! He's all over the shop, is Steve.

Philip: I see what you're getting at. Howell and his colleagues, Jordan Moore and Daniel Folkinshteyn, professors of finance at the same institution, have a plan. They have a project to figure out what a derivatives market in recycling might look like. Such a market would enable buyers and sellers to transact for products at some point in the future at a specified price.

Exchange: Exactly! Just like the farmer who needs to know his winter wheat will be worth something even if the harvest is bountiful, or the miller who wants to be sure he can buy that wheat at a decent price even if the crops fail and the price shoots up, the recycling industry could start to organize itself around a transparent price made by me, a financial market. I would provide a technical service in managing risk. Sorry, Stevie, move over my son, you're fired. There's lots of evidence to suggest that a steady futures price helps to settle and offer transparency to the underlying commodity price, so the scholars hope that the benefits would feed back into the recycling market proper. Come on, you have to admit this is a great idea – a specialized, technical market to deal with a crucial global challenge.

Philip: I suppose so, you could persuade me. It's not going to magically solve problems on its own though. Paired with a legislative regime that cuts back packaging, and improved recycling technologies, it might. But if we have the right laws and good technology, why do we still need you?

Exchange: Mark my words sonny, you'll need all the help you can get on this one. Have you looked in the ocean? Glad I'm not a dolphin, that's all I'm saying.

Philip: I'm not convinced. Give me another example.

Exchange: I'm good at nation building. Look at England. It never would have got off the ground if it wasn't for me, helping to pay for all those wars and colonial exploits. I do feel a bit guilty sometimes about how that worked out. I mean, those railways in India, and those rubber plantations in Malaya. Perpetual dividends of 20 per cent! That wasn't right.

Philip: Most certainly not. But they were your fault!

Exchange: Not my fault. Not my fault at all. If I had been allowed to do my job properly, they would have been traded away. But those English merchant adventurers, with the soldiers and the bureaucrats, sniffed out inequality and weakness and turned it into a hundred years of rents.

Philip: But you were the fulcrum! You provided the mechanism. Besides, that sounds very like the dog-eat-dog world you were just talking about.

Exchange: I'm just a tool. Does a gun kill people by itself? I thought not. …

Philip: Come on, that's a playground argument!

Exchange: Well, look. The thing is, I'd like to make amends. The English regions are always complaining that London sucks capital and investment away from them, so why not have regional exchanges? These flourished in 19th-century Britain when regional investors backed regional enterprises. Scotland boasted markets in Aberdeen, Dundee, Edinburgh, Glasgow and Greenock. In 1962 there were 20 exchanges across the UK, but regulators pushed for amalgamation and rationalization in the name of transparency and investor protection. In 1964 the four city exchanges joined together into the Scottish Stock Exchange, a notional umbrella organization, and then in 1971 centralized in the Glasgow Stock Exchange building. In 1973, in living memory.

Philip: For some maybe. But yes, the Scottish Exchange was wound up and its business transferred to London. An increasing concentration of capital in the city of London, together with greatly improved communications, offered economies of scale and efficiencies that the small regional exchanges simply could not match. I know, I wrote all this. Memories of the old exchanges and regional economic identities persisted. Even the AIM founders toured the UK to build links between these wells of capital and the new market in London.

Exchange: For years there have been calls for independence in Scotland. Brexit and COVID-19 have brought these to the fore again. Even among those less keen on ending the Union, I sense something more fundamental at play: a desire to do things differently, to implement a kind of economic social justice that seems increasingly out of reach in England. Capital seems willing to stay put and circulate more locally.

Philip: Hmmm. You're wearing an England football shirt. Are you sure you believe all this?

Exchange: I don't believe. I know. Besides, I don't have to agree with everyone I work for. That would never get me anywhere. It's just what people are saying: perhaps the time is once again right for a Scottish Stock Exchange as a vehicle to facilitate a different kind of financial geography.

Philip: Go on.

Exchange: Well, there are a few ventures I've heard of. One looked promising. But it got off to a shaky start. The papers said its founding chief executive burned through £2 million of start-up funding with a 'jet-set lifestyle'.[4] It's under new management. We'll see how it goes.

Philip: Aren't you supposed to stop that kind of thing from happening? I mean, when Jensen and Meckling wrote about agency theory and aligning the interests of chief executives and shareholders, the whole point was to put a stop to jet-set lifestyles. No more flying the CEO's dog into hiding on the company jet, that kind of thing. It was supposed to make companies lean and focused. I've been blaming you for all sorts of things, from gig work to environmental destruction, all consequences of these incentives.

Exchange: It just all goes to show, doesn't it, how people make the best of any opportunity. I'm just a mirror of your own worst selves. I am, as you so nicely put it, a social technology. What does that even mean?

Philip: Science and technology studies have long recognized that elements of the social are worked into technological systems as they are developed. Complicated technological systems need lots of organization and so things like rituals, routines and practices become essential for their maintenance and function. Even with all your algorithms you depend on those kinds of things. And vice versa. A stock exchange isn't just a room full of people. The room matters too, the furniture, the desks, all that.

Exchange: I'm a cyborg?

Philip: I'm afraid so. That's how historical unfairness got encoded into your structures. It's in your technological DNA. Even agency theory, which is supposed to be neutral and legalistic, encodes all kinds of privileges for some, usually at the expense of others. Does that make sense?

Exchange: Hang on, I'm just coming to terms with my new identity. It's not every day you realize that you're part man, part machine.

Philip: That's not the worst. There's another thing you are terribly good at. You are a sort of cleaner. You take the messiest, most gritty situations, like exploited labour or unfair contracts, or even slavery, and you clean them up. You wash out all the bodily nastiness, all the suffering and injustice, and turn it into nice, predictable revenue streams that can be chopped up and sold and passed around while everybody else's hands stay clean. That's the most unforgivable thing.

Exchange: But that's your fault, surely? If I am just what you say I am, some strange kind of hybrid people-machine made up of all your history and politics and technology, it's not fair to go blaming me for what I am now. I'm just a reflection of you. It sounds like I'm a reflection of all your worst bits, as well. What about the magic of the market? I like those ideas. Even there, you lot can't agree. I've got half of you singing the praises of the magic of freedom and how market transactions make good citizens, and the other half talking about zombies and black magic. Sometimes a bit of both: that Jesse Livermore reckoned that I warned him about the San Francisco earthquake a day in advance, and he knew what he was talking about, if anyone did.[5]

Philip: There's the problem. What are we to make of you? Or make you into?

Exchange: What did Polanyi say? Market, redistribution, or reciprocity. Reciprocity is fine in the household but can never work with six billion people. And redistribution, that sounds ominous to me.

Philip: The way I see it, you're all about redistribution. Taking from the poor and giving to the rich. Your friends say you're peaceful, a model of bourgeois virtue, but everywhere I've looked I see violence underneath. You're built on strife.

Exchange: The thing is, I'm in business myself. I don't work just for fun, you know. Supply and demand – stock exchanges are businesses and change what we supply to satisfy a changing market. If global financial markets all seem to be organized on principles dictated by efficient market theory, that is because it sells in the market for exchange services. If we now seem to disrupt the very structure of the nation state, that is because they are a reflection, as well as a cause, of globalization, intertwined with and embedded in global capital flows. If you're right and we're extractive and polluting in nature, we're simply a reflection of a high capitalism that extracts and pollutes. If, in the years leading up to the credit crisis of 2008, we gazed more and more at our reflection in the mirror – became increasingly self-referential, in your words – that's just another reflection of a broader shift from production to finance as the source of value, from enterprising opportunity-seeking to riskless rent-seeking. Like you say, a social technology.

Philip: You aren't making a good case for yourself. Besides, I think you're more cause than effect.

Exchange: I know something you don't. You business school types think selling is easy. Every MBA business plan I've ever seen looks at the global market, written up in some report or other, and says we only seek to capture one per cent. What a conservative assumption that is! We'll make a better kind of suitcase and after 10 years one in every hundred suitcases in the world will have been made by us. Easy to say, but how are you going to do that? Get it in shops, pay for adverts, get it on Instagram with some influencer or other. Easier said than done.

Philip: But Peter Drucker, the grandfather of business gurus, says true entrepreneurship is always risk-free because it shifts resources to higher value parts of the economy.[6]

Exchange: What does that even mean? And how could you tell until afterwards? Of course, if something is successful you can claim you are adding value to the economy, but you can't tell that upfront. Look at Amazon: one of the biggest corporations in the world, but when it first appeared the analysts were arguing about what kind of a thing it was. A bookshop? An internet business? Is it a dog or is it a cat? People jump straight in and worry about the technology and the system: about clearing and settlement and those kinds of things. Look at Tradepoint, or PLUS, that's exactly what they did. And neither succeeded. I make my living selling services to customers who actually want them. New exchanges succeed where there are already customers clamouring at the door. AIM was founded when the London Stock Exchange's customers forced its hand, voting with their feet, moving their business to a rival that suddenly became substantial enough to pose a threat. That rival was John Jenkins' Newstrack service, soon to become OFEX, which itself only came into being after customers petitioned Jenkins to offer them trading facilities.

Philip: I accept that you have to earn a living. The better mousetrap strategy might have worked for Amazon, but somebody had just invented the internet. How should we proceed when there aren't any customers? Of course, there are potential customers, but how are we to overcome their inertia? In the case of the recycling industry, dealers are used to trading over the phone with counterparties they know and carrying commodity risk on their books. Your friend Steven has it all sorted out already, or most of it. In the case of the Scottish small company investment world, there are already strong social networks, institutional routines and material practices pulling business down towards London.

Exchange: You need a good story. Let me tell you. Stories do more work than you would think. It's easy for you to say that London's market emerged in the 18th century to service the national debt and the stockholders of the new corporations, but believe you me, it never would have got off the ground without the tremendous work of narration that accompanied it. Daniel Defoe – he was a character – he was in the thick of it. He just forced people to believe. He bombarded them with stories until they just got used to the idea that things you read could be real without being, you know, physically there.[7]

Philip: That's true. The founders of AIM seemed to know intuitively that this was the case. They didn't just forecast and launch. They talked. They went for long meetings, sat through lunches, jawed on and on into the night. Their conversations flowed into the new market's unexpected and novel shape. I have the sense that when the market finally opened it was already there, conjured into existence by so much talk and conversation, like the yet-to-be-built house that has achieved such concrete reality in the minds of its future owners that they find themselves choosing furniture before the foundation has been poured.

Exchange: Throughout the 300-year history of modern finance experts, pundits, academics and pamphleteers have assisted in the sheer effort of make-believe required to make it possible. You're part of that.

Philip: Maybe. I remember in the year 2000 my small research outfit was commissioned to produce a report on OFEX's remarkable commercial success, and it was presented at a shindig celebrating the market's fifth anniversary. I remember a big crowd, colleagues and friends enjoying the Jenkins' hospitality. John Jenkins made a speech about his market's success and waved the report around, getting our name wrong in the process. Another chief executive leaned over and whispered, 'You'll never hit him with a glass from here. …'

Exchange: More than that, you've just written a book about it. About me. The all-knowing, all-conquering stock exchange, taking what it wants from anyone it wants. A victor's history, that's what you've written.

Philip: I have not! At least, I tried not to. I wanted a gentle critique, not one that lionises by accident. That's the point of all the gonzo stuff. The stories and anecdotes. The people.

Exchange: Aha! People. It's not just technology and history, after all. These efficient market hypothesis type exchanges are based on a sleight of hand, to be honest. They go to great efforts to purge social relations, saying these get in the way of price formation. But I'm always embedded in a great spider web of social relationship and reputation. I'm a social animal, me. You know the story about those precarious moments for the Chicago Board of Trade following Black Monday, October 1987. Losses were so huge that the clearing system, where giant banks guarantee individual customer accounts, failed. Leo Melamed, the chairman, spent the night making calls to the senior executives of banks, using all his personal capital to make sure the exchange could open. He's quoted as saying to one account manager, a few minutes before the opening bell, 'Wilma, you're not going to let a stinking couple of hundred million dollars cause the Merc [Mercantile Exchange] to go down the tubes, are you?' At that moment, the chairman walked into Wilma's office and agreed to put up the money. That's what friends are for.[8]

Philip: A stinking couple of hundred million dollars, yes, ha! Nice friends you have. It's true, though, that making efficient markets depends on the very inefficiencies those markets are trying to get rid of.

Exchange: It doesn't have to be that way. AIM decided not to go down that route. They made social relations the backbone of market supervision. It works.

Philip: Up to a point. There are still some exploitative firms listed on that market.

Exchange: Of course. But is that my fault? Change the people! Educate them about their responsibilities. Find new ways of reporting, so some of the grit and misery gets through. Make those advisers work a day in the mines they finance! That would sharpen their judgement. I still think the mechanism works. So do you – you've written that it does.

Philip: You have me there.

Exchange: It's all about the story. Talk it up. What really matters is the collaborative production of a market narrative among those who are going to use the exchange, making it so real and so theirs that when the time comes to move in, they will be unpacking crates and popping champagne corks.

Philip: Okay. At some point, though, you are going to have to build that mousetrap. You are going to trading systems and settlement – wires and screens and all that jazz. Not once have the builders of markets been casual in their approach to the physical and technological spaces. Generations of buildings in Chicago and London evolved to house the great markets of the time, their massive halls with open lines of sight and cutting-edge communications built to support the operation of trade. Architects fretted over such minutiae as floor coverings.

Exchange: They did. I fancied marble, but the traders couldn't hear. Too hard.

Philip: The new electronic markets arrived as projects driven by technologists who sought to rethink how markets might work, following the aesthetic of the engineer rather than the broker. These structures are political. There are electronic order books and market-makers offering buy and sell prices. Lined up behind these are two competing social orders and sets of moral norms, efficiency versus intervention, transparency of price versus transparency of person.[9]

Exchange: So there *are* morals in markets if you know where to look! Don't throw the good bits away with the bad. I admit, if you go down the route prescribed by the dominant understanding of market organization, you end up with electronic order books, anonymous buyers and sellers, and engineering solutions focused on time and speed. It's a matter of logic. Do you really want more speed-of-light traders? And it makes a closed shop: the machinery needed to set up such a system is incredibly expensive. PLUS sunk tens of millions of shareholders' funds sunk into a system capable of rivalling the London Stock Exchange, a vast spider's web of orders, prices, settlement, reporting and surveillance, the chief executive called it.

Philip: You could buy it in, I suppose, approach another exchange company and ask them to supply you with technological services badged up under your start-up's name. That seems to be the default option for the stock exchange entrepreneur.

Exchange: That's what Tradepoint did, and even PLUS bought its exchange from an external provider. But you're never going to beat the London Stock Exchange on its own turf. Why bother? You can't compete on price and efficiency with a global giant, or reliability. Get your business school hat on. Less gonzo, more five forces. You need a niche. Look at the recycling futures market. It aims to create stable prices as reference points for large organizations and their long-term planning. It would shift risk away from the recycling firms into the hands of those whose business is managing risk, leaving the recyclers to the important job of managing rubbish. Steve would have to up his game. He would need professional speculators who would use instruments attuned to the Fama paradigms. He would need to think about transparent prices and the rest, a Fama-type set-up with anonymous participants.

Philip: But a move to anonymous dealing is the greatest obstacle facing the market! The recyclers are used to dealing over the counter, by phone or email, with people they know and trust.

Exchange: I agree. They are also used to dealing with the risk attached their rubbish and worry that if they lose one they might lose the other. It makes no sense to go full Fama on this one. Steve's not up to it. To be honest, I'd have to take over. There's another issue as well.

Philip: Go on, all-knowing market. Elaborate please.

Exchange: While there's lots of evidence to suggest that efficient futures markets help set the price of the underlying commodities, futures need underlying prices to get going in the first place. But there aren't any! One suggestion is an industry board, in order to get prices going, something like London's LIBOR. You could organize something like that for the recycling industry – get these over-the-counter traders to estimate their prices day on day and publish these more widely.

Philip: But if this were enough – if the problem is lack of stable prices in the industry – then perhaps you don't need an elaborate Fama market after all, just strong organizational protocols, social networks, some whiteboards and some phones. Do you need the whole shebang of order books and clearing houses, or could you persuade an existing dealer to offer contracts based on the industry's published prices? If you needed prices at all.

Exchange: I agree. I'm talking myself out of a job here, but I don't think you need me at all. Good regulations and good organization are the solution. Get Steve back on his feet. A failing market needs to be sorted out from the inside, by people who know what's going on. All your business school theory makes it seem as if another market can just be bolted on from the outside and it will make everything right. That isn't always the way things work.

Philip: What about that possible Scottish exchange, the one you mentioned earlier? If they can't compete on price, or speed, or technology, what should they do?

Exchange: They shouldn't even try. They should build a different kind of market for the local needs. They want to raise capital for businesses located in Scotland, with a social and environmental slant, to keep capital circulating locally, and to provide an effective secondary market in the stock, so that investors can sell their holdings at a fair price and sink their money into new ventures.

Philip: That sounds like a market with low volumes and intermittent trading. What inspiration do we have for that?

Exchange: Well, there was Sixtus and his magazine. Or John and Paul on their sofa with phones and notepads.

Philip: Really? You must be joking.

Exchange: Obviously it would be a bit more high-tech these days. But my point is that I don't always have to look the same. I can be whatever you want me to be. Investors and companies will use me because they are Scottish and green – if they cared about trimming commissions or accessing the giant wells of capital available in London, they would be elsewhere. You could build a structure that was really fit for purpose, whatever your purpose was. You'd never make a return on £10 million of start-up costs trying to beat the global giants at their own game, but would you want to?

Philip: The medium matters. As Marshall McLuhan never said, the medium is the matter, and it's precisely because social and material arrangements lock us into certain kinds of social practices that we need to think carefully about the structures we choose.

Exchange: Haha, very droll.

Philip: My history suggests that a functioning Scottish Stock Exchange will come not from the efforts of disruptive, etic entrepreneurs, observing transcendental rules of finance and attempting to apply them at the local level, but from local participants in the finance sector who decide to expand their narratives, their aspirations and their offerings bit by bit until they find that they have – almost by accident – started a stock exchange.

Exchange: Absolutely. I'd like that. Another version of me, a more useful one.

Philip: [Sighs] Nothing is easy, is it? When I started on this adventure, I thought there might a blueprint, a Platonic ideal of a stock exchange that I could set out, and anyone could rush off and build, saving the world by doing so. I thought that you might build a stock exchange in the same you build a car, engineering the machinery to a preordained plan. It turns out the plans are as much a historical artefact as the stock exchanges themselves. You say you can be anything we want, that you are just a reflection of ourselves. That just makes it harder. There's no quick fix. We have to make some real choices about how we want the world to be.

Exchange:	But you've had an adventure. Has it been a bad trip, on balance, a bummer?
Philip:	It's had its ups and downs. I didn't get to where I thought I was going. Perhaps that's how all trips work out.
Exchange:	Are you equivocating?
Philip:	Possibly. I don't know.
Exchange:	Look, you've done your job. You've told your story, made the familiar strange, shone a light into some gloomy corners. Some choices are just too big for one person.
Philip:	I suppose so.
Exchange:	Come on, let's have a nice cup of tea.

Notes

Prologue

1 For accounts of the Zong Massacre see, among others, Baucom (2005) and Walvin (2011). Walvin also begins his narrative with Turner's painting.
2 Rupprecht (2008).
3 Quoted by Rupprecht (2008: 269).
4 Rupprecht (2008: 268).
5 Roscoe (1831: 232–5). The primary and secondary sources for historians are listed by Baucom (2005: 336, note 12).
6 Walvin (2011: 20).
7 Fletcher (2016).
8 From Roscoe (1787).
9 Chandler (1953).
10 Mellor (2019).
11 Here and following, Baucom (2005: 61). Baucom's source for this account is an anonymous pamphlet in the Liverpool archives.
12 Baucom (2005: 92).
13 Arrighi (1994).
14 Chandler (1953).
15 Roscoe (1831).
16 See, for example, the accounts in Dymski et al (2013) and Steil et al (2018).
17 MacKenzie (2011).
18 MacKenzie and Spears (2014).
19 Lewis (2010: 129).
20 The quotation is from Nelms (2012: 238). Nelms compares the 'first zombie movie … a 1932 Bela Lugosi vehicle entitled *White Zombie*, presents a group of zombified workers trudging around a Haitian sugar mill, performing turn-of-the-nineteenth-century fears of alienation' with 'Romero's parody of consumerism in *Dawn of the Dead* – which sees a group of survivors defend a suburban shopping mall against hordes of hungry zombies, enacting "a fantasy of purchase power' that displays 'the zombifying power of commodity fetishism"' (2012: 236).
21 The phrase 'neoliberal fairy story' is borrowed from Mellor (2019), the sentiment from Ho (2009).

Chapter 1

1 The original paper is Jensen and Meckling (1976). The ideas reached a broader audience through Michael Jensen and Kevin Murphy's 1990 article 'CEO incentives – it's not how

much you pay, but how' in the *Harvard Business Review*. For an account of Wall Street's preoccupation with shareholder value, see Ho (2009).

2 Weber (1978).

3 Again, from Jensen and Murphy (1990).

4 Davis and Kim (2015: 211).

5 See *The New York Times*' expose of Amazon's HRM practices in Kantor and Streitfeld (2015). For the increased disciplining of academic researchers under the UK research assessment exercise, see Pardo-Guerra (2022).

6 Lamont (2020).

7 Christophers (2022: 22).

8 Piketty (2017).

9 Monbiot (2022).

10 Quoted in Arrighi (1994: 6).

11 Arrighi (1994: 6)

12 Jameson (1997: 251)

13 Jameson (1997: 251).

14 Quoted in Arrighi (1994).

15 MacKenzie (2018).

16 The ethical nature of markets can be seen, in different ways, in the work of Kimberly Chong (2017), Daniel Beunza (2019) and my own research (Roscoe, 2022).

17 I am here indebted to Marieke de Goede and her reading of Isabelle Stengers, for suggesting that laughter lightens its object of critique rather than fortifying it. Stengers writes that 'the laughter of someone who has to be impressed always complicates the life of power' (see de Goede, 2020: 109).

18 A longer version of this reflection appears as Roscoe (2021).

19 Muniesa (2021), quoting Horatio Ortiz' sharp phrasing.

20 Nordström, K.A. and Ridderstråle, J. (2002).

21 Haiven (2011: 107).

22 La Berge (2015); Benke (2018); Crosthwaite (2019).

23 Clune (2014: 195). See also Fisher (2009).

24 For a critique of cost-benefit analysis and scientific management, see Roscoe (2014).

25 For a lengthy philosophical critique of this approach, see MacIntyre (1981).

Chapter 2

1 Sinclair (1985 [1906]: 44).

2 Zaloom (2006: 16).

3 Sinclair (1985 [1906]: 36).

4 Poitras (2009).

5 Poitras (2009).

6 Preda (2006).

7 Preda (2006: 759–60)

8 Norris (1994 [1902]). For the Taiwanese context, see Chen and Roscoe (2018).

9 Lefèvre (1993); Knight (2013).

10 Knight (2013: 49).

11 Preda (2001a).

12 Preda (2006: 771–2, for the anecdote below).

13 Preda (2006: 772)

14 Knight (2013: 52, 56).

15 Zaloom (2006).

16 Zaloom (2003: 264).
17 Norris, quoted in Borch et al (2015: 1088).
18 Zaloom (2003: 261).
19 Baker (1984).
20 MacKenzie (2015: 654).

Chapter 3

1 Rentoul (2018).
2 Porter, Winnett and Kirkup (2010)
3 Parker and Barker (2010)
4 The following historical section draws on Murphy (2009) and Michie (2001).
5 Michie (2001: 15).
6 Murphy (2019).
7 Carruthers and Stinchcombe (1999)
8 Michie (2001: 18).
9 D. Defoe, (1719: 8) *Anatomy of Exchange Alley*, quoted by Murphy (2009: 183).
10 Hennessy (2001).
11 Michie (2001: 23).
12 Michie (2001: 31).
13 Murphy (2017).
14 Mirowski (1981: 576–7).
15 Levy (2006).
16 Hochfelder (2006: 349).
17 Zelizer (1994).
18 Levy (2006: 316).
19 The following section draws on Levy (2006) and Hochfelder (2006).
20 Hochfelder (2006: 351).

Chapter 4

1 The background detail in this chapter comes from varied sources: my own research into London's markets (Roscoe, 2017) and Michie's history (2001). In 1990 Dr Bernard Attard of the University of Leicester conducted a series of oral history interviews with former jobbers, capturing the details of what was by then a vanished world. The quotations are from Attard's histories. Transcripts and recordings can be found at https://sas-space.sas.ac.uk/view/collections/lseoh.html [accessed 6 December 2022].
2 Pardo-Guerra (2010: 90).
3 Clemons and Weber (1990: 50).
4 Attard (1994: 46).
5 This episode comes from Attard's interview, see note 1.
6 From my own interview notes.
7 Vander Weyer (2012).
8 Michie (2001: 453f).
9 To be precise, the application was rejected on the basis that the firm's accounts did not meet UK standards.
10 Morrison (2015).
11 Here and below, taken from Attard (1994: 45).
12 Michie (2001).
13 Gribben (2012).
14 Cornish (2017).

Chapter 5

1 Quotations are from Bernard Attard's interview with Anthony Jenkins, and my own oral histories (Roscoe, 2017). The chapter title references a comment by one of my interviewees; as the chapter shows, Margaret Thatcher served this group of market participants well.
2 This short political history draws on Sargent (2013).
3 Shaxson (2011).
4 Sargent (2013: 403).
5 Judge (2020).
6 For detailed accounts of the Big Bang see, among others, Poser (1988), Clemons and Weber (1990) and Michie (2001).
7 https://en.wikipedia.org/wiki/Exchange_Controls_in_the_United_Kingdom [accessed 14 May 2019].
8 Krippner (2001: 785). Emphasis in original.
9 For further commentary on the development of the housing market under Thatcher, see Chapter Two in Roscoe (2014).
10 This quotation comes, via Vander Weyer (2012), from David Kynaston. As Vander Weyer points out, Hoare Govett has an interesting and rather circular history. Security Pacific collapsed in 1992 and was bought by Bank of America; the broker was then sold to ABN AMRO, which was taken over by RBS and then found its way back to the British government.
11 Michie (2001: 555).
12 I follow Bryan Appleyard's (1986) characterization, drawn in three very prescient columns.

Chapter 6

1 There is a huge literature here. See, for example, Pickering (1992); Knorr Cetina (1999) and Latour (1999, 2017).
2 MacKenzie (2009).
3 Latour (2007).
4 The following relies on MacKenzie's account (see, in particular, MacKenzie, 2009).
5 Andrew Bailey, then Chief Executive of the Financial Conduct Authority (FCA), setting out policy via a speech on the future of LIBOR (Bailey, 2017).
6 Hall (2009).
7 MacKenzie and Millo (2003).
8 Preda (2009: 99).
9 Fama (1970).
10 MacKenzie (2006).
11 MacKenzie and Millo (2003: 121).
12 Quoted in MacKenzie (2011: 1792).
13 Lewis (1989: 103).
14 The lenders' problem is a variant on George Akerlov's Nobel prize-winning 'markets for lemons' thesis. Akerlov demonstrates that in a market where buyers cannot distinguish quality, they will protect themselves by offering low prices. Sellers of high-quality goods will react by leaving the market and soon only the 'lemons' will be left.
15 The FICO® score has been documented by Poon (2007, 2009).

Chapter 7

1 Forsyth (1996 [1974]: 39)
2 Forsyth (1996 [1974]: 39, 146).

3 Souleles (2017: 397), here and below.
4 Hall (2009)
5 Souleles (2017: 397)
6 Burrough and Helyar (2010: 92–6).
7 Jensen and Murphy (1990), following Jensen and Meckling (1976)
8 Ho (2009: 190, 128).
9 Ho (2009: 128).
10 Wolfe (1987: 58).
11 Poovey (2008).
12 Hamilton and Parker (2016: 3)
13 Hamilton and Parker (2016: 11).
14 Poovey (2008: 89).
15 Poovey (2008: 19).
16 de Goede (2005).
17 La Berge (2015: 875).
18 La Berge (2015: 88), here and below.
19 La Berge (2015: 93)
20 Benke (2018).
21 All these are examples collected by empirical sociologists, things I have observed or stories heard in the field. 'Scalping' is trading on one's own account, as opposed to executing trades for clients.
22 Quoted in Brassett and Heine (2020: 13).
23 Lilley and Lightfoot (2006).
24 Murphy (2019). See also de Goede (2005).
25 Preda (2001a).
26 Salzinger (2016: 15).
27 Salzinger (2016: 17).
28 Prügl (2016: 26–7).
29 Ho (2009: 41)
30 Ho (2009: 66).
31 Prügl (2016: 25).
32 Brassett and Heine (2020).

Chapter 8

1 John Jenkins made his 'grand a day' in the early 1980s trading unlisted stocks by way of a London Stock Exchange exemption, but in Britain it was more usual for these to be dealt by a 'licenced dealer' recognized by the Department of Trade and Industry.
2 Wilmot (1985). This section has been compiled from media coverage of the affair.
3 Brierley (1988b).
4 Leonard (1988).
5 Brierley (1988c).
6 Eadie (1986).
7 A Mr M. Bennett, writing in the *Stock Exchange Journal* of 1959, and quoted by Pardo-Guerra (2010: 93).
8 The illustration is reproduced in Beunza et al (2012: 30).
9 The details of automation are complex and are exhaustively covered in Pardo-Guerra (2019).
10 Pardo-Guerra (2019: 128).
11 Poser (1988: 327).
12 Hennessy (2001: 184).

13 Clemons and Weber (1990: 49).
14 Poser (1988: 325). The quotation and detail are from Clemons and Weber (1990: 49).
15 Lewis (1989: 279).
16 Vulliamy (1987).
17 Brierley (1988a; 1988b).
18 Leonard (1989); BBC News (2011). A 'boiler room' is an operation pressure-selling worthless or imaginary stock to private investors. For some reason they are often based in southern Spain.

Chapter 9

1 Defoe is quoted by Hamilton and Parker (2016: 3).
2 Thrift (2000).
3 This account draws on my own research (Roscoe, 2017).
4 This claim is based on my analysis of interview conversations. It is supported by Posner's (2009) account of strategic rivalry among exchanges.
5 Here and following detail Beunza and Garud (2007).
6 See *The Scotsman* (2018) and *Daily Mail Online* (2018).

Chapter 10

1 Coyle (2000: 14).
2 De Bondt (1998: 832).
3 Tversky and Kahneman (1974).
4 de Long et al (1990).
5 Hardie and MacKenzie (2007).
6 Hardie and MacKenzie (2007: 66). The term 'distributed cognition' was coined by Hutchins (1995).
7 Beunza and Stark (2004).
8 Harrington (2008).
9 Harrington (2008: 48).
10 Roscoe (2013).
11 Harrington (2007).
12 Knorr Cetina and Bruegger (2000: 150). The paper is quoting an interviewee.
13 For a full discussion, see Roscoe (2015).
14 Roscoe (2015: 202–3); Chen and Roscoe (2018).
15 Jegadeesh and Titman (2001).
16 Roscoe (2015: 206). See also Roscoe and Howorth (2009).
17 https://docs.house.gov/meetings/BA/BA00/20210218/111207/HHRG-117-BA00-Wstate-GillK-20210218.pdf [accessed 5 December 2022].
18 Scott (2021).
19 See Gill's testimony to the House, note 17.

Chapter 11

1 Impressions of the breakfast meeting are from memory, and details of the deal from the archives. It was extensively reported in May and June 2000. See notes 2 and 3; see also Cowell (2000).
2 *The Mining Journal* (2000).
3 Business Wire (2000)
4 Bridgland (2000).
5 Frank (2000).

6 Posner (2009: 66).
7 This market offered much lighter admission rules including a three- rather than a five-year trading record, no minimum capitalization or pre-vetting of listing particulars, and a smaller public float. See Arcot et al (2007).
8 Buckland and Davis (1989).
9 Much of this and what follows is drawn from my narrative history of these markets (see Roscoe, 2017).
10 Investors Chronicle (1992)
11 Posner (2009: 66).
12 Cisco (1993a: 8; 1993b: 5–16)
13 Kay (1993: 8)
14 This, and subsequent material, is drawn from my own account of the markets (see Roscoe, 2017). Sources are extensively referenced therein. Additional material comes from my own unpublished interviews.
15 London Stock Exchange plc (2000: 11).
16 BRICS – Brazil, Russia, India, China and South Africa – the 'emerging' powerhouse economies of the 2000s.
17 Essick (2001).
18 Carter et al (2011).
19 Michie (2001: 64–5).
20 Attard (2013: 94).
21 Thomas (1998: 740).
22 Attard (2013).
23 Bear (2020: 53).
24 Bear (2020: 53).
25 Thomas (1998); Kaur (2014).
26 Thomas (1998: 743).
27 Thomas (1998: 747).
28 Thomas (1998: 744).
29 Kaur (2014: 196).

Chapter 12

1 Beckert (2013).
2 Gilbert (2020: 31).
3 Tsing (2001: 158).
4 Tsing (2001: 175).
5 Tett (2009).
6 MacKenzie (2011: 1827).
7 Kish and Leroy (2015: 641).
8 This section draws my own account of the markets (see Roscoe, 2017).
9 Pain (2004: 5).
10 Klinger (2004); Wheatcroft (2004).
11 Foley (2004).

Chapter 13

1 This observation is drawn from Beunza et al (2012).
2 Jameson (1997: 251).
3 Pardo-Guerra (2019: 189). The following section draws on Pardo-Guerra's account.
4 Pardo-Guerra (2019: 191)
5 Roscoe (2022).

6 Pardo-Guerra (2019: 201)
7 Pardo-Guerra (2019: 201).
8 Michie (2001: 616).
9 This next section draws on my own research (Roscoe, 2017).
10 OFEX (2005).
11 Waller (2005).
12 The SEC (Securities and Exchange Commission) eventually launched a huge antitrust action against the broker-dealers, with damages reported to be $910 million in total. See MacKenzie and Pardo-Guerra (2014).
13 Quoted by MacKenzie and Pardo-Guerra (2014: 162).
14 MacKenzie (2017).
15 Hayes (2021).
16 MacKenzie (2018: 518).
17 Bondo Hansen (2020).
18 Borch (2020).

Chapter 14

1 Quotations from my interview with Theresa Wallis (see Roscoe, 2017).
2 Mendoza (2008).
3 Roscoe and Willman (2021).
4 According to Gerakos et al (2013), firms listing on AIM underperform peers listed on more regulated exchanges, less regulated exchanges (eg, the American 'Pink Sheets' over-the-counter [OTC] market) and even private equity, and are more likely to fail than firms on other markets. On the other hand, Nielsson (2013) argues that AIM-listed firms are of equivalent quality to those listing in more regulated markets, and simply do not meet the listing criteria of more established markets. Scholars do agree that AIM offers a successful fundraising venue for smaller companies.
5 Anbleyth-Evans and Gilbert (2020: 579).
6 I am quoting from Sixtus' own account of this start-up. Sixtus is a pseudonym.
7 I would not usually cite Wikipedia, but on such a facile point, where better?
8 See also www.cbinsights.com/research-unicorn-companies
9 Geiger (2019: 14).
10 Barbrook and Cameron (1996).
11 Beck et al (2016).
12 Barbrook and Cameron (1996: 14)
13 Langley (2016).

Epilogue

1 Chiapello (2013).
2 Thompson (2011 [1967]: 284).
3 Wozniak (2014: 453).
4 Grieg (2019).
5 Knight (2013).
6 Drucker (1999).
7 Poovey (2008).
8 MacKenzie and Millo (2003).
9 Roscoe (2022).

References

Anbleyth-Evans, J. and Gilbert, P.R. (2020) 'The oxygenation of extraction and future global ecological democracy: The City of London, the alternative investment market and oil in frontiers in Africa', *ACME: An International Journal for Critical Geographies*, 19(2): 567–99.

Appleyard, B. (1986) 'A year after the Big Bang', *The Times*, 19–21 October.

Arcot, S., Black, J. and Owen, G. (2007) *From Local to Global: The Rise of AIM as a Stock Market for Growing Companies: A Comprehensive Report Analysing the Growth of AIM*, London: London School of Economics and Political Science.

Arrighi, G. (1994) *The Long Twentieth Century: Money, Power, and the Origins of Our Times*, London: Verso.

Attard, B. (1994) 'The jobbers of the London Stock Exchange: An oral history', *Oral History*, 22(1): 43–8.

Attard, B. (2013) 'The London Stock Exchange and the colonial market: The City, internationalization and power', in C. Dejung and N.P. Petersson (eds) *The Foundations of Worldwide Economic Integration: Power, Institutions, and Global Markets, 1850–1930*, Cambridge: Cambridge University Press, Chapter 5 pp.89–111

Baker, W.E. (1984) 'The social structure of a national securities market', *American Journal of Sociology*, 89(4): 775–811.

Bailey, A (2017) 'The future of LIBOR', Financial Conduct Authority, 27 July, www.fca.org.uk/news/speeches/the-future-of-libor [accessed 24 November 2021].

Barbrook, R. and Cameron, A. (1996) 'The Californian ideology', *Science as Culture*, 6(1): 44–72.

Baucom, I. (2005) *Specters of the Atlantic: Finance Capital, Slavery, and the Philosophy of History*, Durham, NC: Duke University Press.

BBC News (2011) 'Father and sons boiler room scam sent to prison', 22 August, www.bbc.co.uk/news/business-14623571 [accessed 15 August 2022].

Bear, L. (2020) 'Speculations on infrastructure: From colonial public works to a post-colonial global asset class on the Indian railways 1840–2017', *Economy and Society*, 49(1): 45–70.

Beck, R., Bruntje, D., Dardour, A., Gajda, O., Marom, D. and Pais, I. et al (2016) 'Introduction', in D. Bruntje and O. Gaida (eds) *Crowdfunding in Europe: State of the Art in Theory and Practice*, Cham: Springer, pp 1–7.

Beckert, J. (2013) 'Imagined futures: Fictional expectations in the economy', *Theory and Society*, 42(3): 219–40.

Benke, G. (2018) 'Humor and heuristics: Culture, genre, and economic thought in the big short', *Journal of Cultural Economy*, 11(4): 303–14.

Beunza, D (2019) *Taking the Floor: Models, Morals, and Management in a Wall Street Trading Room*, Princeton, NJ: Princeton University Press.

Beunza, D. and Garud, R. (2007) 'Calculators, lemmings or frame-makers? The intermediary role of securities analysts', *The Sociological Review*, 55(2): 13–39.

Beunza, D. and Stark, D. (2004) 'Tools of the trade: The socio-technology of arbitrage in a Wall Street trading room', *Industrial and Corporate Change*, 13(2): 369–400.

Beunza, D., MacKenzie, D., Millo, Y. and Pardo-Guerra, J.P. (2012) *Impersonal Efficiency and the Dangers of a Fully Automated Securities Exchange*, Government Office for Science Foresight Driver Review, DR11.

Bondo Hansen, K. (2020) 'The virtue of simplicity: On machine learning models in algorithmic trading', *Big Data & Society*, 7(1), https://doi.org/10.1177/2053951720926558

Borch, C. (2020) 'Ten years after the flash crash, we still need to make algorithmic trading less risky. Can culture save the day?', *Socializing Finance*, 6 May, https://socfinance.wordpress.com/2020/05/06/ten-years-after-the-flash-crash-we-still-need-to-make-algorithmic-trading-less-risky-can-culture-save-the-day [accessed 22 August 2022].

Borch, C., Hansen, K.B. and Lange, A.-C. (2015) 'Markets, bodies, and rhythms: A rhythmanalysis of financial markets from open-outcry trading to high-frequency trading', *Environment and Planning D: Society and Space*, 33(6): 1080–97.

Brassett, J. and Heine, F. (2020) '"Men behaving badly"? Representations of masculinity in post-global financial crisis cinema', *International Feminist Journal of Politics*, 23(5): 763–84.

Brierley, D. (1988a) 'DTI takes flak over Harvard', *The Sunday Times*, 10 July.

Brierley, D. (1988b) 'Harvard dealers turn to minister', *The Sunday Times*, 18 September.

Brierley, D. (1988c) 'The quest for approval that sank Harvard', *The Sunday Times*, 2 October.

Bridgland, F. (2000) 'Mugabe seeks hard cash from "blood diamonds"', *The Sunday Herald*, 11 June, p 15.

Buckland, R. and Davis, E.W. (1989) *The Unlisted Securities Market*, Oxford: Clarendon Press.

Burrough, B. and Helyar, J. (2010) *Barbarians at the Gate: The Fall of RJR Nabisco*, New York: Random House.

Business Wire (2000) 'Oryx Diamonds Ltd to be Listed on London Stock Exchange', 6 June.

Carruthers, B.G. and Stinchcombe, A.L. (1999) 'The social structure of liquidity: Flexibility, markets and states', *Theory and Society*, 28: 353–82.

Carter, C.A., Rausser, G.C. and Smith, A. (2011) 'Commodity booms and busts', *Annual Review of Resource Economics*, 3: 87–118.

Chandler, G. (1953) *William Roscoe of Liverpool*, London: B.T. Batsford Ltd.

Chen, Y.-H. and Roscoe, P. (2018) 'Practices and meanings of non-professional stock-trading in Taiwan: A case of relational work', *Economy and Society*, 46(3–4): 576–600.

Chiapello, E. (2013) 'Capitalism and its criticisms', in P. Du Gay and G. Morgan (eds) *New Spirits of Capitalism?*, Oxford: Oxford University Press, pp 60–81.

Chong, K. (2017) *Best Practice: Management Consulting and the Ethics of Financialization in China*, Durham, NC: Duke University Press.

Christophers, B. (2022) 'The rentierization of the United Kingdom economy', *Environment and Planning A: Economy and Space*, https://doi.org/10.1177/0308518X19873007

Cisco (1993a) *Newsletter*, February.

Cisco (1993b) *Newsletter*, April.

Clemons, E.K. and Weber, B.W. (1990) 'London's Big Bang: A case study of information technology, competitive impact, and organizational change', *Journal of Management Information Systems*, 6(4): 41–60.

Clune, M. (2014) 'Beyond realism', in A. Shonkwiler and L.C. La Berge (eds) *Reading Capitalist Realism*, Iowa City, IA: University of Iowa Press, pp 195–212.

Cornish, C. (2017) 'Winterflood', *Financial Times*, 30 April.

Cowell, A. (2000) 'African Diamond concern to sell shares in London', *The New York Times*, 26 May, p C2.

Coyle, D. (2000) 'Following the tracks of the new economy', *The Independent*, 25 April, p 14.

Crosthwaite, P. (2019) *The Market Logics of Contemporary Fiction*, Cambridge: Cambridge University Press.

Daily Mail Online (2018) 'Duchess of Cornwall's aristocratic cousin "claimed housing benefit under Brad Pitt's Fight Club character's name Tyler Durden and duped Highland walkers into thinking he was a doctor as he charged them for refreshments"', 16 January, www.dailymail.co.uk/news/article-5275083/Camillas-aristocratic-cousin-claimed-housing-benefit.html [accessed 19 August 2022].

Davis, G.F. and Kim, S. (2015) 'Financialization of the economy', *Annual Review of Sociology*, 41(1): 203–21.

De Bondt, W. (1998) 'A portrait of the individual investor', *European Economic Review*, 42: 831–44.

de Goede, M. (2005) *Virtue, Fortune and Faith: A Genealogy of Finance*, Minneapolis, MN: University of Minnesota Press.

de Goede, M. (2020) 'Engagement all the way down', *Critical Studies on Security*, 8(2): 101–15.

de Long, J., Shleifer, A. and Waldman, R. (1990) 'Positive feedback investment strategies and destabilising rational speculation', *Journal of Finance*, 45(2): 379–95.

Drucker, P. (1999) *Innovation and Entrepreneurship*, Oxford: Butterworth.

Dymski, G., Hernandez, J. and Mohanty, L. (2013) 'Race, gender, power, and the US subprime mortgage and foreclosure crisis: A meso analysis', *Feminist Economics*, 19(3): 124–51.

Eadie, A. (1986) 'OTC dealers plan exchange to rival SE's third market', *The Times*, 13 August.

Essick, K. (2001) 'Guns, money and cell phones', *Global Issues*, 11 June, www.globalissues.org/article/442/guns-money-and-cell-phones [accessed 22 August 2022].

Fama, E. (1970) 'Efficient capital markets: A review of theory and empirical work', *Journal of Finance*, 25(2): 383–417.

Fisher, M. (2009) *Capitalist Realism*, Ropley: Zero Books.

Fletcher, S. (2016) *Roscoe and Italy: The Reception of Italian Renaissance History and Culture in the Eighteenth and Nineteenth Centuries*, Abingdon: Routledge.

Foley, S. (2004) 'Spiralling losses spell crisis for OFEX', *The Independent*, Business, 30 September, p 46.

Forsyth, F. (1996 [1974]) *The Dogs of War*, London: Arrow.

Frank, J. (2000) 'A question of ethics', *Accountancy Age*, 22 June.

Geiger, S. (2019) 'Silicon valley, disruption, and the end of uncertainty', *Journal of Cultural Economy*, 13(2): 169–84.

Gerakos, J., Lang, M. and Maffett, M. (2013) 'Post-listing performance and private sector regulation: The experience of London's Alternative Investment Market', *Journal of Accounting and Economics*, 56(2–3), Supplement 1: 189–215.

Gilbert, P.R. (2020) 'Speculating on sovereignty: "Money mining" and corporate foreign policy at the extractive industry frontier', *Economy and Society*, 49(1): 16–44.

Gribben, R. (2012) 'The City 60 years ago: Bowler hats, financial feudalism and no brown shoes or Big Bang', *The Daily Telegraph*, 3 June, www.telegraph.co.uk/finance/newsbysector/banksandfinance/9308913/The-City-60-years-ago-bowler-hats-financial-feudalism-and-no-brown-shoes-or-Big-Bang.html [accessed 5 October 2022].

Grieg, C. (2019) 'Scottish stock exchange: "Jet-set life" of boss Tomas Carruthers', *The Times*, 23 November, www.thetimes.co.uk/article/scottish-stock-exchange-jet-set-life-of-boss-tomas-carruthers-j2skf9wsq [accessed 22 August 2022].

Haiven, M. (2011) 'Finance as capital's imagination? Reimagining value and culture in an age of fictitious capital and crisis', *Social Text*, 29(3): 93–124.

Hall, S. (2009) 'Financialised elites and the changing nature of finance capitalism: Investment bankers in London's financial district', *Competition & Change*, 13(2): 173–89.

Hamilton, V. and Parker, M. (2016) *Daniel Defoe and the Bank of England: The Dark Arts of Projectors*, Ropley: Zero Books.

Hardie, I. and MacKenzie, D. (2007) 'Assembling an economic actor: The agencement of a hedge fund', *The Sociological Review*, 55(1): 57–80.

Harrington, B. (2007) 'Capital and community: Findings from the American investment craze of the 1990s', *Economic Sociology, European Electronic Newsletter*, 8(3): 19–25.

Harrington, B. (2008) *Pop Finance: Investment Clubs and the New Investor Popularism*, Princeton, NJ: Princeton University Press.

Hayes, A. (2021) 'The active construction of passive investors: Roboadvisors and algorithmic "low-finance"', *Socio-Economic Review*, 19(1): 83–110.

Hennessy, E. (2001) *Coffee House to Cyber Market: 200 years of the London Stock Exchange*, London: Ebury Press.

Ho, K. (2009) *Liquidated: An Ethnography of Wall Street*, Durham, NC: Duke University Press.

Hochfelder, D. (2006) ' "Where the common people could speculate": The ticker, bucket shops, and the origins of popular participation in financial markets, 1880–1920', *Journal of American History*, 93: 335–58.

Hutchins, E. (1995) *Cognition in the Wild*, Cambridge, MA: The MIT Press.

Investors Chronicle (1992) 'USM closure', Business Notebook, 23 December.

Jameson, F. (1997) 'Culture and finance capital', *Critical Inquiry*, 24(1): 246–65.

Jegadeesh, N. and Titman, S. (2001) 'Profitability of momentum strategies', *Journal of Finance*, 56: 699–720.

Jensen, M. and Meckling, W. (1976) 'Theory of the firm: Managerial behaviour, agency costs, and ownership structure', *Journal of Financial Economics*, 3: 305–60.

Jensen, M. and Murphy, K. (1990) 'CEO incentives – it's not how much you pay, but how', *Harvard Business Review* (May–June): 138–53.

Judge, B. (2020) '27 October 1986: The City's Big Bang', *Money Week*, 27 October, https://moneyweek.com/353587/27-october-1986-the-citys-big-bang [accessed 13 October 2021].

Kantor, J and Streitfeld, D. (2015) 'Inside Amazon: Wrestling big ideas in a bruising workplace', *The New York Times*, 15 August, www.nytimes.com/2015/08/16/technology/inside-amazon-wrestling-big-ideas-in-a-bruising-workplace.html [accessed 4 March 2022].

Kaur, A. (2014) 'Plantation systems, labour regimes and the state in Malaysia, 1900–2012', *Journal of Agrarian Change*, 14(2): 190–213.

Kay, W. (1993) 'Profile: Enter the man from the Pru', *The Independent*, 14 November, Business p 8.

Kish, Z. and Leroy, J. (2015) 'Bonded life', *Cultural Studies*, 29(5–6): 630–51.

Klinger, P. (2004) 'Shares in Ofex dive as it fights imminent collapse', *The Times*, Business, 30 September, p 53.

Knight, P. (2013) 'Reading the ticker tape in the late nineteenth century American market', *Journal of Cultural Economy*, 6(1): 45–62.

Knorr Cetina, K. (1999) *Epistemic Cultures: How the Sciences Make Knowledge*, Cambridge, MA: Harvard University Press.

Knorr Cetina, K. and Bruegger, U. (2000) 'The market as an object of attachment: Exploring postsocial relations in financial markets', *Canadian Journal of Sociology*, 25(2): 141–68.

Krippner, G. (2001) 'The elusive market: Embeddedness and the paradigm of economic sociology', *Theory and Society*, 30(6): 775–810.

La Berge, L.C. (2015) *Scandals and Abstraction: Financial Fiction of the Long 1980s*, Oxford: Oxford University Press.

Lamont, D. (2020) 'Causes and consequences of the dramatic changes in ownership of the UK stock market in the past 55 years', *Schroders, In Focus*, November, https://prod.schroders.com/en/sysglobalassets/digital/insights/2020/november/global-britain/2020-november-stock-market-ownership.pdf [accessed 5 October 2022].

Langley, P. (2016) 'Crowdfunding in the United Kingdom: A cultural economy', *Economic Geography*, 92(3): 301–21.

Latour, B. (1999) *Pandora's Hope: An Essay on the Reality of Science Studies*, Cambridge, MA: Harvard University Press.

Latour, B. (2007) *Reassembling the Social: An Introduction to Actor-Network-Theory*, Oxford: Oxford University Press.

Latour, B. (2017) *Facing Gaia: Eight Lectures on the New Climatic Regime*, Cambridge: Polity Press.

Lefèvre, E. (1993) *Reminiscences of a Stock Operator*, Chichester: John Wiley & Sons.

Leonard, C. (1989) 'Wilmot's old banger; City Diary', *The Times*, 12 January.

Levy, J.I. (2006) 'Contemplating delivery: Futures trading and the problem of commodity exchange in the United States, 1875–1905', *The American Historical Review*, 111(2): 307–35.

Lewis, M. (1989) *Liar's Poker*, London: Coronet.

Lilley, S. and Lightfoot, G. (2006) 'Trading narratives', *Organization*, 13(3): 369–91.

London Stock Exchange plc (2000) 'Third response to OMX's offer', October.

MacIntyre, A. (1981) *After Virtue: A Study in Moral Theory*, London: Duckworth.

MacKenzie, D. (2006) *An Engine, not a Camera: How Financial Models Shape Markets*, Cambridge, MA: The MIT Press.

MacKenzie, D. (2009) *Material Markets: How Economic Agents Are Constructed*, Oxford: Oxford University Press.

MacKenzie, D. (2011) 'The credit crisis as a problem in the sociology of knowledge', *American Journal of Sociology*, 116(6): 1778–841.

MacKenzie, D. (2015) 'Mechanizing the Merc: The Chicago Mercantile Exchange and the rise of high-frequency trading', *Technology and Culture*, 56(3): 646–75.

MacKenzie, D. (2017) 'A material political economy: Automated trading desk and price prediction in high-frequency trading', *Social Studies of Science*, 47(2): 172–94.

MacKenzie, D. (2018) '"Making", "taking" and the material political economy of algorithmic trading', *Economy and Society*, 47(4): 501–23.

MacKenzie, D. and Millo, Y. (2003) 'Constructing a market, performing theory: The historical sociology of a financial derivatives exchange', *American Journal of Sociology*, 109(1): 107–45.

MacKenzie, D. and Pardo-Guerra, J.P. (2014) 'Insurgent capitalism: Island, bricolage and the re-making of finance', *Economy and Society*, 43(2): 153–82.

MacKenzie, D. and Spears, T. (2014) '"The formula that killed Wall Street": The Gaussian copula and modelling practices in investment banking', *Social Studies of Science*, 44(3): 393–417.

Mellor, M. (2019) *Money: Myths, Truths and Alternatives*, Bristol: Policy Press.

Mendoza, J.M. (2008) 'Securities regulation in low-tier listing venues: The rise of the Alternative Investment Market', *Fordham Journal of Corporate & Financial Law*, 13: 257–328.

Michie, R.C. (2001) *The London Stock Exchange: A History*, Oxford: Oxford University Press.

Mining Journal, The (2000) 'Petra's DRC deal takes shape', 26 May, p 418.

Mirowski, P. (1981) 'The rise (and retreat) of a market: English joint stock shares in the eighteenth century', *The Journal of Economic History*, 41(3): 559–77.

Monbiot, G. (2022) 'Britain faces crisis upon crisis, and our leaders are absent. This is how a country falls apart', *The Guardian*', 10 August, www.theguardian.com/commentisfree/2022/aug/10/crisis-britain-leaders-inflation-energy-wages-conservative [accessed 18 August 2022].

Morrison, C. (2015) 'How Winterflood's founder went from Freemason to gangster', *CityAM*, 15 October, www.cityam.com/226688/how-the-winterflood-founder-went-from-freemason-to-gangster [accessed 5 October 2022].

Muniesa, F. (2021) 'Finance: Cultural or political?', *Journal of Cultural Economy*, https://doi.org/10.1080/17530350.2021.1927151

Murphy, A. (2009) *The Origins of English Financial Markets*, Cambridge: Cambridge University Press.

Murphy, A. (2017) 'Building trust in the financial market', *Critical Finance Studies Conference*, Leicester: University of Leicester, 3–5 August.

Murphy, A. (2019) ' "We have been ruined by whores": Perceptions of female involvement in the South Sea Scheme', in C. Stefano and M. Daniel (eds) *Boom, Bust, and Beyond: New Perspectives on the 1720 Stock Market Bubble*, Oldenbourg: De Gruyter, pp 261–84.

Nelms, T.C. (2012) 'The zombie bank and the magic of finance', *Journal of Cultural Economy*, 5(2): 231–46.

Nielsson, U. (2013) 'Do less regulated markets attract lower quality firms? Evidence from the London AIM market', *Journal of Financial Intermediation*, 22(3): 335–52.

Nordström, K.A. and Ridderstråle, J. (2002) *Funky Business: Talent makes Capital Dance*, Pearson Education.

Norris, F. (1994 [1902]) *The Pit: A Story of Chicago*, London: Penguin Twentieth Century Classics.

OFEX plc (2005) 'Interim statement', 6 September.

Pain, D. (2004) 'No pain, no gain: I've changed my mind about OFEX. I may even buy shares', *The Independent*, Features, 10 January, p 5.

Pardo-Guerra, J.P. (2010) 'Creating flows of interpersonal bits: The automation of the London Stock Exchange, c. 1955–90', *Economy and Society*, 39(1): 84–109.

Pardo-Guerra, J.P. (2019) *Automating Finance: Infrastructures, Engineers, and the Making of Electronic Markets*, Oxford: Oxford University Press.

Pardo-Guerra, J.P. (2022) *The Quantified Scholar: How Research Evaluations Transformed the British Social Sciences*, New York, NY: Columbia University Press.

Parker, G. and Barker, A. (2010) 'Cameron closer to No 10 after 'very positive' talks with Clegg' *Financial Times*, 10 May, p 1.

Pickering, A. (1992) *Science as Practice and Culture*, Chicago, IL: University of Chicago Press.

Piketty, T. (2017) *Capital in the Twenty-First Century*, Cambridge, MA: Harvard University Press.

Poitras, G. (2009) 'From Antwerp to Chicago: The history of exchange traded derivative security contracts', *Revue d'Histoire des Sciences Humaines*, 1(20): 11–50.

Poon, M. (2007) 'Scorecards as devices for consumer credit: The case of Fair, Isaac & Company incorporated', *The Sociological Review*, 55(s2): 284–306.

Poon, M. (2009) 'From new deal institutions to capital markets: Commercial consumer risk scores and the making of subprime mortgage finance', *Accounting Organizations and Society*, 34(5): 654–74.

Poovey, M. (2008) *Genres of the Credit Economy*, Chicago, IL: University of Chicago Press.

Porter, A., Winnett, R. and Kirkup, J. (2010) 'Hung parliament: Clegg and Cameron "close to agreeing economic deal"', *The Telegraph*, 9 May https://www.telegraph.co.uk/news/election-2010/7702768/Hung-parliament-Clegg-and-Cameron-close-to-agreeing-economic-deal.html [accessed 03/11/22]

Poser, N.S. (1988) 'Big Bang and the financial services act seen through an American's eyes', *Brooklyn Journal of International Law*, 14(2): 317–38.

Posner, E. (2009) *The Origins of Europe's New Stock Markets*, Cambridge, MA: Harvard University Press.

Preda, A. (2001a) 'In the enchanted grove: Financial conversations and the marketplace in England and France in the eighteenth century', *Journal of Historical Sociology*, 14(3): 276–89.

Preda, A. (2001b) 'The rise of the popular investor: Financial knowledge and investing in England and France 1840–1880', *Sociological Quarterly*, 42(2): 205–30.

Preda, A. (2006) 'Socio-technical agency in financial markets: The case of the stock ticker', *Social Studies of Science*, 36(5): 753–82.

Preda, A. (2009) *Framing Finance: The Boundaries of Markets and Modern Capitalism*, Chicago, IL: University of Chicago Press.

Prügl, E. (2016) 'Lehman brothers and sisters', in A. Hozic and J. True (eds) *Scandalous Economics*, Oxford: Oxford University Press, pp 21–40.

Rentoul, J. (2018) 'What if Nick Clegg had gone into coalition with Labour, not the Tories, in 2010?' *Independent*, 13 November, www.independent.co.uk/news/long_reads/nick-clegg-coalition-lib-dems-2010-labour-gordon-brown-conservative-david-cameron-a8586046.html [accessed 18 August 2022].

Roscoe, H. (1831) *Reports of Cases Argued and Determined in the Court of King's Bench, 1782–1785*, London.

Roscoe, P. (2013) 'Economic embeddedness and materiality in a financial market setting', *The Sociological Review*, 61(1): 41–68.

Roscoe, P. (2014) *I Spend Therefore I Am: The True Cost of Economics*, London: Viking.

Roscoe, P. (2015) '"Elephants can't gallop": Performativity, knowledge and power in the market for lay-investing', *Journal of Marketing Management*, 1–2: 193–218.

Roscoe, P. (2017) *The Rise and Fall of the Penny-Share Offer: A Historical Sociology of London's Smaller Company Markets*, St Andrews: University of St Andrews, https://research-repository.st-andrews.ac.uk/handle/10023/11688 [accessed 5 October 2022].

Roscoe, P. (2021) 'Shouldn't we all be doing cultural economy?', *Journal of Cultural Economy*, doi:10.1080/17530350.2021.1986112.

Roscoe, P. (2022) 'How "matter matters" for morality: The case of a stock exchange', *Human Relations*, 75(3): 475–501.

Roscoe, P. and Howorth, C. (2009) 'Identification through technical analysis: A study of charting and UK non-professional investors', *Accounting, Organizations and Society*, 34(2): 206–21.

Roscoe, P. and Willman, P. (2021) 'Flaunt the imperfections: Information, entanglements, and the regulation of London's Alternative Investment Market', *Economy and Society*, 50(4): 585–69.

Roscoe, W. (1787) *The Wrongs of Africa, A Poem. Part the First*, London: R. Faulder.

Rupprecht, A. (2008) '"A limited sort of property": History, memory and the slave ship Zong', *Slavery & Abolition*, 29(2): 265–77.

Salzinger, L. (2016) 'Re-marking men: Masculinity as a terrain of the neoliberal economy', *Critical Historical Studies*, 3(1): 1–25.

Sargent, D. (2013) 'The Cold War and the international political economy in the 1970s', *Cold War History*, 13(3): 393–425.

Scotsman, The (2018) 'Camilla's royal cousin jailed after claiming disability benefit', 21 February, www.scotsman.com/news/people/camillas-royal-cousin-jailed-after-claiming-disability-benefit-347273 [accessed 19 August 2022].

Scott, B. (2021) 'The real lesson of the GameStop story is the power of the swarm', *The Guardian*, 30 January, www.theguardian.com/commentisfree/2021/jan/30/gamestop-power-of-the-swarm-shares-traders [accessed 17 December 2021].

Shaxson, N. (2011) *Treasure Islands: Uncovering the Damage of Offshore Banking and Tax Havens*, Basingstoke: Palgrave Macmillan.

Sinclair, U. (1985 [1906]) *The Jungle*, London: Penguin.

Souleles, D. (2017) 'Something new: Value and change in finance', *Journal of Cultural Economy*, 10(4): 393–404.

Steil, J.P., Albright, L., Rugh, J.S. and Massey, D.S. (2018) 'The social structure of mortgage discrimination', *Housing Studies*, 33(5): 759–76.

Tett, G. (2009) *Fool's Gold: How Unrestrained Greed Corrupted a Dream, Shattered Global Markets and Unleashed a Catastrophe*, London: Hachette.

Thomas, W. (1998) 'An intra-empire capital transfer: The Shanghai rubber company boom 1909–1912', *Modern Asian Studies*, 32(3): 739–60.

Thompson, H.S. (2011 [1967]) *Hell's Angels*, London: Penguin Classics.

Thrift, N. (2000) 'Performing cultures in the new economy', *Annals of the Association of American Geographers*, 90(4): 674–92.

Tsing, A. (2001) 'Inside the economy of appearances', in A. Appadurai (ed) *Globalization*, Durham, NC: Duke University Press, pp 155–88.

Tversky, A. and Kahneman, D. (1974) 'Judgement under uncertainty', *Science*, 185: 1124–31.

Vander Weyer, M. (2012) 'Any other business: Third time lucky? Hoare Govett is the history of the modern City writ small', *The Spectator*, 4 February, www.spectator.co.uk/article/any-other-business-third-time-lucky-hoare-govett-is-the-history-of-the-modern-city-writ-small [accessed 5 October 2022].

Vulliamy, E. (1987) 'Darkening clouds as the little yuppies go to market', *The Guardian*, 21 October.

Waller, M. (2005) 'OFEX meets brokers in attempt to poach trade from LSE', *The Times*, Business, 10 November, p 54.

Walvin, J. (2011) *The Zong: A Massacre, the Law and the End of Slavery*, New Haven, CT: Yale University Press.

Weber, M. (1978) *Economy and Society: An Outline of Interpretive Sociology*, Berkeley, CA: University of California Press.

Wheatcroft, P. (2004) 'AIM's appeal is Ofex's problem', *The Times*, Business, 30 September, p 45.

Wilmot, T. (1985) *Inside the Over-the-Counter Market in the UK*, Westport, CT: Quorum Books.

Wolfe, T. (1987) *The Bonfire of the Vanities*, New York: Macmillan.

Wozniak, J.S.G. (2014) 'When the going gets weird: An invitation to gonzo sociology', *The American Sociologist*, 45(4): 453–73.

Zaloom, C. (2003) 'Ambiguous numbers: Trading technologies and interpretation in financial markets', *American Ethnologist*, 30(2): 258–72.

Zaloom, C. (2006) *Out of the Pits: Traders and Technology from Chicago to London*, Chicago, IL: University of Chicago Press.

Zelizer, V.A. (1994) *The Social Meaning of Money*, New York: HarperCollins.

Index

Note: References to endnotes show both the page number and the note number (231n3).